# The Forgotten History of Lake County, Illinois

# THE FORGOTTEN HISTORY OF LAKE COUNTY, ILLINOIS

James D. Lodesky

Copyright © 2020 by James D. Lodesky.

| Library of Congress Control Number: | | 2020920336 |
|---|---|---|
| ISBN: | Hardcover | 978-1-6641-3703-5 |
| | Softcover | 978-1-6641-3704-2 |
| | eBook | 978-1-6641-3702-8 |

All rights reserved. No part of this book may be reproduced or transmitted in any form or by any means, electronic or mechanical, including photocopying, recording, or by any information storage and retrieval system, without permission in writing from the copyright owner.

The views expressed in this work are solely those of the author and do not necessarily reflect the views of the publisher, and the publisher hereby disclaims any responsibility for them.

Any people depicted in stock imagery provided by Getty Images are models, and such images are being used for illustrative purposes only.
Certain stock imagery © Getty Images.

Print information available on the last page.

Rev. date: 10/23/2020

**To order additional copies of this book, contact:**
Xlibris
844-714-8691
www.Xlibris.com
Orders@Xlibris.com
619861

# CONTENTS

Introduction ................................................................. vii

Chapter 1   Robert Dady ........................................................ 1
Chapter 2   Violence in Lake County ..................................... 31
Chapter 3   Lake County Fights ............................................ 36
Chapter 4   Lake County Mobs and Riots ............................. 41
Chapter 5   Ethnic Waukegan/North Chicago ...................... 67
Chapter 6   Self-Made Men in Early Lake County History ..... 144
Chapter 7   Famous Lake County Women ............................ 151
Chapter 8   Lake County Women Acting Badly ..................... 156
Chapter 9   The All-Time Worst Lake County Woman .......... 165
Chapter 10 Miscellaneous Lake County Women .................. 175
Chapter 11 Miscellaneous Lake County Stories .................. 182
Chapter 12 Lake County Hermits and Squatters .............. 206

Epilogue ..................................................................... 209
Notes ........................................................................ 211
Author Bio ................................................................ 237

# Introduction

The following stories were first published in the *Waukegan Gazette*, *Waukegan Daily Sun*, or *Waukegan News Sun* newspapers. Articles from the Lake County independent newspaper, *Libertyville*, were also used. The period mainly takes place from the 1890s to the 1920s.

Some readers might be shocked by the amount of violence taking place in the county during this time. Our ancestors had different priorities from the current state of affairs. Moderate levels of violence were tolerated and penalties light. People (judges included) agreed that some people actually deserved a punch in the nose. Major violent acts were more harshly punished.

Chapter 1 tells the story of Robert Dady and his daughter, Nellie Dady Conrad. Robert started out in life with nothing and never learned to read or write but became the county's first great landowner. His daughter, Nellie Dady Conrad, was probably one of Waukegan's greatest builders, constructing an opera house, roller rink, apartment buildings, and subdivisions.

Chapters 2 to 4 concern violence by mobs, riots, and individuals in the county. Police response to violence, and court-ordered punishments are included.

Chapter 5 informs about the various ethnic groups living in the Waukegan/North Chicago area.

Chapters 6 and 7 highlight some of the county's most successful men and women.

Chapters 8 and 9 take a look at Lake County women acting badly. The case for female toxicity can be made here.

Chapter 10 contains miscellaneous stories about Lake County women.

vii

Chapter 11 presents miscellaneous Lake County articles, including the county's strongest man, greatest consumer of alcohol, Fats baseball team, lynching record, gypsies, and so on.

Chapter 12, the final chapter, writes about Lake County hermits and squatters. These people have always been with us, and Lake County was no exception.

# CHAPTER 1

## Robert Dady

Any list of the county's greatest characters would have to include Robert Dady. Starting with nothing, he acquired a vast amount of wealth during his lifetime, mainly in real estate. Pretty impressive for someone who never learned to read or write. He memorized all his business transactions until his daughter Lorena was old enough to write them down for him.[1] Robert considered himself a capitalist and seemed to have been a ruthless businessman. He was definitely not a people person. His tough business practices led to the estrangement of his son and a daughter. He also engaged in almost constant feuding with neighbors and business associates. Robert grew increasingly eccentric with age, making things even worse for those living around him. Your author has a special reason for writing about Robert—he was a relative. Robert was married to my great-grandfather's sister, Mary Wlodeski.

Robert seemed to be in and out of a courtroom his whole life, and it's amazing he had anything left after paying for attorney's fees. He was a part of the longest court case in Waukegan's history up to the time. The Condit-Dady lawsuit lasted from 1891 to 1904. During his lifetime, he was either being punched out, suing someone, or being sued himself.

Robert was born in LaSalle County, Illinois, in 1841,[2] but the family moved to Libertyville Township, Lake County, soon afterward. He was a son of Owen and Margaret Dady, immigrants from County Kerry, Ireland. Owen and Margaret settled in Massachusetts in 1838 but were living in Illinois by 1841. The Dadys were Catholic, and Owen was a farmer by trade. Besides Robert, there were four other children: James, born on August 7, 1842; Jeremiah (JR), born on January 22,1844; Mary, born in 1846; and Eugene (Owen Jr.), born in 1848. Both Robert's parents died at a young age. His mother died when she was just thirty-three years old and his father at thirty-nine years of age, dying about 1859.[3]

After Owen died, the Dady family was split up.[4] Robert was the eldest son but had already left home and was already a master blacksmith by the age of nineteen. According to the 1860 census, Robert was living in Waukegan at the home of George and Sebina Bub. Bub was his employer and taught Robert the blacksmith trade. Later, they would become business partners.

Seventeen-year-old James Dady ended up living in Waukegan with the Steven Drew family. The 1860 census shows that Steven Drew was a blacksmith and taught James the trade. The Drews were Irish immigrants and had five children of their own.

Fifteen-year-old JR went to live and work at the Michael Connolly farm in Benton Township. On the 1860 town of Benton census, Connolly and his wife, Alice, are shown to be Irish immigrants. They had one daughter, Margaret, aged eleven, and another hired man named Joseph Wall, an Irish immigrant. JR stuck around the Connolly farm for only a couple of years and then moved to Waukegan and learned the blacksmith trade from his big brother Robert.

I can't find out who took in Mary or Eugene. Eugene also became a blacksmith and later went into business with his brothers. All four Dady brothers worked at the Dady Carriage Shop for a time. Eugene eventually settled in Chamberlain, South Dakota. Mary went on to marry John Powers and spent her life in Scribner, Nebraska.[5] The Dadys remained close to one another their entire lives. Their children also had a close relationship with their cousins. My grandfather and his siblings were cousins with Robert's family, but I don't know how close they actually were. I do remember them mentioning the Dady name on occasion. One thing I noticed in my research was that my great-grandfather and his brother Ansel rarely had any business relations with Robert despite both parties engaging in the same types of business. I think they realized it was much easier to get along with Robert when not in business with him.

Robert married Mary Wlodeski on April 6, 1861, at St. Mary's Catholic Church in Waukegan.[6] St. Mary's name was later changed to

Immaculate Conception. Your author went to school there for six years. According to the 1870 census, Robert and Mary were the parents of Nellie, born in 1863; Eugene (Frank) born in 1865; and Lorena, born in 1870. They also had a daughter named Genevieve, who was born on May 5, 1867, but died two years later on June 5, 1869.[7]

Sometime after 1860, Robert Dady and George Bub became business partners in a blacksmith shop. Their business was located in Waukegan near the City Hotel, which Robert would later own. They sold and repaired wagons, buggies, sleighs, and cutters. In addition, general blacksmithing and horseshoeing were performed.[8] Robert's business partnership with Bub didn't last long. The *Waukegan Gazette* published their dissolution of partnership on November 29, 1862.[9]

Robert was already engaged in building his own wagon/blacksmith shop on South Genesee Street before the partnership was officially ended.[10] He also formed a new partnership, this time with brothers James, JR, and Eugene, making it a real family affair.[11] The Dadys were now Bub's competitors.

The Dady Carriage Shop offered something new in town. Bub only repaired and sold old and new wagons, but the Dadys offered more. They built wagons by hand. Known as the Dady wagon, hundreds were built and sold throughout the county.[12]

The *Waukegan Gazette* described one of Robert's wagons in 1867. Robert had entered the lumber wagon he made for Ezra Yager in the 1867 Lake County Fair. According to the September 28, 1867, *Waukegan Gazette*, "The wheels were oak, varnished and striped with blue. The body was scarlet, covered with a heavy coat of English varnish, and on either side was the American shield emblazoned with gold leaf. Its cost was $125 and was a creditable specimen of wagon making. Mr. Dady also exhibited a round bowl body top buggy and a side spring or denary buggy."[13] The lumber wagon captured first place, and Robert was awarded a $4 prize.[14] Besides wagons, Robert usually entered livestock in the fair as well.

James was the first to leave the partnership. Sometime in the 1860s, he started his own blacksmith shop in Gurnee. It was located on the west side of the Des Plaines River on the northwest corner of Route 132 and Route 21. James practiced the blacksmith trade in Gurnee until 1920. He was known to be an extremely friendly person, on good terms with everyone in town. His shop was the hangout for many of the local youngsters who liked to watch him work. James married Margaret Welch of Millburn on November 21, 1865. They were the parents of four sons—Ralph, Robert, Eugene, and Charles. Margaret died on February 3, 1921,[15] and James died on April 7, 1924.[16]

The book *Historical Highlights of the Waukegan Area* by Osling wrote that James's son Ralph became a Lake County state's attorney and circuit court judge. Although he grew up in Gurnee, Ralph attended Waukegan High School. Warren High School did not exist at the time. After high school, he went to the Chicago-Kent College of Law, graduating in 1904.[17]

Over the years, Ralph prosecuted a number of big cases. The Orpet murder case in Lake Forest made national headlines. Ralph also prosecuted Illinois governor Len Small in 1923. Another time, he was pitted against the famous Clarence Darrow in a Chicago school board case.[18]

Robert's brother JR bought him out of the carriage shop in 1864.[19] The book *Portrait and Biographical Album of Lake County, Illinois* claimed JR bought out Robert in 1870.[20] Whichever year it was, JR became the sole owner of the Dady Carriage Shop and operated it until the year 1909. There is no information as to when Eugene Dady left the carriage shop and moved to South Dakota. Under JR's control, the business grew even larger. The March 14, 1874, *Waukegan Gazette* reported, "He employs eight hands and does everything pertaining to the trade. His business for the year 1873 may be summed up as follows: 35 lumber wagons; 75 light buggies, skeletons and sulkies; 25 cutters; 15 pair bob-sleds, which, together with his repairing brings his total receipts up to the handsome figure of $16,000."[21] The January 14, 1909, *Waukegan Daily Sun* wrote, "Mr. Dady had a two story blacksmith and wagon making shop at 114 South Genesee Street, a three story brick building used for harness making, and painting shops, for the storage of finished vehicles and supplies and for offices, numerous other buildings attached to the plant."[22] The plant ran from 114 to 118 South Genesee Street and was the largest blacksmith shop in town.

JR was known about town as a real straight shooter. He took pride in being a self- made man and a fair, reputable businessman. Like Robert, JR invested in much Waukegan real estate. He also served on the school board for fourteen years and was an alderman on the city council for a time. His funeral in 1909 was one of the largest in Waukegan history. Over two hundred carriages and buggies took part in the procession.[23]

After selling his interest in the carriage shop, Robert switched occupations and became a farmer. He started buying land west of Waukegan around Belvidere (Route 120) and Green Bay roads. He owned 390 acres by 1880.[24] Robert added more acreage to the farm on Belvidere Road when possible. By 1882, he owned 1,200 acres.[25] Later, he bought other farms in and around Waukegan. Robert occasionally sold some farms but usually liked to hold on to them. Robert also bought quite a few lots mainly on the south side of Waukegan.[26]

The *Waukegan Gazette* rarely mentioned anything about Robert during the early 1870s. When they do, it is usually about some accident. In 1873, his team of horses spooked and ran from the Dady Carriage Shop straight at the Robert Douglas home. Douglas's front gate stopped the horses, but the gates were completely destroyed. In describing the accident, the *Daily Sun* was surprised that Robert and his team were not seriously hurt.[27] Robert survived a number of accidents during his lifetime. In 1878, he sustained a serious head wound when a binding pole from a hay wagon broke loose and hit him in the head. I'm not sure what a binding pole is, but it nearly killed him.[28] Robert's wagon overturned on him in 1905. He was trapped underneath and saved by a stranger. Robert had broken his collarbone and suffered a shoulder injury but still managed to drive his four-horse team home, accompanied by the stranger who had saved him.[29] Robert was kicked by a horse in 1910 and laid up for weeks before going to a hospital in Milwaukee for medical care. His injuries were so bad weeks after the accident that he had to be carried to the train station.[30] Robert managed to get in an automobile accident in 1915. He had complained about automobiles for years but surprised everyone in 1913 when he bought one. Robert loved horses and stuck with them as long as possible but finally saw the writing on the wall. He bought a brand-new forty-horsepower Kissell automobile. His daughter Loretta did most of the driving and chauffeured him around town.[31] Robert finally learned to drive and was in the market for a new car by 1915. He took a new Scripps-Booth car from the Ford dealership for a test-drive and drove it right into a ditch. He claimed he had done it to avoid a collision. The front end sustained enough damage that the dealership had to send it away for repairs.[32]

Robert was content to operate his farm until the year 1877. He added a new aspect to his farm that year, one that would make him possibly the most well-known man in the county. He became a horse trader. I doubt if anyone even knows what a horse trader is nowadays. A horse trader buys and sells livestock and farm equipment. Robert would take horse trading to a whole new level in the county. The *Waukegan Gazette* announced in 1877

5

that a huge livestock and farm equipment auction sale would be held at the Robert Dady farm on February 16. A total of 90 to 100 cows, 2 bulls, 175 sheep, 6 sows, and 1 boar plus a team of oxen and farm equipment would all be auctioned off.[33] This was the first of many auctions to come. The *Gazette* usually described them as immense, mammoth, colossal, and so on. All through the late 1870s and 1880s, Robert went on trips to Wisconsin, Minnesota, and South Dakota, buying livestock. His trips usually averaged about two weeks in length, and he made three or four a year.

His auction in the fall of 1880 listed 2,500 sheep, 32 cows, 150 heifers and steers, 25 pigs, and 6 horses for sale.[34] Robert made two trips up north in the spring of 1882. He returned home from Wisconsin on March 4, 1882, with twelve train cars loaded with cattle.[35] A month later, he came back with eight more cars of stock.[36] Robert acquired 407 head of cattle in Wisconsin and Iowa for his auction in the fall of 1882.[37]

Robert was becoming well-known in other parts of the country as well. The April 15, 1882, *Waukegan Gazette* published a story written about Robert by the Sparta, Wisconsin, Chronicle in 1882.

### *"Stock Buying"*

> Mr. Dady, *the eccentric and enterprising stock buyer, who introduced himself to the farmers in this vicinity during the winter, has again been heard from. Farmers are beginning to look for him as eagerly as children are represented to cry for "Winslow's soothing syrup." His eruptions thus far have invariably been followed by seasons of prosperity among farmers, and hence the desire for his reappearance. The gentleman seems to be a traveling bank, possessing unlimited cash and distributing it with a free hand. Yesterday six car loads of stock were shipped from the Milwaukee stock yards, 109 head of cattle coming from Cole's Valley alone. This makes the third trip of Mr. Dady to these parts, during which time he has diminished the sum total of our stock by twenty-seven car loads, shipping nine the first trip, ten the second and eight the third. His operations are not confined to cattle, but he now has in town a team and a mare purchased of Col. May. Possessing*

*a farm of 1,200 acres at Waukegan, he ships his stock to the latter place and disposes of it by auction sale.*[38]

Robert conducted auctions through most of the 1880s. Then he switched directions again and started keeping most of the livestock for himself. Robert had always kept some of the livestock he had bought up north. In 1882, he had over 600 head of cattle on his farm as well as large numbers of sheep.[39] He still engaged in horse trading until the early 1900s but on a much smaller scale and dealing mainly in horses. By the 1890s, Robert had converted his farm on Belvidere Road into one giant sheep farm. He claimed sheep were the most profitable of livestock and went into the business in a big way. Robert did not completely stop fattening cattle but kept them on his other farms in Waukegan located on the north side of town. In 1902, he drove 250 head of cattle from one of his farms through the streets of Waukegan to another farm. The whole procession was four city blocks long, and the November 29, 1902, *Waukegan Daily Sun* wrote, "It was a sight to see."[40]

The Lake County independent newspaper reported in 1897 that Robert bought enough sheep in Montana to fill thirty-three double-decker cars and had just shipped them home to his farm in Waukegan.[41] The December 14, 1897, *Waukegan Daily Sun* described unloading the cars and driving the large flock to the farm. Then the *Daily Sun* mentioned that Robert was the owner of 16,000 head of sheep, more than all the other farmers in the county combined.[42] Robert's obituary in 1919 stated that on one of his trips to Wisconsin, he bought 10,000 sheep and brought them home to fatten. The amount of money he made from this one transaction would have made the average man very wealthy. By this time, the whole state had found out about Robert's large sheep farm and was interested in his operation.[43] Robert announced at the end of 1897 that he was retiring from the sheep business. According to the December 27, 1897, *Waukegan Daily Sun*, "Mr. Dady says he will lay aside the crook of the shepherd, hand up his broad brimmed hat in the garret and not object if his neighbors refer to him as a capitalist."[44] He had been raising sheep for twenty-five years and was spending $100 a day to feed 10,000 head of sheep on his farm. Robert claimed he was not getting out of the business because of the cost of feed since he would get more money the heavier the sheep were. He also advised anyone thinking of fattening sheep on the same scale as he did to be very careful. Only those with a lot of experience raising sheep should try.[45] He gave this advice because so many people in the state were planning to copy his operation.

Most likely, Robert was quitting the sheep business because his health was getting the best of him. His rheumatism bothered him so much in 1905 that he started going to Florida every winter.[46] Robert started to cut back on farming by at least 1903; that year, he rented out three of his farms.[47] He decided to quit farming altogether by 1910. It looks like he had already rented out his farm on Belvidere Road and was living at one of his farms on North Sheridan Road. Robert also auctioned off most of his horses in 1910.[48]

According to the 1911 *Waukegan Daily Sun*, Robert owned more land than anyone else in the county. He owned a total of 1,300 acres of farmland, most but not all in Waukegan Township. He also owned land in Deerfield, Shields, and Vernon Townships. Robert owned anywhere from twenty-five to thirty lots, most on the south side of Waukegan.[49] This is just what he owned in Lake County. He also owned lots in Cook County, Illinois, 500 acres in Wisconsin, and 1,760 acres in Kansas.[50]

Robert retired from farming but not from work. In the late 1890s, he started paying more attention to his lots on the south side and his buildings in Downtown Waukegan. Sometime in the late 1890s, he bought the City Hotel. According to *Historical Highlights of the Waukegan Area* by Osling, the hotel was located on County Street, next to Immaculate Conception Catholic Church, and was one of the oldest and most historic hotels in town. Built in 1845, the hotel catered to the upper classes when first built. In the early days, there were seldom any vacancies, and it was just about impossible to find a place to park your buggy in its lot. Their Sunday dinners cost 50¢ and always brought in a large crowd.[51] By the 1890s, the hotel had fallen on hard times. It was closed for a time, reopened, and then almost closed again before Robert bought it. The previous owner was suffering from low occupancy rates and had resorted to drastic measures to keep the hotel going. The new city jail just happened to be under construction, and there was not enough space to hold all of Waukegan's tramps. The hotel and police department came to an agreement. The police would now take all their tramps to the City Hotel instead. In return, Mrs. Wiggins, who ran the hotel, was paid 25¢ per night for every tramp. Unfortunately, the appearance of the tramps scared away most of the regular customers still living there.[52] Robert began remodeling the hotel in March 1901. He sunk

The Forgotten History of Lake County, Illinois

$3,000 into the place and managed to increase its value and then leased it to a Mr. Schimmerhorn.[53] The hotel later became a source of friction between Robert and his son-in-law. I'll write more about that later.

Robert's most ambitious building project never got off the ground. In 1900, he planned to build a three-story combination apartment/store with an opera house located in the back of the building.[54] The first floor would contain four stores while the two upper floors would be apartments.[55] The proposed site was located at Water and Genesee streets, and Robert's architects were already drawing up the plans by January 1901. The city needed an opera house, and it looked like the project would be a slam dunk.[56]

One small problem held up the project. The sidewalk grade was not up to code. Robert petitioned the city council to change it, but the council refused. Robert, in turn, said he would not build on it until it was changed.[57] Despite the grade problem, Robert still planned to build. The *Daily Sun* reported throughout the year that Robert would soon start construction, but nothing ever happened. Something always seemed to interfere. Robert's son, Frank, surprised everyone by getting married in 1901.[58] The same year saw the renewal of the Dady-Condit trial, one of the longest trials in the county's history.[59]

The project dragged on for years. Robert had the go-ahead to build in 1904 but did not start because the price of building materials was too high.[60] Robert told the *Daily Sun* that he would start building in the spring of 1905. The plans had been changed a little, apartments on the first two floors and business rental apartments on the third floor, opera house still in the back. Robert had supposedly placed an order for four or five million bricks from the Zion brickyards. The cost to construct the building was estimated to be $65,000 but could easily run to $75,000.[61] For whatever reason, construction never started. The site was still empty in 1907. The federal government considered building on the site, but that didn't work out either.[62] Robert's daughter Nellie Conrad finally managed to erect a building on the site in 1920.

The year 1903 saw Robert's next building venture. He began constructing houses on the twenty-five to thirty vacant lots he owned on the south side of Waukegan, but he soon ran into problems. He awarded a contract to the Charles Goodrich Company to build twelve houses for him. Goodrich used nonunion carpenters and bricklayers. Most of the bricklayers just happened to be from Zion. Robert seems to have done quite a bit of business in Zion. Soon, a union representative showed up to confront Goodrich about joining the union. Goodrich told him where to go and said he would hire whoever he wanted.[63] His response didn't go over well with the union rep. That night, all the masonry work done on three houses was torn down. None of the carpentry work was touched, however. The incident set Robert back $600. The episode only provoked Robert, who went out and hired armed guards to patrol the building sites.[64]

Two weeks later, four union representatives showed up at the job. Goodrich confronted them with a shotgun and demanded they leave, or else he would shoot them.[65] The union reps didn't stay around long enough to find out if he meant business and left in a hurry.

Two more weeks passed, and the situation was still tense. Waukegan's city council met to find a solution. They planned to arrange a meeting among Robert, Goodrich, and the labor union. It was hoped they could talk Robert into sending the nonunion Zionites home.[66] The meeting was soon arranged, but Robert and Goodrich didn't show up. Robert later claimed he hadn't been told about it until it was too late to attend. He also said he was happy with the work being done and was not making any changes. Robert was also disappointed with the city council. He had asked the council to appoint a certain policeman he trusted to patrol the building site, but they refused, even though Robert told them he would pay his salary.[67] It looks like Robert never did give in to the unions. When he died in 1919, he owned twenty to thirty houses on the south side.

## People Problems

Robert had more than his share of trouble with people over the years. He was in and out of court most of his life and involved in the county's longest court case. Robert must have rubbed some people the wrong way, for he managed to get punched out or sued many times over during his lifetime. Here are some records of Robert's court appearances:

The 1870 circuit court records show James Grimes suing Robert Dady, Joseph Tonigan, and Patrick A. Brown.[68]

In 1877, it was James Grimes vs. Robert Dady, Joseph Tonigan, and Patrick A. Brown again.[69]

Also in 1877 was Kratz vs. Dady. The case was dismissed.[70]

In 1882, it was Dady vs. McCann in chancery court.[71]

In 1885, it was J. B. Gordon vs. Robert Dady in chancery court.[72]

There were two cases in 1898: John B. Arno vs. Robert Dady[73] and Riley vs. Dady.[74]

In 1899, it was Kelly vs. Dady. In this case, Robert had foreclosed on the Kelly farm. A combination of hard feelings by the Kellys and bad timing by Robert put him in the wrong place at the wrong time. Robert had driven in to his brother's carriage shop from his farm. As soon as Robert got out of his buggy, John Kelly confronted him. Robert told him to go away, but Kelly was in no mood to listen. Kelly swung at Robert's head and connected, sending Robert sprawling to the ground at the doorway of the carriage shop. Robert was pushing sixty years old while Kelly was much younger and stronger. William A. Melody was nearby and came to Robert's aid. Kelly swung at Melody, but Melody beat him to the punch. Kelly's brother then joined the battle. About the same time, Officer Tyrrell heard the commotion and was soon on the scene.[75] Kelly was arrested and fined $10 plus court costs, which came out to $22.15.[76] Robert had taken a hard blow to the head and was laid out for a while.

Robert foreclosed on George S. Hill in 1914. Hill was able to control his temper, and Robert escaped without a scratch.[77]

W. A. Melody, who came to Robert's rescue, was a longtime friend of his. According to *Historical Highlights of the Waukegan Area* by Osling, W. A. Melody was born on April 8, 1843, in Chicago. Soon afterward, his family moved to a farm near Libertyville. They moved to Waukegan in 1846. William went to school in Waukegan until he was sixteen years of age. After leaving school, William learned the tinner's trade, working first in Waukegan and then a number of years in Chicago. He returned to Waukegan in 1870 and established a hardware store. The store was very successful, and William, like Robert, was able to invest in extensive real estate holdings in Waukegan.[78] Robert was a sponsor for William's son Francis when he was baptized in 1880.[79]

Another incident occurred in 1901. A man claimed that Robert owed him $1,000. Robert had bought some land from the man in 1886, so maybe this was the source of the problem.[80] The April 4, 1901, *Waukegan Daily Sun* claimed that the man showed up at Robert's door and demanded that Robert give him his money, or he would "blow his brains out."[81] Robert told him to leave and warned him not to come back, or else he would "blow *his* brains out instead."[82] The man later claimed that some of his friends had put him up to the stunt. He was arrested, and a bond of $300 was set.

This man had once been a wealthy businessman in Waukegan. He made a fortune on the board of trade but lost it all on the same board of trade. He was broke ever since and seemed to have lost his mind. He was married for a time, but his wife divorced him and left town with his son. The man was highly educated for his time, well read and well known around town, but dressed like a bum after losing his fortune. He lived like a hermit in the back of one of Robert's farms in a dugout he had built. Robert let him live on his property and permitted him to grow vegetables to support himself. Upon conclusion of the case for threatening Robert, the man went to Decatur to live with his son. He came back to Lake County in 1910, claiming to be sick, and petitioned Supervisor Ed Conrad to be admitted to the poor farm in Libertyville and died a few days after being admitted.[83]

A peculiar incident occurred in 1904. Robert was hauling two-and-one-half tons of hay from Winthrop Harbor to Waukegan. Just south of Winthrop Harbor, a wheel fell off the wagon, and it tipped over, blocking the street. Robert unhitched his team, left the wagon right where it broke down, and went home, intending to come back the next morning for the hay. After Robert had left, someone drove their car right into the pile of hay. The upset driver went to the nearest farmhouse, demanding to know whose pile of hay it was. The farmer said it was Robert Dady's. The next thing the farmer saw was the motorist driving away, laughing to himself, the pile of hay on fire. The next day, all Robert found was the iron trappings of the wagon.[84]

This was not the first time something like this had happened. In 1880, someone set fire to a vacant house on one of Robert's farms.[85] The following year, a barn on the same property was set on fire, destroying between twenty to thirty tons of hay. It was thought that someone with a grudge had set both fires.[86]

A great commotion took place in 1911 near Robert's farm on Belvidere Road. A mock battle was held on the west side of Waukegan by soldiers from Fort Sheridan. No one bothered to notify the nearby farmers about it. All at once, two opposing armies overran the neighborhood, shooting at each other. The army was only conducting maneuvers and using blanks, but no one knew. The police were flooded with calls from frightened citizens. When the battle ended, the troops formed up on Robert's farm and then left.[87]

## Working for Robert

County farmers always had trouble finding hired help. If Robert's idea of a normal workday was practiced by other farmers, it's not hard to see why. In 1908, one of Robert's employees named George Tucker sued Robert for $5.30 in back wages. Tucker had come up from Tennessee to work for Robert. Tucker had been working for only seven days when they got into an argument. Robert jumped all over Tucker for not getting up until five thirty in the morning. The usual starting time was four thirty. Tucker maintained that he always got up at four o'clock and worked until nine o'clock. That's only a seventeen-hour workday—what's Tucker got to complain about? Tucker told Robert where to stick the job, whereas Robert refused to pay him.[88]

Robert might have had his faults, but he had a charitable side too. In 1902, Waukegan was in the running for an institute for homeless boys. Robert offered to donate the land if Waukegan was awarded the home.[89] He also let the city of Waukegan use his vacant lots for carnivals, circuses, and plays. Robert willed $4,000 to Immaculate Conception Church to help pay for the construction of a new church.[90]

## The Condit-Dady Court Case

The Condit-Dady court case started in 1891 and ended in 1904, the longest case in Lake County history up to that time. The episode started when Robert signed a contract to sell James Condit his 160-acre farm on Dugdale Avenue for $150/acre. Condit was supposed to pay $3,000 in 1891. The remaining sum was to be paid in four different payments, the last one in 1903. Soon after signing the contract in 1891, Waukegan experienced a land boom. Land prices went up dramatically. Robert soon realized he had sold the property too cheap and backed out of the contract. Condit then sued Robert for breach of contract. Condit claimed that he could have turned around and sold the property for $300/acre, doubling his money in a short time. Condit said he was suing not so much for breach of contract but for the money he would have made if Robert had lived up to his part of the bargain. The lawsuit started in 1891 but was in and out of court several times. The year 1898 marked a new chapter in the case.[91]

Both sides had the best attorneys money could buy, and the first trial was like a clash of titans. The audience was composed of a large number of local attorneys who were expecting to see a first-class trial. Many of the county's real estate agents showed up as well.[92] Robert was represented by Joseph Quarles, one of the best trial lawyers in Wisconsin. Quarles was known as a brilliant orator, and his law firm was the preeminent practice in Milwaukee. At the time of the trial, it was thought that Quarles would someday replace John L. Mitchell as state senator. Quarles did become a state senator shortly after the trial.

Quarles's brother Charles was also a lawyer. The *Daily Sun* published an interesting story about the Quarles brothers after the trial. Someone from Central Wisconsin needed a lawyer and contacted the Quarles Law Firm, looking for one. According to the December 22, 1898, *Waukegan Daily Sun*, the receptionist asked him, "Which one of the Quarles do you want?" The person said he didn't know, and the receptionist responded with "Do you want guff or law? If you want guff, we will send Joseph, but if you want law, we will send Charles."[93] Joseph Quarles's strategy in the Dady case was to try to prove that the property was not worth as much as Condit claimed.

Condit was represented by John O'Conner of Chicago. A verdict was reached on December 9, 1898. Robert lost, but the amount awarded Condit was small. The jury spent all night trying to decide on an amount, and a sum of $4,920 was found sufficient. Condit, however, was not satisfied with the settlement and made a motion for a new trial.[94] Local attorneys were shocked at the low settlement. One Waukegan lawyer complained that Lake County was the worst place in the state to get a jury to award large settlements.[95] On December 19, 1898, Condit's attorney petitioned the circuit court for a new trial and was successful.[96]

The second trial started on March 6, 1899. This time Robert used the Cooke and Upton Law Firm.[97] Joseph Quarles was a senator by this time.[98]

An amusing incident occurred during the second trial. The jury was thirsty, so the bailiff went out to get some water. Usually, lake water was provided to the jury, but this time the bailiff returned with some expensive bottled water. The bailiff walked among the jury, pouring water into their cups from the elaborate-looking bottles of water. The March 13, 1899, *Waukegan Daily Sun* wrote that the judge, not used to seeing such bottles in his court, thought the bailiff was serving alcohol to the jury and asked, "Is that water?" He waited until assured that the fluid was nothing else and then had one for himself.[99] The jury took seventeen hours to reach a verdict. Condit won again and was awarded $15,000, the largest amount ever awarded to anyone in Lake County. Some thought the amount should have been even higher.[100] Condit was satisfied with the settlement.

Robert, however, was not satisfied, and now it was his turn to appeal for a new trial. His request was denied. Next, he appealed to the appellate court but was also denied. Robert then went to the Supreme Court, who overturned the verdict and cleared the way for another trial.[101]

The third trial began in circuit court on December 9, 1901. Condit was represented by John L. Griffiths of Indianapolis and Hoyne, O'Connor and Hoyne of Chicago. Robert was represented by P. C. Haley of Chicago.[102] The *Daily Sun* remarked that it was now the most expensive case in the county's history. The trial was still closely watched by attorneys from around the county.[103] Robert lost again. After intense debate, the jury awarded Condit $16,000. Robert was outraged and told the December 13, 1901, *Waukegan Daily Sun*, "I will fight it as long as I have a dollar in the world. It is so unjust a verdict."[104]

A controversy arose three weeks after the verdict. One of the jurors committed suicide. A note was found in his pocket, which claimed that someone had attempted to bribe him during the trial. The juror wrote the suicide letter the day he killed himself. Here's part of the note published in the January 4, 1902, *Waukegan Daily Sun*:

> *Some stranger tried to bribe me on 12 December 1901, during the Dady trial and in a unguarded moment I took a cigar after I had refused to let him pay for my shave, this has broke my mind.*[105]

Doesn't seem like much of a reason to kill yourself over. Nothing more was ever written about the attempted bribe, so it doesn't look like anyone was very much worried about it.

Robert spurned the verdict and would not hand over any money. He appealed again in 1902, the case going to the appellate court. Judge Fuller considered the $16,000 verdict too high an amount and thought $8,000 a fairer amount. He told both parties he could sustain the verdict if both sides agreed to settle for $10,000. He also declared that this would be the last trial.[106]

Robert still would not give up. He appealed to the Supreme Court again in 1903.[107] The Supreme Court took the case and ruled that a sum of $8,000 should be awarded to Condit plus $1,000 court costs. Robert threatened to appeal to the highest court in the country but soon changed his mind and announced that he was done fighting the case. It was finally over. Robert still thought he was right and said if it was not for the fact that his rheumatism was bothering him, he might still fight on.[108]

Four days later, Robert sent his daughter Lorena to the courthouse with a check for $9,000. To everyone's surprise, Condit did not show up for the check. Lorena spent most of the day sitting around the courthouse, waiting for him.[109]

The case had almost bankrupted Condit. It was thought that most of the $8,000 settlement would go to pay for his lawyers. Robert stated that the whole thing had cost him $28,000. He had spent $19,000 in court costs and paid Condit $9,000.[110]

> John Heinrichs, Robert's real estate agent, also sued Robert
> over the property. He had sold the Dugdale farm to Condit
> in 1892, and Robert had failed to pay him his commission.
> A Chicago jury awarded Heinrichs $7,500 in 1899.[111]

## The Waukegan Baseball Grounds

In 1914, Robert leased some land on the south side of Waukegan to Thomas McCann. The land was actually owned by one of Robert's brothers, possibly Eugene. Robert took care of the field for him. The place was also used by the circus when it came to town. McCann organized and managed his own baseball team but needed a baseball park.

McCann leased the field for five years. He was to pay $75/year for the first two years and $100/year for the last three years. The first thing McCann did was to build a 1,600-foot-long fence around the field. Then he erected an 800-seat grandstand with 50-foot-high bleachers on each side. It was considered the best baseball field in the county.

McCann had a top-notch team, and the baseball park proved to be very popular. At the end of the first season, McCann's team played for the city and Lake County championship at the park against a team from the west side of Waukegan. The two teams played three games: best of three the winner. A total of three thousand people showed up to watch the first game. They cheered so loudly the whole city could hear them. The south siders won the first game, 2 to 1. The second game was supposed to have been a real raucous affair with the west siders winning 8 to 3. An overflow crowd attended the third game won by the south siders, 4 to 2. The book *Historical Highlights of the Waukegan Area* by Osling claimed that McCann hung a sign at the entrance to the field, saying, "Waukegan Baseball Grounds. Thos. H. McCann, manager, Champions of Lake County."[112] Osling noted that McCann's team played the Chicago Cubs in 1915, losing 9 to 3.[113]

The McCanns and Dadys had a good thing going. Unfortunately, it only lasted one year. The *Daily Sun* reported that Robert had revoked the lease. McCann offered to pay $250/year, but Robert refused. McCann claimed that Robert wanted $300/year and ownership of the fence at the end of the second season. McCann had paid $600 for the fence the previous year. McCann was understandably upset and began taking down the fence, grandstand, and bleachers.[114]

Robert told his side of the story three days later. According to him, the fence was supposed to become Dady property after the five-year lease was over. He further stated that McCann was told to build the grandstands in the northeast corner of the field, but McCann had built the grandstands in the wrong location. As a result, the circus was not able to use the field and looked elsewhere for a place to set up. Robert also said that McCann kept trying to write to his brother when he had been told to deal directly with him. The final straw was when the Dadys found out that McCann was digging up part of the field to build a skating pond. They ordered him to stop digging immediately. Despite everything, Robert said he was still willing to lease the field for $300/year.[115]

McCann might have been the godson of Robert's wife, Mary. Aunt Mary was a sponsor at the baptism of Thomas McCann on May 8, 1859.[116] I am not sure if it was the same Thomas McCann.


## Getting Old

Robert was really losing it by 1914. He was living on North Sheridan Road in the wealthiest part of town, but his property was an eyesore. His neighbors must have had an opinion of him similar to what Lake Forest's residents thought of Mr. T (of *The A-Team* fame). Mr. T cut down all his trees on his Lake Forest property in 1987. Robert had been collecting manure in Waukegan and stockpiling it at his home on Sheridan Road, planning to use it for fertilizer on his farms. It should be remembered that Robert was one of the richest men in the county at the time, worth $2 million.

Robert went over the line when he built a monster pile of manure next door to John Sutherland's house. Sutherland was fit to be tied as was everyone else in the neighborhood. The smell was nauseating, and complaints to the board of health fell on deaf ears. The neighbors went to the police next, and Robert was given a notice to clean up the mess within twelve hours or be charged with maintaining a nuisance.[117]

An unexpected tragedy befell Robert in 1914—his wife, Mary, died. I mentioned earlier that she was my great-grandfather's sister. Not much is written about Aunt Mary. The only information I have about her is what's written about her in her obituary. The December 14, 1914, *Waukegan Daily Sun* wrote that "she was very unassuming and quite a home-woman, having helped greatly in her husband's career which has been marked by acquisition of extensive farm property in Lake County."[118] She had been sick for about six weeks with what seemed to be a minor case of pneumonia. No one had thought it was serious, and her death shocked everyone. I wish I could write more about her, but this is all I've been able to find out.

Robert was back at it again in 1915. He left two big wagonloads of manure right next to John Sutherland's house. Next, a northwest wind blew the stench right into neighborhood homes. The smell was so overpowering that the whole neighborhood was in an uproar. The chief of police showed up with the entire force, expecting a riot. Dr. Foley, superintendent of the Department of Health, was called. Even the *Daily Sun* newspaper sent a reporter over to see what all the commotion was about. The police ordered Robert to remove the wagons, and he agreed to move them in the morning.

It was not only the manure wagons that riled the neighbors. Robert's yard was full of assorted piles of lumber, bricks, and miscellaneous debris.[119] The piles butted up to within inches of John Sutherland's house. Robert must have really hated his neighbors, Sutherland in particular. Sutherland might have been hard to get along with too. One time, Sutherland refused to pay two real estate agents their commission for selling some land for him. They came over to collect their fee, but Sutherland kicked them out of his yard instead. It turns out that they had sold the land to Robert Dady.[120] The police claimed they had no authority to make Robert clean up his yard but pleaded with him to at least tidy the place up to the standards set by the rest of the neighborhood.[121]

A bizarre accident occurred in 1915, which sent Robert into court the following year on April 5, 1916. A woman alleged that Robert purposely ran her over with his buggy and was suing him for $20,000.

The whole incident started when the woman agreed to pay Robert $4/month to pasture her cow in one of Robert's pastures. Robert rented out the use of his pastures to a number of people. She only used the pasture for a few days and then stopped. There was an epidemic of hoof-and-mouth disease at the time, and she decided to keep her cow closer to home. At the end of the first month, Robert drove over to the woman's house to collect the pasture fee. Robert thought he was owed the full amount, but she thought she should only pay for a few days of grazing time.

Robert never left his buggy as he and the woman went back and forth over the amount. On the first day of the trial, she claimed that Robert had lost his temper and had shoved her to the ground so hard that she rolled underneath the wheels of his buggy. Then he whipped his horses and ran over her. She had to be helped into her home and was unable to work for six weeks. She suffered two broken ribs plus a number of bruises. According to the woman, Robert left the scene, not bothering to see if she was hurt or not.

Robert said he was driving a young, inexperienced team that day. He claimed that she had fallen on her own and spooked the horses, causing them to run. According to Robert, it was all a freak accident.[122]

On the second day of the trial, the woman testified that the incident had left her bedridden for six or seven weeks. Her daughter had witnessed the whole incident and verified the story. The woman also changed her story some, claiming that Robert had thrust the bill so hard in her face that she fell down and rolled under his buggy.[123]

On the third day of the trial, Robert's attorney disputed the woman's story. He produced witnesses who had seen the woman in her yard two weeks after the incident. Someone also had seen her walking to town at about the same time. Robert took the stand on the third day of the trial and got so upset that he stopped answering any more questions.[124]

The trial ended on April 10, 1916. The jury believed it was an accident but awarded the woman $500 to pay for her doctor and attorney's fees.[125] It looks to me that the woman exaggerated her injuries and was looking to win the lottery at Robert's expense.

Robert managed to anger his neighbors again in 1917, if he had ever stopped angering them at all. He was no longer stockpiling manure, but now there were other complaints. The neighbors' complaint, published in the May 29, 1917, *Waukegan Daily Sun*, wrote that Robert's place looked "like a pigpen."[126] Robert's yard was full of piles of lumber, and hundreds of rats called it home. Robert was periodically served notices to clean up his yard. He had actually been abiding by the notices, but his yard always reverted to its old form after a short time. He made the mistake of ignoring his most recent notice, and the police came to arrest him. Robert, however, wasn't backing down and soon became very argumentative and disrespectful to Officer Tyrrell. He told Tyrrell that he did not have any time for his BS. The May 29, 1917, *Waukegan Daily Sun* reported Officer Tyrrell's response: "He's a—old nuisance and a bluffer, and it is high time that we found out whether Bob Dady or Waukegan is in the right in this matter. The people tell me I am afraid of Bob Dady and his money and that for this reason I hesitate to have him arrested."[127]

Robert was sitting in his wagon the whole time the exchange occurred and refused to get down. He couldn't get down anyway because he had forgotten to bring his stepladder, which he needed to get down. The police were afraid to pick him up and take him off the wagon because of his age, so they decided to bring the police magistrate there instead. Bond was set at $200, which Robert scoffed at, even though he did not have even $1 on him. His friend William Melody had to bail him out.[128]

Toward the end of his life, Robert had to use a cane or crutch to walk.[129] He had had severe bouts of rheumatoid arthritis for almost half of his life. The local newspapers frequently noted the fact.[130] He was in and out of Sacred Heart Hospital in Milwaukee a number of times for various illnesses. In 1918, Robert spent a few weeks at Sacred Heart Hospital. Upon returning home, he got an unstoppable case of hiccups. Everything was done to stop the hiccups, but nothing would work. It was feared that Robert would soon die. His brother Eugene came back from South Dakota, expecting the worse. Brother James frequently came out from Gurnee to visit. Even his son, Frank, came to see him. (Robert and Frank had been estranged for a number of years.)[131] Robert, however, recovered and lived another eight months. He was never able to live a normal life, though, as he was sick most of that time. Robert died on June 9, 1919, at the age of seventy-eight.[132]

## Family Issues

Robert seems to have had as many problems with some of his own children as he did with everyone else. Lorena (Rena) was the only one who managed to stay on his good side, becoming his right-hand man, or woman, if you prefer. Not so with Nellie and Frank. Robert disowned Frank, and they had nothing to do with each other for years. Nellie's relationship with Robert seems to have been on and off.

Both Rena and Nellie seem to have had Robert's disposition, Nellie more so. Frank seems to have taken after the Wlodeski side. Rena assisted Robert in his business affairs and ran everything when Robert was unable to. She could read and write so became invaluable to Robert. Rena was always the one who took care of her mother and father when they could not take care of themselves. According to the March 29, 1919, *Waukegan Daily Sun*, Rena was "one of the most robust women in the county; large of frame, of sturdy physique and unusual physical strength."[133] It also looks like she conducted business as aggressively as Robert. Once she wrote a letter to the *Daily Sun* and asked them to print it. The editor remarked in the September 30, 1913, *Waukegan Daily Sun*, "It was too libelous, defamatory and malicious to permit its publication."[134]

Robert left almost everything to Rena. He thought she needed it more than Nellie or Frank; both were already wealthy. Robert, however, outlived Rena. She had to will it all back to Robert on her deathbed.[135] Robert never changed his will. Frank and Nellie got everything because they were the closest relatives, and each one inherited a million dollars.[136]

Rena died on March 29, 1919, about two and a half months before Robert. She was fifty years old, and the cause of death was blood poisoning. The end came about because of an infected tooth. She had waited too long to see a doctor, and a rare type of blood poisoning set in. She spent three weeks in critical condition at McAllister Hospital in Waukegan before she died. They sent for the best doctors from Chicago to save her, but by then, it was too late.[137] Rena's death really hurt Robert and Nellie. Robert was bedridden at the time, and the loss really tore him up. Nellie had been sick herself for two years and was still grieving over the death of her husband, who had died four months earlier.

## Frank Dady

Frank was born on September 11, 1867, at the farm on Belvidere Road. There is not a lot written about Frank. He had had a falling-out with Robert and left town for almost fifteen years. Frank seems absolutely tame compared with Robert, Rena, and Nellie. There are no records of any fights, arrests, or lawsuits except when his own sister Nellie sued him. I remember hearing his name mentioned on occasion at family get-togethers when I was young.

A foreclosure caused all the trouble between Robert and Frank. Frank was operating his own bakery in one of Robert's buildings on South Genesee Street when Robert foreclosed on it.[138] Frank was so upset he left town, going to Milwaukee, where he eventually started a roofing business.[139] Frank and Robert had nothing to do with each other for years, and Frank didn't return to Waukegan for a long time.[140] Robert disowned Frank during this time, cutting him out of his will.[141] Frank, meanwhile, started his own roofing business and became a millionaire on his own.[142] Frank did see Robert when he was sick and dying, so they must have buried the hatchet at the end.

Frank was a real hands-on businessman and was always more comfortable around blue-collar workers as opposed to the upper classes. He prided himself on working alongside his workers rather than sitting in an office. He believed in hard work and took a great amount of pride in the fact that he earned every penny he had.

Although Frank had been cut out of Robert's will, he inherited half of Robert's wealth anyway because he was the nearest relative, Nellie being the other. After receiving his portion of the inheritance, he told the *Daily Sun* that despite all his wealth, he would continue to live the way he always had. He planned a trip to California but only because his wife had always wanted to go there.[143]

Despite Frank's wishes, the inheritance did change his life. Taking care of his new properties took more time than he thought it would, and he had to move back to Waukegan. Frank was married twice, but no children were born from either marriage. He died of complications from a stroke on May 22, 1929.[144]

## Nellie Dady-Conrad

Nellie was born on Robert's farm on July 5, 1861. Robert had no education himself, but he made sure Nellie did. She was educated first at Immaculate Conception grade school in Waukegan and then at a private school for girls in Chicago. Your author attended Immaculate Conception for six years. Nellie was also an accomplished musician and artist.

Nellie was probably Waukegan's greatest businesswoman. Besides owning much real estate in Waukegan, she built the Valencia Ballroom, the Roller Rink, and developed at least two subdivisions.[145] Those readers who remember the Times Theater will be interested to know that it was at one time the Valencia Ballroom. My grandfather used to play the organ at Nellie's Roller Rink, which was located at the corner of Jackson and Belvidere streets. Nellie inherited one-half of Robert's estate, a total of $1 million.

Nellie seems to be as hard to get along with as Robert. She was also in and out of court her whole life. Nellie even let her vacant lots become overgrown with weeds just like her father did.[146] She was either suing someone or being sued herself for not paying bills. Even the Archbishop of Chicago once sued her. Another time, she sued her own brother, Frank.

Nellie married John Conrad on July 11, 1894.[147] John was a self-made man. He started his working life as a clerk for the W. H. Werden produce house in Waukegan. Later, John and his brother Albert established a grocery store in town. Next, he bought a seat on the Chicago Board of Trade.[148] John also founded the Central Garage in Waukegan.

The Central Garage was situated on South Genesee Street and did a very successful business. They sold Chevrolet and Mitchell automobiles in addition to repairing and storing cars.[149] The garage had the capacity to store one hundred cars. John went out and hired one of the best mechanics in the state to service cars.[150]

Robert Dady and John Conrad were business partners for a time. I mentioned earlier that Robert bought the old City Hotel in the late 1890s. At some point, the name was changed to the Arlington Hotel. Conrad became half owner when he married Nellie in 1894. Robert sold him one-half interest in the hotel for $4,000.[151] It was worth $50,000 by 1917. The partnership had not gone smoothly, and Robert filed a lawsuit against Conrad in 1917. John collected the hotel profits, but Robert said he had not received his share since 1909. In addition, Robert had to pay all the taxes and insurance; Conrad paid nothing.[152] I found some of the hotel records in Nellie Conrad's personal papers at the Waukegan Historical Society. It appears to me that John was paying his bills at first. In 1905, John paid his share of the monthly tax payment of $42.50.[153] It also looks like John was paying his share of the taxes in 1909. He paid Robert for half of the taxes, which amounted to $152.97.[154]

Robert had had enough of the partnership by 1917 and petitioned the circuit court for a partition of interests. His suit named, besides John Conrad, C. O. Ames, D. L. Shales, L. O. May, and Millie Milhizer.[155] The hotel was put up for sale. The sale was held on August 22, 1917, with only two bidders showing up, Robert and John Conrad. Conrad started off the bidding with a bid of $25,000. The bidding went back and forth until Conrad offered $31,000. The auctioneer turned to Robert and told him he might want to have another drink of water before making another bid. Robert took his advice and, after another drink of water, bid $31,100. Conrad threw in the towel, and the hotel was sold to Robert. Robert paid Conrad $15,555 for his half and was now sole owner.[156]

You would think that Robert and Nellie's relationship would have been strained after all the problems with the hotel, but it doesn't seem to be the case. John and Nellie started building a new house right next door to Robert's home on North Sheridan Road the same year. Before the house was completed, John took a nasty fall, breaking his leg at the ankle. He was laid up for three months while the leg healed. Soon after his leg mended, he was found to have pernicious anemia. John spent the next seven months either in the hospital or at home, recovering from blood transfusions. He had twelve in all, the blood all donated by his friends and relatives. Finally, Dr. A. J. Ochsner, considered one of the best surgeons in the world, was brought in. Dr. Ochsner did his best, and for a short time, it looked like John might recover. John did not recover, however, and died two days later on December 1, 1918. Nellie was sick herself at the time and took it hard. She never remarried.[157]

Nellie displayed some of her father's stubbornness in 1911. A tailor had rented an apartment at Robert's building on South Genesee Street. He skipped out before paying the rent and owed her dad $9. The man had left all his furniture behind, having bought it all on credit. The furniture dealer sent a policeman named Hicks with papers to seize all the furniture. The furniture dealer was none other than Meyer Kubelsky, comedian Jack Benny's father.

Hicks started to remove the furniture when Nellie came on the scene and stopped him from taking it. She told Hicks that because the man had not paid his rent, the furniture belonged to her father. Then she barred the doorway, defying the officer to act. Nellie and Officer Hicks went back and forth at each other for hours. Nellie would rage at Officer Hicks, who would just laugh at her. Then the argument would reverse itself, and Officer Hicks would be in a rage with Nellie laughing at him. According to the February 11, 1911, *Waukegan Daily Sun*, at one point, Nellie shouted out, "Strike me or take the stuff out if you dare."[158] Incredibly, she managed to halt the proceedings for three hours.

By this time, the building's residents were all on the scene and making no effort to conceal their laughter over the whole episode. Finally, Nellie agreed to let the chief of police decide the matter. The chief came down on Meyer Kubelsky's side. Nellie gave up and let Hicks take the furniture.[159]

Nellie was in trouble with the law about a month after Rena died in 1919. She was trying to terminate the lease of a tenant in her father's building on South Genesee Street. The tenant operated a store in the building. Nellie showed up, demanding to see canceled rent checks. The tenant showed her the checks, but she wanted to see some older checks. The tenant had to leave for some reason, and after he was gone, Nellie started an argument with the tenant's wife. Then Nellie went behind the counter and opened the cash register, looking for older canceled checks. The wife and one of her male employees tried to stop her, but Nellie attacked both of them and got into a hair-pulling contest with the wife. Then Nellie swore she'd kill her husband.[160] The police were called, and three warrants were sworn out against Nellie.[161] I know Nellie sounds like she was crazy, but remember, her husband and sister had recently died, and her father was close to death. In addition, she had been sick for two years herself. Nellie was fined $50 and court costs for attacking the tenant's wife and employee. She was also put under a $500 peace warrant. The tenant's wife then filed a civil suit against Nellie for $2,000.[162] The case was settled out of court and never went to trial. The aggrieved wife settled for a few hundred dollars.[163]

Nellie ran into someone with as bad a temper as herself in 1921. A couple of boys had been damaging the cellar doors at some of her houses. She thought the vandals were two boys who lived nearby. Nellie went to the boys' home and confronted their mother and accused her sons of the deed. The mother blew her top and attacked Nellie, pushing her off the porch.

Nellie went away with two missing teeth and covered with scrapes and bruises. The woman was charged with assault and battery and fined $15 and court costs. She claimed she had only given Nellie a light push. The November 15, 1921, *Waukegan Daily Sun* wrote that Nellie then uttered to the judge, "She pushed harder than the kick of forty mules."[164]

The Catholic Church sued Nellie in 1932. Robert Dady had willed $4,000 to his daughter Lorena. She was supposed to hold on to it until Immaculate Conception built a new church.[165] Since Lorena had died before Robert and Robert never changed his will, Nellie and Frank got the money instead. Nellie wouldn't part with the money and managed to keep it out of the church's hands for years, thirteen to be exact. Her nephew, Circuit Court Judge Ralph J. Dady, heard the case. Wouldn't that be a conflict of interest?[166]

In 1921, a year and a half after Robert's death, Nellie sued her brother, Frank. She charged him with breach of contract. She accused him of acting like the whole Robert Dady estate was his own. Furthermore, she stated that he was making the rounds to all her properties and collecting rent from the tenants.[167]

A Waukegan man named George Clark mentioned in his memoirs that he lived next door to Nellie when he was a kid and had some interesting things to say about her. George claimed that Nellie had a volatile temper and used to take it out on her chickens almost every week. Something would always set her off, and she would come running out of the house with a shotgun and shoot at her chickens. Nellie also kept half-a-dozen Doberman pinschers in her yard, who probably knew to run for their lives when Nellie was mad.[168]

## Nellie's Building Boom

One thing I have to say about Nellie, she didn't sit on her new fortune. Her first building project began in 1920. She planned to build a three-story building at the corner of Water and Genesee streets. This was the same site her father had tried to build on in 1900. Even the plans were similar, the first floor containing a store and the two upper floors business offices. The estimated cost was $65,000.[169] The residents of Waukegan were surprised at how fast the new building went up and how modern and beautiful it was. Waukegan considered itself lucky to have such a building.[170]

Her second project was building a subdivision on a forty-acre pasture at Belvidere and Jackson streets in September 1923,[171] on the site known as the "Dady Pasture."[172] The plans called for 135 lots. The *Daily Sun* claimed it was a beautiful piece of land, flat, with a ravine running through the middle.[173] A strange incident happened at the subdivision in 1924. A twenty-foot-high cross was set on fire. Hundreds of people and over fifty cars stopped to watch. Nellie was Catholic, but the KKK was never a suspect. The police thought it was not meant as a threat to Nellie but to a local bootlegger instead.[174]

Nellie decided to build another subdivision in 1923. Known as the circus grounds, the site had hosted circuses and carnivals for years. Located on South Sheridan Street, it had enough space for thirty lots.[175] She also made plans to build a public parking lot between County and Genesee streets. The lot had enough space for one hundred cars and was badly needed in town. Nellie also treated herself to a new Pierce Arrow car in 1923.[176] She did not drive it herself. A chauffeur had been driving her around since at least 1920.[177]

She built herself a new house on North Sheridan Road in 1924, a two-story house with eight rooms and a price tag of $15,000.[178] The house is still there; the address is 936 North Sheridan Road. It was included in the June 26, 2016, Tour of Homes by the Waukegan Historical Society. I toured Nellie's house and was very impressed with it. I recommend the tour.

Nellie tried to start construction on her theater, the future Valencia Ballroom, in 1924. The site was located at the corner of Water and Genesee streets. She was denied a permit by the city commission, however. The disagreement was over an alley. The city wanted to build a twelve-foot-wide public alley on the site of the ballroom. Nellie protested that there would not be enough room to build a ballroom there.[179] It was the last block in Downtown Waukegan without a public alley. She must have figured, "What's the use of taking on city hall?" and didn't even bother to even show up to the city council meeting.[180] The alley was built, but it turned out that Nellie still had enough room to build her ballroom on the site.

Nellie was also sued in 1924. She had never paid the architect who drew up the plans for the theater and owed him $3,500.[181] This reminds me of when her dad refused to pay the real estate agent who had sold the Dugdale farm to Condit.

Nellie took a break from building in 1925 but still managed to get her name in the newspaper. Both Nellie and her brother, Frank, had succeeded in not paying any taxes that year. They had so many write-offs that they did not owe the government anything.[182]

Nellie went back to work in 1926 and remodeled her building at 29 South Genesee Street. This is the same building her father owned when she argued with Officer Hicks over furniture. It was here that she attacked the former tenant's wife. The bottom floor was turned into a store and the two upper floors made into eight three-and four-bedroom apartments.[183]

Later in the year, Nellie applied for a permit to build her ballroom. She still planned to build it at the corner of Water and Genesee streets, the site next to the new alley. This time she succeeded, and construction started immediately.

Named the Valencia Ballroom, the estimated cost was $150,000. The building was 163.4 feet long by 74 feet wide. The round dance floor was 110 feet by 57 feet with enough room for 1,800 dancers. The entrance was two-and-a-half stories high and resembled a tower. Upon entering, there was a lounge and two shops and then the dance floor. The outside was modeled after a Spanish-style building, Spanish roof tiles included. In addition, there was a women's lounge and a men's smoking room. The *Libertyville Independent* newspaper stated that it should be one of the outstanding ballrooms in the Midwest.[184] The inside was designed to look like Chicago's Aragon Ballroom. The architect was William Dady, associate designer of the Aragon Ballroom.[185] I am not sure if William Dady was a relative or not.

A total of two thousand people showed up for the Valencia's grand opening on New Year's Eve, December 31, 1926. They came from all over the North Shore. The music was furnished by Heinie's ten-man orchestra. The lights were arranged so that Heinie could control them while on stage.[186]

Nellie had a stairway built between the ballroom and the Pantheon Ice Cream Parlor next store. She owned the ice cream parlor too.[187] Her right-hand man, Gus Gorgan, ran the store for her. More about Gus later.

In 1933, the Pantheon Ice Cream Parlor and Valencia Ballroom were merged together and remodeled into a bar/restaurant.[188] Known as Valencia Gardens, the restaurant had room for five hundred customers and two thousand dancers on the dance floor. Gus Gorgan ran the ballroom while L. N. George managed the restaurant.[189] After all the work and money that Nellie had poured into the Valencia Ballroom, it was only open for a little over seven years. She leased the building out in 1935, and it was turned into a movie theater.[190] The man who leased the theater declared bankruptcy in 1938 and stopped making lease payments.[191]

The Valencia's last dance on January 13, 1935, attracted so many people that there was no room to dance. The Orrin Tucker band provided the music. During its time as a dance hall, such bands as "Wayne King, Duke Ellington, Hal Kemp, Art Kassel, Clyde McCoy, Paul Whiteman, Jan Garber, Cab Calloway, Louis Panico, Dan Russo and others played there."[192] C. H. Penikoff bought the ballroom in 1937 and changed the name to the Times Theater.[193] Penikoff, however, was not able to make his mortgage payments, and Nellie got the Valencia back. Some of you readers might remember the Times Theater. The theater showed only "B" movies when your author was in high school. Nellie would have rolled over in her grave if she only knew. The building is gone now, and the site is a parking lot.

Nellie was sued by the Tobey Furniture Company of Chicago in 1929. She had bought $30,000 worth of furniture and other household goods for her new house but never paid for them.[194] Nellie wasn't going to let any lawsuits slow down her building projects, and it was still full speed ahead. Nellie had two more projects in the works, but I am not sure of the exact dates when she started them. She either purchased or built a gas station in the late 1920s. It was in operation at the corner of County and Water streets by 1930.[195]

Her other project was the Roller Rink located at the corner of Jackson and Belvidere streets. The estimated price tag to build it was $32,000. It was still in the planning stage in 1930.[196] The Roller Rink opened in 1931 and was a big hit in town. The four-foot-thick maple floor was two hundred feet long and ninety-two feet wide. The article says four-foot thick but must mean four-inch thick. Lighting for the floor came from three giant chandeliers. A dance there on Easter Sunday in 1932 brought in 1,806 people. Roller skating was done on Tuesday, Wednesday, and Friday nights. Thursdays, Saturdays, and Sundays were reserved for dancing. Dancing the waltz on roller skates took place on Wednesday. A total of twenty-one-mile-long races were held there once a week. Friday was ladies' night; women paid a smaller entry fee and got their skates for free.[197] When the rink first opened, a contest was held to find a name for the place. The May 26, 1930, *Waukegan News Sun* mentioned that Anita Cliff won $10 for submitting the name "Marathon."[198] Gus Gorgan managed the rink. I mentioned earlier that my grandfather used to play the organ at the Roller Rink. My dad and uncle used to go there too. They said Nellie took tickets at the door and was so cheap that despite my grandfather being her cousin, they still had to pay the full price to get in.

Nellie kept a business office in Downtown Waukegan until 1947. She still owned the Times Theater, the Roller Rink, and much real estate in Waukegan when she died at the age of eighty-eight on July 29, 1949.[199]

## Gus Gorgan

Gus Gorgan's real name was Constantine Peter Korakas. He was born in Greece on December 2, 1897,[200] and immigrated to America when he was about ten years old. He settled in Waukegan in 1919.[201] My uncle claimed that Gus was selling newspapers on Genesee Street when he first met Nellie. He was soon working for her and became her right-hand man. He moved into Nellie's house sometime in the 1920s. Later, he married Irene Canelakes. They were both shown to be living in Nellie's house on the 1940 census. On the census, Irene's occupation is listed as assistant manager to Gus. Also living with Nellie was a gardener named Charlie Gilan. Gus's marriage to Irene was the first Greek marriage in Lake County. They were the parents of one son, Patrick.[202] Gus continued to manage the Times Theater until he sold it on May 26, 1950. The Roller Rink closed in 1967.[203]

Gus died in 1981. Illinois state senator Adeline J. Geo-Karis thought Gus was one of Waukegan's most prominent residents. On June 24, 1981, she sponsored Resolution Number 79 in the Illinois Senate. Part of the resolution reads, "Truly, he was an outstanding citizen with an outstanding record of service, whose name should endure for posterity."

# CHAPTER 2

## Violence in Lake County

Here's a topic to get your attention. Those who think it strange to write about a topic like this might be surprised at how common violence was in the county. It seemed to permeate much of the culture, especially among the newly arrived immigrant groups living on the south side of Waukegan and in North Chicago. The north side of Waukegan was relatively quiet, but the area around Genesee Street had its share of excitement. The February 28, 1905, *Waukegan Daily Sun* wrote about the violence in the foreign district or what was called Little Europe in 1905.

> *Every week there are fights and brawls, to say nothing of the extra big ones which are pulled off at every christening, wedding and funeral. The appearance of these people with heads bandaged, black eyes, etc. are enough to bear out this statement. Knife scars are plentiful enough also.*[204]

A friend of mine remembers seeing her father regularly coming home from bars all beaten up. It seems like everyone in Little Europe carried knives. The sheer volume of fights and brawls there gave the newspaper plenty to write about, and no doubt some of the stories are sensationalized. It's also possible that the newspaper got some stories wrong. Getting the right story during a riot or from a mob during a riot is not always an easy endeavor. The period for most of this chapter takes place from the late 1890s to the early 1900s.

The rural areas of the county were almost as bad as the city. Most people didn't carry knives there, but most of them owned guns. Most of their fights seem to have been fistfights rather than gunfights. Getting hit over the head with the nearest object wasn't at all uncommon. The October 25, 1897, *Waukegan Daily Gazette* wrote about a dance in Wadsworth in 1897.

> *Wadsworth should be proud of the improved condition of its social gatherings. A few years ago it was almost impossible to have a hop without trouble of some kind being brewed among the participants.*[205]

Not to exclude any group, the January 3, 1906, *Waukegan Daily Sun* printed an interesting article about some of Waukegan's Black citizens in 1906.

> *The times in Waukegan are certainly getting strenuous as far as Negro troubles are concerned. The colored gentry here have been given lots of lee-way and it is regretted that they have lately shown a disposition to create disturbances, through cutting and shooting affrays.*[206]

The January 3, 1906, *Waukegan Daily Sun* went on to write that the people living in those neighborhoods were scared to death that they'd get killed, and "[t]here is no getting around the fact that some whites of the north are acquiring the feeling of their southern brethren."[207]

Translation: Your actions are creating white racists.

The Jews managed to get themselves scolded in the January 17, 1899, *Waukegan Daily Sun,*

> *The numerous "scrapes" into which the Jews of this city have been indulging lately is certainly becoming monotonous and a great nuisance to the authorities.*[208]

Waukegan's Jewish community was split into two opposing camps at the time and engaged in some type of feud.

Great Lakes sailors and Fort Sheridan's soldiers were no saints either and caused their share of trouble. I will write more about that later.

The south side of Waukegan and the city of North Chicago was home to a vast number of ethnic groups, most being immigrants or first generation. They usually lived in neighborhoods of the same ethnicity but not always. My father lived in a mixed neighborhood of Irish, Croats, Polish, and other nationalities on the south side of North Chicago. The south side of Waukegan and North Chicago was home to Albanians, Armenians, Blacks, Bohemians, Bulgarians, Croats, Finns, Germans, Greeks, Hungarians, Irish, Italians, Lithuanians, Macedonians, Poles, Romanians, Russians, Serbs, Slovaks, Slovenians, Swedes, and Turks. I think I named them all. Mexicans came in the 1920s. Austrians (Slovenians, Slovaks, and Croats), Blacks, Finns, Germans, Irish, Polish, Lithuanians, and Swedes were the largest ethnic groups.

More fights seem to have occurred among members of the same ethnic group, but fights among different ethnic groups were not uncommon. Some ethnic fights carried over from Europe, like Armenians versus Turks. Other times, an ethnic group fought with the nearest other ethnic group. Poles and Greeks never fought in Europe but almost got into a small war in North Chicago. The Lithuanians were not always on good terms with the Austrians living to their east or the Finns to their west. Taverns located at the boundaries of two different ethnic neighborhoods always seemed to be troublesome places. The Turks had it pretty tough. Every Greek, Armenian, Albanian, Macedonian, Bulgarian, and Romanian in town probably hated them. These groups had all endured bad treatment by the Turkish army in Europe, and some of their relatives back home were still being treated badly. There was never a large number of Turks in town, but they never backed down from anyone and participated in a long feud with the Armenians. They also had occasional mix-ups with Greeks, Bulgarians, and Macedonians. Actually, none of the various ethnic groups put up with any guff and always protected their turf.

I always heard that you risked getting beaten up by going into another ethnic group's neighborhood. A friend told me that in the 1930s, it was better to stay out of another parish. The parishes were mostly ethnic, so both statements hold true. Parishes would have been in the Catholic parts of town where the Irish, Polish, Lithuanians, Germans, and Austrians lived. The Finns and Swedes were all members of the Lutheran Church. The Greeks, Armenians, Macedonians, Bulgarians, and Russians were all Orthodox Christians. The Turks and some Albanians were the only Islamic people in town. It was probably best to just stay out of everyone else's neighborhood. A friend told me that you could go into another neighborhood if you knew someone who lived there.

It seems like everyone carried knives on the south side of Waukegan and North Chicago. I was surprised to find out that groups like the Finns and Lithuanians carried knives. No doubt some groups from South and Southeastern Europe had carried knives in their former countries. The others might have begun carrying them here as part of a mini arms race. Most of the immigrants arrived here with little or nothing, and knives were a lot cheaper to buy than guns. The knife fights themselves could be bloody affairs but were usually stopped before anyone got killed. A few gunfights and gun crimes did take place, but knives seem to be more common.

Fighting seems to have been taken for granted. Penalties were often light, usually a night in jail with fines ranging from a day's to a week's wages. A particularly violent act could result in more time. Smart alecks, cheats, and a-holes got what was coming to them. They could expect a punch in the nose or get hit over the head with the nearest loose object. The judge and jury might also be more sympathetic to the perpetrator.

Attacking the police was also common. The police themselves restored order with billy clubs, and no one gave it a second thought. It was almost impossible to get the death penalty in Lake County, and sometimes cases from Cook County were tried here to avoid the death penalty.

No place was off-limits for fights: sporting events, churches, trains, schools, bars, and restaurants. I will give a sample of some brawls shortly. Their priorities were somewhat different from the present times. One thing that was really unacceptable was swearing in public. Everyone seemed more concerned about swearing than fighting. In 1901, Henry Domski of Hainesville made the mistake of swearing in public. The American flag was being hoisted at the Fourth of July festivities in Grayslake. It was a windy day, and the flag was getting damaged by flapping against a telephone wire. Domski was a proud and patriotic army veteran who had served in the Civil War. He lost it when he saw the flag being torn to shreds and yelled for someone to take down the flag, inadvertently swearing out loud. He was arrested and charged with disorderly conduct. He was found not guilty after enduring an eighteen-hour trial.[209]Henry was involved in a much different episode at the 1877 Lake County Fair. Two men attacked a Lake County marshal named Ballard on the fairgrounds racetrack right in front of the judges' stand. One of the men was supposedly hitting the marshal with a hammer. Henry jumped in and disarmed the man with the hammer. Some claimed that the attacker was only holding the hammer and just used his fists. Marshal Ballard's face was cut up pretty badly. What type of punishment was meted out? One offender was escorted off the fairgrounds while the other was told he could stay but not to cause any more trouble.[210]

One more thing I've noticed a lot—troublemakers were often escorted to the city limits and told not to come back. Man or woman, white or black, it made no difference.

# CHAPTER 3

# Lake County Fights

In this chapter, I'll write about some individual altercations. There were so many fights that I will just give a sampling of my favorites.

Two justices of the peace fought it out on the streets of Waukegan in 1917. Their practices were at the opposite ends of Genesee Street. One justice was upset because his rival was soliciting business on the street as well as working too cheaply. He thought a justice of the peace should stay in his office and wait for business. The man was obviously cutting into his profits as well. The April 10, 1917, *Waukegan Daily Sun* wrote that one day the two ran into each other on the street, and the upset justice called the other one a scab.[211] His rival hauled off and punched him in the head five or six times. Our upset justice, though, was able to get a chokehold on his rival and almost strangled him to death. An onlooker finally stopped the fight.

Two Greek tailors entertained the passengers on the Chicago and Northwestern Railroad with a good old-fashioned scissors fight in 1911. They were taking the train to Chicago when one of the tailors did something to upset the other tailor. According to the August 3, 1911, *Waukegan Daily Sun*, the offended tailor screamed, "I'll kill you,"[212] at the other tailor and then pulled out his pair of scissors and attacked. The other tailor drew his own pair of scissors and stabbed his attacker, and the fight was on.

The other passengers were shocked by the bloodletting. Neither tailor would give in as they stabbed each other repeatedly. The scissors did not penetrate very deeply but left small bleeding cuts instead. Both men were covered in blood by the time the train arrived at the station. There, the police pulled them apart. They were weak from loss of blood, but each one lived to alter garments again.

In 1908, a Macedonian immigrant named John passed another Macedonian immigrant named Pete on the street. The December 20, 1908, *Waukegan Daily Sun* claimed John called Pete the Macedonian word for "dead one."[213] The offended Pete grabbed John's suspenders and broke them. Not to be outdone, John quickly found a six-foot-long two-by-four and hit Pete over the head a half a dozen times. Each one was fined $20 and court costs.

A Waukegan attorney battled an attorney from McHenry inside a McHenry County courtroom in 1905. It started as a fistfight but ended up a wrestling match. They rolled around the floor for a few minutes as Judge Wattles shouted for order in the court. Finally, the Waukegan attorney pinned the McHenry attorney to the floor. Both attorneys realized the seriousness of their actions and apologized to Judge Wattles. Judge Wattles was really upset and fined each one $25. Both attorneys apologized again, and Judge Wattles relented, canceling the fine.[214]

A fight over payment for some apples and bananas occurred in 1910. A Highland Park businessman accused two other businessmen from Highland Park of cheating him. The May 9, 1910, *Waukegan Daily Sun* wrote that one of the accused businessmen was known by the nickname Yom Pots.[215] The two parties started to argue. The argument evolved into a fistfight and, finally, a battle with horsewhips.

In 1908, an old woman let her cow graze on a lot owned by a Waukegan junk dealer. A driver for the junk dealer grabbed ahold of the old woman as a joke. But his real mistake was when he threw bottles at the old woman's son. The son soon fixed him. He grabbed a baseball bat and hit the driver over the head, knocking him out.[216]

A fight between a one-armed man and a one-eyed man took place in Deerfield in 1906. The one-armed man owned the Deerfield Inn. One of his employees only had one eye. One day the one-armed man went down to the Des Plaines River to go fishing. His employee was supposed to be working, but when the one-armed man got back, he found the one-eyed employee sleeping in his favorite chair. The one-armed man blew his top and pushed the one-eyed man out of the chair. The one-eyed man got up and charged at his one-armed employer. The one-eyed man was getting the worst of it and ran outside with the one-armed man close on his heels. When they got to the street, they both began throwing whatever objects they could find at each other, including old shoes, bricks, and any loose objects available. Bricks finally became the weapon of choice and were flying around everywhere. Their aim started getting wild, and soon, onlookers were also dodging bricks. Finally, Police Officer Curry stepped in before anyone got hurt and arrested them both.[217]

In 1914, the Lake Forest School Board was unable to decide whether the large iron gates at the entrance to the John J. Halsey School should be locked when school was not in session. The school was completely surrounded by an iron fence. Some wanted the gates locked; others did not. Finally, those in favor of locking the gate won out.

Wouldn't you know it? As soon as the decision was made to lock the gates, the school caught on fire. The fire department showed up but could not get near the school because the gates were locked. Someone was sent for the key while the rest of the firemen watched helplessly as the fire burned.

Then an argument broke out between one of the firemen and a member of the school board who had been in favor of locking the gate.

The school board member had just walked over to watch the fire with his wife and daughters when the fireman approached. He was upset about the gates being locked and read the board member the riot act. The board member soon became annoyed with the fireman and smarted off to him. Then the fireman hauled off and belted the board member. The board member responded by punching the fireman, and the fight was on.

Everyone crowded around the two fighters and cheered on their man. Might as well watch the fight; it was impossible to put the fire out anyway. The battleground itself was all lit up by the flames from the burning school. More Lake Forest residents soon showed up to watch the fire, and they took it upon themselves to separate the fighters.

Both men filed charges against the other. The fireman accused the board member of slander and disorderly conduct. The board member charged the fireman with assault and battery. Everyone thought the matter would be settled out of court. Both men were upstanding members of the community, and a court appearance would be too embarrassing.

The newspaper never did mention if the school burned down or not. It had taken fifteen minutes just to find the key. I doubt if the school's gates were locked after that.[218]

In 1925, two men, one forty-eight years old and the other seventeen years old, fought a four-day battle. I don't see how a fight could last four days, but that is what was reported. It is more likely they fought at times over a four-day period. The older man had hired the young guy to help him at the Highland Park City incinerator. Soon after hiring the young man, the older man noticed he was missing $125. While they were in the coal bin, the old guy accused his helper of stealing the $125 from him. The helper took exception, and the fight was on. The combatants began the first day's fighting by throwing chunks of coal at each other. The fight moved out of the coal bin the next day and seems to have taken place over a number of days. Outside the coal bin, the fighters used anything available, including hammers, milk bottles, and crowbars. City Marshal Edward J. Moroney found out about it and paid a visit to the incinerator later that week. They had beaten each other up so badly that Moroney could barely recognize them. Almost all their clothes were ripped off. The older man had numerous wounds all over and had almost been scalped. The young guy's body was in the same condition, but he claimed his wounds were from bite marks. He also said that the older man tried to chew his feet off.

Both were arrested. A doctor had to attend to the older man's wounds. Then they were led to Justice of the Peace Smith. They were both barely clothed. Marshal Moroney thought he might want to find something for them to wear before going before Justice Smith but decided to let them face the justice of the peace just as they were. They were each fined $200. Neither could pay, so they were escorted to the Lake County Jail in Waukegan.[219]

A liquor store was the location for this fight. In 1915, two soldiers from Fort Sheridan walked into a liquor store on South Genesee Street and asked the store employee which the best liquor was. A black customer happened to be in the store and tried to be helpful by telling one of the soldiers which liquor was the best. The soldier smarted off to him, saying something to the effect of who asked you? The answer didn't sit well with the black customer, who began swearing at the soldier. The soldier told him not to swear in front of the store's employee (a woman).

That was too much for the black customer, and he belted the soldier in the face, knocking him down. The woman called the police. Next, the black customer jumped on top of the soldier. The other soldier tried to pull the man off his friend, but the black customer bit his arm and held on like a bulldog for a good three minutes. The soldier finally broke loose and ran out to find a cop. When the police came on the scene, the black customer was beating the other soldier over the head with an iron paper weight. Besides his other injuries, the soldier had one of his fingers bitten off. Both the soldier and the black customer were covered in blood. The black customer might have received a skull fracture as the back of his head had been split open. The black man was fined $15 and court costs because he threw the first punch.[220]

# CHAPTER 4

## Lake County Mobs and Riots

This 1906 mob was the result of the police roughing up a street preacher, named Captain Cook, and his family. The *Daily Sun* estimated that about two thousand people attended a gospel meeting at the corner of Genesee and Washington streets. Captain Cook must have been one popular preacher to attract the attention of two thousand people on a street corner.

At eight o'clock that night, Police Chief Swanbrough ordered one of his officers to inform Captain Cook to move his gospel wagon to Gilbert's Corner. Cook's two thousand listeners were making it difficult for customers to shop at the nearby stores. Cook refused to leave and declared that he had permission from the mayor to set up shop there. Cook claimed that all the sinners were at Genesee and Washington streets, and it made no sense to preach at Gilbert's Corner. Another officer then approached Cook and told him to leave. Cook again refused to leave. Chief Swanbrough came next and told Cook for a third time to leave but to no avail.

One of Swanbrough's officers lost his patience and took hold of Cook's horse by the bridle and led Cook's buggy away. The sudden movement of the buggy knocked all its shrieking occupants to the floor of the buggy. Then Cook's seven-year-old daughter fell out of the buggy and hit her head on the road. The police officer leading the horse did not bother to stop for the girl, instead carelessly steering the buggy over a curb. The buggy almost overturned, and the remaining passengers were all thrown out.

The crowd went crazy, shouting insults at the chief of police. Captain Cook was arrested, but before the police could take him to the station, the crowd attacked them and tried to free Cook. The police had to fight their way out of the crowd with their billy clubs. The crowd, more like a mob by then, followed the police all the way back to the police station, hurling insults at them the whole time. At the police station, the mob shouted and pounded on the station doors. Swanbrough came out and tried to speak to them, but it was no use. All they did was curse at him.

The mob stayed until Cook was freed. They cheered wildly when he appeared and rushed over to congratulate him on his release. The gospel meeting resumed but this time at Gilbert's Corner. His followers cheered for so long that Cook was unable to speak for ten minutes.

Meanwhile, police reinforcements had arrived, and everything got ugly again. This time Cook and one of the newly arrived officers had words with each other. Suddenly, Cook leaped out of the buggy and hit the officer over the head with his guitar. The policeman warned him to stop or be arrested. (Stop or be arrested? See what happens to you nowadays if you hit a policeman over the head with a guitar!) According to the July 5, 1906, *Waukegan Daily Sun*, one of the new police officers then exclaimed, "Is the fellow going to walk over the police department?"[221]

The disgusted police officer then moved in on Cook's buggy. Cook's horse reared up as soon as the officer grabbed him. Then all the women in the buggy freaked out and began to scream. Cook dropped his guitar and began to run around the buggy. His wife tried to stop him and grabbed hold of his coat but got pulled along for the ride instead. At the same time, the daughter was holding on to her mother. She, however, was not strong enough to hold on and fell down into the mob. A soldier from Fort Sheridan picked her up and put her back in the buggy. Cook's wife had seen enough and now began to berate Cook. Then Cook's daughter fell out of the buggy again. Cook went berserk after seeing his daughter fall out of the buggy and attacked the police. The mob charged the police as well, and another free-for-all occurred. Using fists and billy clubs, the police restored order long enough to take Cook back to the station. Once again, the police were subject to curses and insults all the way there, and the mob surrounded the police station again.

Swanbrough and his officers were starting to get a little nervous. The large mob outside was getting increasingly unruly, and finally, the police decided to just release Cook. The mob broke into cheers at the sight of

Cook while the police were subjected to boos. The mob accompanied Cook back to his wagon, where he addressed the crowd and expressed his gratitude for their coming to his aid. He blamed Chief Swanbrough for everything and asked what kind of police department would attack a preacher.[222]

In 1912, Homer K. Galpin was host to the Long Lake Clambake. Held every year, the clambake was a very popular event that always attracted a large crowd from Chicago. About one thousand people were in attendance that day. Most came out by train from Chicago. It was a hot September day, and many of the clambake's visitors were overdressed. A nearby farmer consented to use his home to store coats for a fee of 25¢ per coat.

Toward the end of the day, about half the crowd was still there. As the clambake was winding down, all the visitors started to gather at the farmhouse for their coats. There was only one more train back to Chicago, the five o'clock, and it was almost five o'clock. The farmer and his family did their best to retrieve their coats, but they could not keep up with the demand. The crowd was getting nervous. The train was right on time and soon pulled up to the station. It was only scheduled to stop for a few minutes. The crowd panicked and turned into a mob when they realized there might not be enough time to get their coats. They stampeded into the farmhouse, crashing through the doors and windows. The farmer and his family were almost bowled over and decided to beat a hasty retreat. In the chaos, no one had time to find their own coats, so they grabbed whichever ones they could find. The house was ransacked of almost every article of clothing.[223]

This 1909 mob story had Waukegan's Lithuanian community in an uproar. It's also one of my favorite mob stories. This story was the toughest and most confusing one that I encountered in writing this book with the exception of the Bender story in chapter 9. The police had a tough time figuring it out too. They had to use interpreters because almost none of the participants could speak English.

Two Lithuanians named Paul Malinowski and Nick Mossis (Ignaeas Mazeviczce) were drinking at Peter Wember's saloon on the south side of Waukegan. It was a Sunday afternoon, and Wember was getting ready to close. All saloons were required to close by seven o'clock.

Mossis and Malinowski were cousins and both single men. Mossis was twenty-eight years old and worked in the nail department at the wire mill. He had immigrated to America six years earlier. Mossis was the type of person who was always looking for trouble. He would find it on this night. Malinowski was thirty years old. Malinowski is obviously a Polish name, but this can be explained by the fact that at one time, Poland and Lithuania were united in a commonwealth. Many Poles settled in Lithuania during that time, mainly around the city of Wilno (Vilna). Before WWI, 75 percent of Wilno's population was Polish.

Also drinking at Wember's that evening were two Croatian immigrants from Bosnia, Steve and Sam. The two Bosnians were known around town as tough characters. Steve and Sam, along with an unnamed Bosnian, had gotten into an argument with Malinowski, Mossis, and another Lithuanian named Gaspartaz Zukas earlier that day at Wember's.

Shortly after closing the bar, Wember noticed two groups arguing at the corner of Ninth and Lincoln streets. He recognized both parties and remembered that they had exchanged words earlier in what had seemed like a minor event. It looked more serious this time.

The May 17, 1909, *Waukegan Daily Sun* reported that Mossis, Malinowski, and Zukas had just left the saloon and were following Sam the Bosnian and told him, "Go home—, The Bosnian answered, Go home yourselves—."[224] The Bosnian then approached Mossis, and they started to argue. Zukas later said the two were arguing in a language he didn't understand. Zukas asked Mossis what they were talking about and was told that the Bosnian demanded that he (Mossis) go to his (the Bosnian's) house. Mossis said no, and they continued arguing. Then the Bosnian grabbed Mossis by the arm and began to pull him down the street. Zukas grabbed Mossis's other arm and pulled him back.

The May 29, 1909, *Waukegan Daily Sun* claimed that Sam's brother, Steve, was heard yelling from across the street. "What are you going to do here, fight? I'll show you how to fight."[225] Then Steve ran across the street and pulled out his knife. He pushed Zukas out of the way and attacked Malinowski, slashing him three times. Next, he turned and stabbed Mossis three times: once right below the heart, once to the left lung, and once to the liver.[226] Mossis instantly collapsed next to a ditch. He was still alive but died within a few minutes. Zukas claimed that he did not see the stabbing, only Mossis falling down. A witness named John Minalaga was standing across the street when the whole event came down and swore that Steve did all the stabbing. Sam had his knife out but had never used it.[227]

Malinowski took off and ran back to his home at a boardinghouse on South Park Avenue. He left a trail of blood all the way to the boardinghouse and was covered in blood by the time he got there. The occupants of the boardinghouse all rushed out to see what all the excitement was about. Malinowski was weak from loss of blood but able to tell them what had just happened. He also was able to spot the two Bosnians running down Ninth Street. Some residents of the boardinghouse kept an eye on the fleeing Bosnians while everyone else took the time to get their guns, clubs, or knives. Then they poured out of the house and ran after the two Bosnians.

Back at Ninth and Lincoln streets, a large crowd had come out to see what happened. Pete Wember was one of the first on the scene and tried to save Mossis with the help of someone named Cooper. A priest just happened to be near the area at the time. He rushed to the crime scene, arriving while Mossis was still alive, and gave him last rites. Two men then came up with burning candles and held them over Mossis's head. This must have been some type of Lithuanian custom. Mossis's shirt was off, and the extent of his wounds sent shudders through all who saw them. A North Chicago police officer named Lux was making his rounds, checking to see if all the saloons had closed on time. Lux heard people yelling and ran down to see what all the excitement was about.[228] Though Lux was not in his jurisdiction, he came anyway. He didn't get far enough to see Mossis's body but saw the mob and joined in the chase. He soon figured out that a murder had just been committed.

The crowd around the dying Mossis was growing by the minute. The area around the crime scene was soon filled with hundreds of shouting, cursing Lithuanians, swearing vengeance on all Bosnians. The May 20, 1909, *Waukegan Daily Sun* wrote, "Little Europe on Tenth Street and for two blocks on each side of it is aroused as never before and at a white heat."[229]

The ambulance soon showed up at Ninth and Lincoln streets, but it was decided instead to take Malinowski to the hospital. Mossis was already dead, and Malinowski could still be saved. Mossis's body was left where it lay until the dead wagon could get there.

The enraged crowd at Ninth and Lincoln streets joined in the search for the two Bosnians. A mob of hundreds of men, women, and children surged down Ninth Street. Some women carried their babies. The boardinghouse residents were also on the trail of the Bosnians. They intended to lynch the Bosnians as soon as they could get their hands on them.

The Bosnians turned right on State Street and headed south. State Street must be the current Sheridan Road. They ran past the cemetery and the envelope factory. (Your author worked at the envelope factory for a short time.) The mob was hot on their trail and never lost sight of them. The Bosnians stayed on State Street until they got to a path leading to the wire mill and then fired at the mob. Luckily, no one was hit. The path led to a vacant lot at the end of Thirteenth Street near the wire mill, about a mile from the crime scene.

Just as the two Bosnians were running through the lot, a southbound freight train rumbled by and blocked their escape. There, two men from Waukegan, Jack Needham and Frank Reardon, caught the Bosnians next to a barbed wire fence. Reardon worked at the wire mill, while Needham worked at the Dow Mill. Police Officer Lux was right on the heels of Reardon and Needham. Steve was able to escape from Needham and Reardon right before Officer Lux got there and ran for the train, intending to jump on.

Needham and Reardon were able to hold on to Sam. Officer Lux was on the other side of the barbed wire fence, and he shouted to Needham and Reardon to bring Sam to him. Lux was able to put his handcuffs on Sam just as the mob arrived. The mob started beating Sam, but Lux was able to pull him through the fence, ripping Sam's pants in the process. The mob started climbing over the fence and began attacking both Sam and Officer Lux. Lux yelled to Needham for help in holding the mob back until he could get Sam away. Just then, Police Officer Harvey Hyde drove up, and Sam was thrown into his car and driven off.

After putting Sam in the car, Officer Lux turned around to see the mob tearing Needham apart. His coat had already been ripped off, and he was fighting for his life. Lux ran back and started busting heads with his billy club. He was able to drive the mob back long enough for Needham to escape. Lux told Needham to run for his life, which he did. The mob mistakenly believed that Needham was involved in the murder and spent all night looking for him. Needham, however, made good his escape and was never found.

Steve was running for the train when he ran right into Clarence Hetrick, a driver for the wire mill who lived nearby. Hetrick had heard all the commotion, grabbed his shotgun, and ran toward the mob. On the way, he ran into the fleeing Steve. Hetrick told him to stop, but Steve pointed his pistol at him and fired. Fortunately for Hetrick, Steve was out of ammo. Steve threw his gun away and started to run for the train. Hetrick fired off a load of number 5 shot from his shotgun, wounding Steve in the hip.

The Forgotten History of Lake County, Illinois

Steve kept running, but the shotgun blast slowed him down some. Hetrick later claimed that Steve's bulky pants and long underwear protected him from a more severe wound. Steve didn't get far before he was captured by North Chicago constable Charles Litchfield and a part-time cop named Mike Babke.

Although the murder was committed in Waukegan, the Bosnians were taken to the North Chicago jail. There, the police chief tried to interview them, but neither one could speak much English, so an interpreter was brought in. The May 20, 1909, *Waukegan Daily Sun* stated that after talking to the Bosnians, the chief claimed, "The two Bosnians are tough customers; they are hard as nails and as imperious to impressions as granite blocks. They are not to be moved."[230] The May 20, 1909, *Waukegan Daily Sun* also wrote that one of the Bosnians had spoken in broken English. "No trouble, just me have fight, kill. No troub."[231] Lithuanian witnesses were also brought in, but the police couldn't get much out of them either. The chief remarked that neither side was talking very much.

The two Bosnians did not stay in North Chicago's jail for long. The North Chicago Police were worried that the mob would attempt to break into the jail and lynch them. They were soon taken to the county jail in Waukegan for safekeeping. The crime had occurred in Waukegan anyway.

Both the Waukegan and North Chicago Police Departments had a new problem to worry about. They feared a feud might break out between the Lithuanian community and the Croatian community. Some Lithuanians were already plotting to get their revenge. A *Waukegan Daily Sun* reporter attended a meeting on May 18 and claimed the Lithuanians were all shouting, "We fix them, the—."[232] A meeting was also held to raise money to hire a good attorney to prosecute the case and to raise money for Mossis's funeral. Not every Lithuanian was on board with raising money for Mossis or planning revenge. They contended that Mossis was always in some kind of trouble and had brought all the trouble on himself.

The arrangements for Mossis's funeral were just as difficult for me to figure out as the rest of this story. The *Daily Sun* reported that the pastor of the Polish church refused to let the funeral take place there. Mossis was Lithuanian, not Polish. He should have had his funeral at St. Bart's, the Lithuanian church. The priest, Father Jananseheck, said that Mossis had not gone to church there in over a year. Nor had he done any type of religious work at the church for over a year. Even Mossis's brother-in-law

47

wanted nothing to do with the funeral, but he finally relented and decided to plan it.[233]

At their trial, the Bosnians claimed that it was a case of mistaken identity. They claimed that they were on the other side of the street when the crime occurred. At the inquest, Clarence Hetrick had identified Steve as the man he captured. At the trial, he said that the man he captured was not in the courtroom. Steve was found guilty anyway and given a sentence of from one to fourteen years in prison.[234] He was sent to Joliet, along with another murderer from Lake County. I will write more about him in my story about black mob violence in North Chicago.

This is another one of my favorite battles I would love to have seen. I also have to mention that I know the relatives of one of the participants. Mother of God Church was the scene for this large brawl in 1923. An unknown incident at a dance at Slovenic Hall caused the melee later that night. At four in the morning, two large groups of men, estimated to be about one hundred individuals, decided to settle the matter and met in front of Mother of God Church on Tenth Street. Most had been drinking all night.

One of the rioters ripped off one of the pickets from Mother of God's picket fence. Soon, other pickets were ripped from the fence, and an arms race ensued. Almost everyone had a picket by now, and the fight was on. By the time police arrived, three men had been stabbed, and many more were lying around, holding their heads. Anyone able to leave scattered when the police arrived. After the affair, Mother of God was in the market for a new fence.[235]

In 1907, the Waukegan Cubs baseball team played the Libertyville town team at Libertyville. Waukegan no-hit Libertyville and won the game 13–0. Toward the end of the game, a Waukegan player trying to score shoved Libertyville's catcher out of the way. Libertyville's fans were already upset with the score, and the shoving incident didn't help any. When the game ended, Waukegan's players kept the ball, refusing to give it back to Libertyville. Waukegan was actually in the right on this issue. The winning team always gets to keep the ball.

That didn't make any difference to Libertyville's two hundred fans, who stormed onto the field to get the ball back. Waukegan's players played keep-away with the ball by tossing it to one another. This just got Libertyville's fans even madder, and they finally attacked a Waukegan player. Waukegan only had twenty-five fans at the game, but they all ran out onto the field to help their players.

Despite being outnumbered, Waukegan's fans put up a tough fight. Two people were knocked out. One person was kicked in the stomach. Others had black eyes or bruises. The fight lasted a couple of minutes and was finally stopped by the employees of the baseball field.[236]

Here's a military mob story. On June 1, 1920, a mob of five hundred sailors attacked the Sherman House on the south side of Waukegan. The Sherman House was a black boardinghouse. The *Waukegan Daily Sun* first reported that the incident was caused by a ten-year-old black juvenile delinquent. The boy and his younger sister were throwing rocks at cars passing by their home. One rock broke the windshield of Navy Lt. A. F. Blasier's car, wounding Mrs. Blasier. Another car, driven by Charles Bairstow of Waukegan, was also damaged, injuring one of Bairstow's passengers.

The incident made the rounds at Great Lakes Naval Base, and the *Daily Sun* printed the story. The only problem was the paper got the story wrong. The Chicago Commission on Race Relations investigated the matter and came to a different conclusion. They found that Navy Lt. A. F. Blasier and Charles Bairstow were actually riding in the same car. The windshield was broken, but no one was injured. They also found out that there was no woman in the car and that Lieutenant Blasier did not even have a wife.[237]

What the sailors had heard was just a rumor, but it set them off. About midnight, a mob of four to five hundred sailors and marines formed outside the Sherman house. The Sherman House also went by the name of the "Blackstone." The rock-throwing crime had occurred a block south of the Blackstone, but the mob chose instead to form up at the Blackstone. There was a lot of speculation as to why the sailors attacked the Blackstone Hotel when the rock-throwing crime had happened a block away. Later, I will reveal the results of a number of investigations into the cause of all the trouble and why the mob picked the Blackstone.

The rock-throwing incident became an excuse to attack any black person unfortunate enough to be nearby. The June 2, 1920, *Waukegan Daily Sun* claimed a black man walking not far from the Blackstone was chased by a gang of sailors who shouted, "Lynch him!"[238] Police officers Lawrence McDermott and Robert Wilson saw all the commotion and ran to the rescue. They held the mob at bay until the man was able to get away.

Meanwhile, the situation at the Blackstone was getting bad. The mob started to pelt the boardinghouse with rocks and bricks, breaking every window in the house. The mob tried to charge the Blackstone, but the six residents inside were armed and opened fire. Just then, the police reached the Blackstone and were able to push the mob back. According to the June 2, 1920, *Waukegan Daily Sun*, the whole time the mob shouted, "Lynch the blacks!"[239]

Just then, Assistant Police Chief Thomas Tyrrell arrived with more officers. The mob did not seem to care about the arrival of the new officers and attacked the Blackstone again. The police were determined to restore order, though, and drew their weapons. The sight of the drawn weapons was all it took, and the mob moved backward. Next, the military police (MP's) came on the scene. Great Lakes trucked in two hundred MP's to help restore order, and the mob soon broke up. Some sailors went down to Market Street to harass Ike Franklin, a black resident of the area. Assistant Chief Tyrrell and his son decided to check Market Street at the same time and were able to drive the troublemakers off. The police also drove off a different group who were menacing two black janitors working the night shift at the post office. After arriving, the MP's were able to round up most of the mob, and that was the end of all the excitement for that night.[240]

Everything was calm the next night but not for long. The following night, a mob of four to five hundred sailors and marines was back. They intended to burn down the Blackstone at 9:30, but the police had been warned and were ready for them. The whole force was called out, along with some auxiliary police. In addition, the navy base sent fifty MP's to help. The mob approached the hotel, only to find it heavily guarded. The police fired a few warning shots in the air to scare the mob.

A different mob of about fifty sailors and marines had formed up in a ravine, five hundred yards west of the Blackstone. One of the sailors carrying an American flag started to advance up the ravine. The rest followed behind, and the group stormed up the ravine. The police were ready this time too. They were drawn up on Lake Street and ordered them to stop when they were seventy-five feet away. The mob ignored the order and kept on coming. One officer drew his weapon and fired two shots in the air. Other shots were heard coming from the ravine, but it was never determined who fired them. Somehow two marines were wounded in the encounter. The police line on Lake Street was too strong, and the mob was stopped in their tracks. Two of the mob leaders were arrested, and the flag was seized from the sailor.

The wounding of the two rioters and the arrests of the two leaders energized the larger mob gathered at the Blackstone. They made a rush for the Blackstone again. A few of them were able to break through the police line and tried to force their way through the entry door. The remaining Blackstone residents turned off the lights and left through the back door. The mob's advance soon petered out, and the police were able to regain control.

Next, part of the Blackstone mob broke off and caught up with the police taking the two arrested marines to the police station. Some of the mob ran ahead of the police and prevented them from entering the station. M. M. Fruchi, the commanding officer at Great Lakes, had been waiting at the police station for the mob. He commanded them to stand down and allow the police to enter the station with their prisoners. A short time later, the police released the two marines to a loud ovation from the mob. Even the flag was returned. The mob broke up, and everyone went their separate ways. A total of two hundred more MP's showed up, but all the excitement was already over.[241]

Both the police and the navy conducted investigations. Rear Admiral Bassett determined that some civilians had instigated all the trouble. Bassett noted that Great Lakes and Waukegan had always had a good relationship, and he intended to keep it that way. The marines claimed that some civilians told them that the windshield-breaking incident occurred at the Blackstone. The civilians left as soon as the attack began. The *Daily Sun* wrote that the Blackstone was an old rundown building situated at a prime location on the south side, and certain people thought there were better uses for the property.[242] The Blackstone might have been the first hotel in town. It was also one of the oldest buildings in Waukegan. The Blackstone was owned by Theodor H. Durst, who was white. Durst was leasing the Blackstone to Sam Durham, who was black. Durham had leased the building for three years as a hotel for blacks only. Soon after the riot, Durst sold the hotel to Dave Webb, who planned to tear it down.[243]

The police investigation concluded that communists (Reds) had a hand in the outbreak. They had recently been seen around town but left when they found out the police were investigating the riot. They were known as Wobblies and had been accused of stirring up trouble between the races before.[244]

Before I go any further, it is necessary to inform you about the state of race relations between blacks and sailors at this time. The two sides had been feuding with each other and not only in Waukegan.

The trouble might have started right after the United States entered World War I. Many white Southerners joined the navy and were sent to Great Lakes for training. The May 29, 1917, *Waukegan Daily Sun* wrote that the white Southerners thought Northerners let blacks "walk all over them."[245] At the same time, Waukegan's black residents complained that the sailors were harassing them. Navy Capt. W. A. Moffett issued orders to all navy personnel to behave themselves. He also ordered navy MP's to patrol train and street cars, looking for troublemakers and drunks.

It looks like there was still some trouble between the two groups. Black employees from Fort Sheridan claimed they were still being harassed on trains. One Saturday, a mob of forty blacks left Fort Sheridan for Waukegan with the intention of tearing up the sailors, but nothing seems to have come of it.[246]

About two months later, a mob of fifty blacks attacked three sailors in Evanston. The sailors had just gotten off a street car when a black man started badmouthing them. The black man was a known troublemaker and had had scraps with the law before. Within minutes, a mob of fifty blacks had congregated nearby and threatened the sailors. The sailors called the police. A few other sailors and some soldiers from Fort Sheridan were nearby and came to their assistance. The black man, who had started everything, had gone into a restaurant but was just then coming back out. The sailors grabbed him and held him for the police. The black mob started closing in on the sailors, shouting at them to let the man go and issuing threats. The August 29, 1917, *Waukegan Daily Sun* wrote that a member of the mob yelled out, "Let's give them what they gave them down in Texas."[247] Some type of racial incident had recently taken place in Houston, Texas.

Just then, the police came. They arrested the black troublemaker and ordered the mob to leave. The mob, however, refused to leave. The police put the troublemaker in their squad car and took off. A vocal group of blacks ran after the squad car, threatening violence. The remaining police were able to disperse the mob.[248]

Now back to the story. George Taylor, "the person accused of starting the whole thing by throwing rocks at cars," gave a taped interview to Curtis

L. Dorsey in 1974. He claimed that the sailors and their girlfriends were being harassed by blacks when they happened to walk by the Blackstone Hotel. The sailors were looking for some reason to go off on the hotel, and the stone-throwing incident was all it took. George also said that neither he nor his family was harmed during the riot.[249] The black areas in North Chicago and the south side of Waukegan were spared as well.

The Chicago Commission on Race Relations wrote that at one time, the sailors patronized the billiard room and bar at the Blackstone Hotel. I previously wrote that the navy had a lot of Southern whites in its ranks, so drinking and playing pool in a black hotel seems like a volatile combination to me. About thirty to thirty-five single black men lived at the hotel. The Chicago Commission on Race Relations also came to the conclusion that the riot was not a race riot.[250]

After the riot, the black residents of the Blackstone collected all their possessions and left, going to a more welcoming part of the city. One marine went missing. He had been married for only three weeks. The police searched everywhere for him but never did find him.[251]

Mobs could be useful at times. In 1913, a mob of fifty sailors volunteered to help the police find a twelve-year-old girl kidnapped by a railway worker. The sailors planned to lynch him if they found him first. Luckily for the railway worker, a policeman found him first.[252]

This North Chicago mob story took place in 1906. A black man named Archie was known around the black community as a bad character. He had been married to his wife, Lottie, for only about five months but already had a serious wife-beating problem. Archie was well-known to the police, and they had been out to his combination store/apartment a number of times for various reasons.

One day Archie had been drinking moonshine and decided to go to the beauty salon where his wife was getting her hair done. He walked in, took a drink of moonshine, drew his pistol, and announced to everyone that he would like to shoot somebody. His wife hastily summoned a cab and took him home, where they got into a long argument.

Next, the upset wife demanded to go to Chicago to see her eleven-year-old son, who lived there. Archie did not feel like going to Chicago and told her so. Lottie was in another part of the house when she lost her cool and called Archie a number of obnoxious names. Archie was in the bedroom and responded to his wife's name-calling by firing his .38-caliber pistol five times through the bedroom door. Two shots hit Lottie in the chest and killed her.

Archie put the pistol in his wife's hand to make it look like a suicide. Police, however, could not find any powder burns on Lottie. The police claimed Archie was drunk when they showed up, and a gallon-sized oil can full of moonshine was found there. Archie was taken down to the police station, where he confessed to the murder. He said that he did not intend to kill her but only shot through the door to scare her.

The black community of North Chicago was outraged over the murder. Soon, a black mob began collecting around North Chicago's jail. The situation was becoming desperate, and a lynching was feared. Police Chief Tiffany decided it best to sneak Archie away and take him to the county jail in Waukegan. The escape was a success, and a lynching was averted.[253] Archie was sentenced to twenty-five years in prison at Joliet.[254]

This 1903 mob story is also a fishing story. Six men from Chicago camped out at Grassy Lake near Barrington. They were on a fishing trip and were seining for fish. Seining is using large nets to catch fish. Some of the local farmers were worried that the campers would fish out the lake.

About midnight, while the fishermen were in their boats, the farmers set fire to their camp. The outraged fishermen drew their guns and shot at the farmers on shore. The farmers returned fire and wounded a Chicago attorney in the shoulder. The fishermen soon realized they were outgunned and rowed for their lives to the other side of the lake. From there, they skedaddled back to town. The farmers not only burned their tents but wrecked their boats and equipment as well.[255]

This riot story took place in 1905. Police showed up to a house on Market Street to investigate a noise complaint. A wedding was taking place at the home, and the place was full of foreigners; we now call them immigrants. This was an Austrian wedding. They were not from the country we now know as Austria but from the present countries of Slovenia, Croatia, and Slovakia. Those regions were parts of Austria at the time.

Two police officers responded to the call and told the partiers to quiet down a little. But the hostile crowd was in no mood to quiet down and instead began screaming obscenities at the police. Feeling outnumbered, the police called for backup. Three more officers came on the scene, and the police were confident that five policemen would be enough to control the crowd.

The five policemen entered the house and split up; some stayed in front, and the rest went to the back. The owner of the home flew into a rage and started hurling insults at the police stationed in the front of the house. They arrested him and were taking him out when his wife ran over screaming and summoning help. A crowd of men and women responded with beer bottles and clubs. The officers ordered them to stop but were met with a shower of bottles instead. The police pulled out their billy clubs and started busting heads. The outnumbered police were getting desperate and finally had to pull out their guns and threaten to shoot. The mob backed down, and the police arrested six men.[256]

This 1903 Russian wedding reception on Nineteenth Street in North Chicago got out of control. The wedding guests had been heavily drinking all night. About midnight, a terrible commotion broke out that was so loud it woke up the whole town. Some people wondered if someone had just been killed.

The party was going strong when the violin player announced that he was done playing. The band had played until the agreed-upon time, but his response didn't sit well with the guests, who still wanted to dance. They told him to play on or else, but the violin player still refused to play. Big mistake! He was soon attacked by the drunken wedding guests. The violin player broke loose and ran away, the wedding guests in hot pursuit, carrying knives and clubs. They caught him at Commonwealth Avenue and beat the sense out of him. The other members of the band came to his rescue, but they got the same treatment. One had his head cracked open. Another was hit over the head with a bottle. All five band members had head wounds, and they all seem to have had Polish last names.[257]

Here's a farm story about how important it is to drink your daily milk. In 1935, there was a milk strike. The farmers were dumping out all their milk instead of taking it to the dairies. The *Chicago Tribune* reported that three unions with a total of fifteen thousand dairy farmers as members went on strike on September 30, 1935. The dairy farmers were paid 3.76¢ per quart but wanted it raised by a penny and a half more. The retail price was 10¢ a quart. Scabs taking milk into Chicago risked getting a good thrashing. Railroad tankers hauling milk were broken into and drained. One railroad bridge was burned down and another set on fire.[258]

Word got out that four trucks hauling milk would take Route 60 through Lake Zurich on Sunday at four o'clock in the morning. From seventy-five to one hundred farmers set up a road block at the junction of Routes 60 and 22 just south of a gas station. They used railroad ties to block the road, and the gas station became their base. (This location is in Half Day.)

As the trucks approached, the farmers noticed that they were accompanied by seven cars. When the drivers of the cars saw the blockade, they passed the trucks and pulled up to the blockade. Next, a gang of armed men exited from the cars. The trucks pulled up and headed for the shoulder of the road. Someone commanded the armed men to fire, and they opened up a barrage, which passed over the farmers' heads. The unarmed farmers, not expecting any shooting, retreated. The bodyguards poured on the lead until three of the trucks drove around the blockade. The other truck veered off the road into the gas station and drove straight for the mass of farmers. The farmers all scattered in time, but the truck almost hit the gas pumps. The bodyguards kept on firing until all the trucks were past the blockade and then drove off and caught up with them.

A convoy of farmers followed, but soon, the bullets began to fly again. The farmers' lead car was hit in the radiator. Then one of the guard cars broke off from the rest and hid on a side road. After the farmers' convoy drove past, the guard car pulled out from its hiding place and shot at the last car.

Some farmers continued to follow the convoy into Cook County. (They claimed that when the road widened to four lanes, each truck driver picked out a lane and drove side by side, next to the others.) The guard cars then took up their positions in the front and back of the convoy.[259]

Being an army veteran, I really didn't want to write this story. I could have buried it, but that would be biased. Most of the soldiers I am about to write about seem to have been infantrymen blowing off some steam.

The towns of Highwood and Waukegan were the favorite destinations for the soldiers of Fort Sheridan. Fort Sheridan was created in November 1887. The late 1800s and early 1900s was a particularly trying time for Highwood and Waukegan. Residents lived in constant dread of drunken soldiers who always seemed to get themselves into some kind of trouble. The majority of each town's police department was kept busy by the soldiers' outrageous conduct. Waukegan's jail was usually filled to overflowing with them on Saturday nights and would sometimes pack them in on weeknights as well.[260] The soldiers also engaged in a long-running feud with the Italian community of Highwood.

One of the soldiers' worst acts was the almost complete destruction of a saloon in Highwood in 1900. The soldiers were upset over the treatment that had been meted out to two drunken soldiers by the saloon's proprietor. He had beaten the hell out of the two soldiers, putting both of them in the hospital. The soldiers thought the battered men were too drunk to put up much of a fight and wanted to teach the man a lesson. The proprietor maintained that the two soldiers had tried to take over his place, and he wasn't about to let them.

Late the next night, about one hundred mostly armed soldiers went into the saloon and sat at the bar. They all ordered drinks, and when everyone had a drink, the signal was given to start the riot. The whole group threw their drinks in unison at the windows, mirrors, or the proprietor's head. The man grabbed his gun and fired off one shot, but two soldiers jumped him before he could get off another shot. No one was hit by the lone bullet.

The proprietor was held down while the soldiers began to demolish the place. All the windows, bottles of liquor, and dinner plates were broken. The proprietor managed to escape and ran upstairs with his son and two bartenders. They armed themselves with shotguns and pistols and barricaded the door. A fierce firefight soon ensued. Some of the soldiers went out in the street and fired at the saloon from there. The proprietor's daughter was almost shot while she was looking out a window. The bullet hit a flowerpot next to her elbow.

The proprietor called Fort Sheridan, pleading for help, but no one came. Someone rang the fire bell, hoping the fire department would come out, but they didn't show up either. The July 13, 1900, Lake County independent newspaper claimed that one of Highwood's citizens declared, "It was so hot, and bullets were so thick, that everybody took to the woods. The streets became deserted in the twinkling of an eye."[261]

The town of Highwood was shocked by the violence. The saloon sustained $2,000 in damages. The proprietor went to Chicago and complained to Fort Sheridan's commander. The commander guaranteed that his saloon would be safe from then on and sent the MP's to periodically check on the saloon. In addition, warrants were issued for four soldiers. More soldiers were later arrested.[262]

The *Daily Sun* wrote in 1906 that paydays were always the worst.[263] Soldiers wandered into Waukegan's downtown saloons and restaurants and caused havoc. Fighting drunken soldiers was routine for the police, and the fights could really get nasty. In 1908, a soldier wrapped a brick in a handkerchief and hit Officer Neally over the head, almost killing him. That was the last straw for Waukegan's citizens. In response to the attack, they turned to vigilantism.[264] A group of about thirty men began hanging out at downtown streetcar stops and refused to let the soldiers get off the cars. The police looked the other way, and there was talk that soldiers would not be allowed in town anymore.[265] Chief Tyrrell disputed the vigilantism story. He claimed that only three men turned the soldiers back and that there was no organized group involved. The three had simply been at the train station when the soldiers arrived and decided to cause some trouble.

The vigilante stories combined with law enforcement by the police must have sent a message to the army. The incidents became fewer and fewer. By 1914, the *Daily Sun* claimed that the soldiers were relatively well behaved. It was thought that the army was recruiting higher-quality men. In fact, the situation reversed so fast that the soldiers became more desirable callers to Waukegan than most other visitors to town.[266]

The soldiers might have been too focused on other problems to cause any more trouble in Waukegan. They were engaged in a long-running feud with the Italian community of Highwood. In 1912, a soldier was attacked and disemboweled by a gang of Italians carrying knives. The trouble started at a blind pig just outside the Highwood city limits.

A blind pig is an unlicensed saloon. Lake County supposedly had more blind pigs than any other county in Illinois. A total of fifty were operating, mainly around Highwood, Lake Forest, and Fox Lake in 1907.[267] Highwood had eleven blind pigs in 1909.[268] The worst blind pig in the county was located in Rondout. It was operated by some Polish people from North Chicago and sat just one hundred feet from the railroad tracks. The January 9, 1908, *Waukegan Daily Sun* wrote that Secretary Quayle, from the Lake County Law and Order League, declared, "The place is the graveyard of Lake County."[269] Libertyville Township and the residents of Rondout in particular were outraged by its existence and threatened to vote the township dry.[270] Crusades against blind pigs took place periodically, but it could be a dangerous undertaking. The mayor of Highwood tried to shut them down in 1913 and got his house burned down for his trouble.[271]

Blind pigs got their name from a saloon in Maine. In 1851, a law went into effect that banned the sale of alcohol in saloons. One saloonkeeper came up with a great idea to get around the law. He rented a small building next to the saloon. Then he installed a door to the building from his saloon and put a live pig in the other building. He put a sign above the door

The Forgotten History of Lake County, Illinois

announcing that a blind pig was on display, and for only 10¢, you could have a look. After paying their 10¢, patrons were given a drink when they entered the other building. There was no evidence that the pig was blind, but the saloonkeeper could not be charged for selling liquor.[272]

Now back to the story. Five soldiers and eleven Italians had words over something at one of Highwood's blind pigs in 1912. According to the August 31, 1912, *Waukegan Daily Sun*, one of the soldiers called the Italians Guineas.[273] The bartender of the blind pig was able to prevent a fight in the saloon, but the Italians waited outside for the soldiers to leave. When the soldiers left, the Italians fell on them with knives, and an army private was disemboweled. One of the soldiers hit the attacker over the head with a club, but the Italian managed to get away. Some of Fort Sheridan's MP told a different story. They stated that the fight actually occurred at a Chicago and Northwestern ticket office at 1:30 in the morning, not at the blind pig.[274]

The Italian-soldier feud was on again in 1916. Two soldiers from the first cavalry were beaten up by Italians in what the November 13, 1916, *Waukegan Daily Sun* called "jealousy assaults."[275] The *Daily Sun* first reported that the soldiers had accompanied some local women home after a dance. Both soldiers were jumped and badly beaten in two different clashes.[276] A week later, the *Daily Sun* published a different account. They claimed the soldiers were beaten up for dancing with two of the Italians' girlfriends.[277] The two soldiers were able to get back to the fort and tell their friends what happened. The first cavalry was out for revenge, and about eighty of them left camp, searching for the offenders. They had left their guns on post but were carrying clubs. The soldiers spent most of the day in Highwood but came up empty and went back to the fort.

The first cavalry was back at it a few hours later. They confronted a young Italian whom they mistook for one of the offenders. The soldiers tried to arrest him, but he fought back. The soldiers beat him to an inch of his life, breaking his jaw. Highwood's police department was too small to handle so many soldiers, so the mayor called Fort Sheridan, asking for assistance. The MP's were dispatched and managed to bring all the soldiers back to the fort. The mayor promised to find the culprits who jumped the soldiers and punish them severely.[278] It was later found that the young Italian who was beaten up had not been involved in the attacks.

The feud was not over yet. The soldiers made plans to wipe out the Italian community of Highwood. The Italians made their own plans as well.

They planned to burn down Fort Sheridan. Fort Sheridan's commander found out, and guards were employed all around the fort with orders to stop any soldier from leaving as well as watching for any suspicious activity. The fort's fire department was put on alert and sentries posted at all the buildings.[279]

More trouble occurred a week later. Two soldiers were attacked outside the fort by a gang of Italians. One had to be carried away on a stretcher. The other one made it back to the fort with his head cracked wide open.[280] The beating was retribution for the earlier beating of the young Italian. Why were the soldiers even outside the fort when they were ordered to stay in it?

The MP's were sent out to look for the attackers but were not able to find them. It was thought that everything would blow over anyways. The first cavalry had already been assigned to a new post, and the whole unit left the next morning. It was decided to overlook the most recent attack, so the perpetrators were never brought to justice.[281]

This 1910 riot was the result of teasing and jealousy. All the most skilled positions at the North Chicago Hardware Foundry were held by Poles. The grunt work was done mainly by Greeks, but some other ethnic groups were also represented.

The Poles amused themselves by teasing the Greeks, while the Greeks were jealous of the Poles. A couple of bloody incidents had occurred previously but not on such a large scale as this time. One day the s— hit the fan. A Polish mold maker was giving his Greek helper his customary teasing. The Greek finally had enough and threw a large casting at the Pole's head, knocking him out. The whole place went up for grabs, and eighty workers were in a brawl. Another Pole was stabbed in the neck during the riot. I would expect more to have been wounded in a fight this size, so the newspaper may have sensationalized this story some.

No one was arrested after the riot, and the management at the foundry tried to smooth everything over. They also made efforts to get the two groups to better tolerate each other. Even so, there was still tension between the two groups.

Rumors began to spread that each side planned to attack the other to decide the matter. Each group supposedly had recruited four to five hundred men for the battle. I doubt if that many Greeks actually lived in North Chicago at the time but could have been brought up from Chicago.

The North Chicago police found out about the upcoming battle and kept a strong presence around town until tempers cooled.[282]

Fights on trains seem to have been a relatively common occurrence in the old days. In 1885, Evanston and some of the other towns north of Chicago were dry. Dry, meaning no alcoholic beverages were sold there. As a result, the young men from those towns had to go somewhere else to drink. The nearest wet town was Rose Hill, near Highland Park. The Saturday northbound train from Chicago was their favorite mode of travel, and the train was always full of them. Business was so good for the bar owners at Rose Hill that they built flophouses for anyone who could not make it back home.

Not everyone wanted to stay overnight in Rose Hill. At 11:30 on an October night, a dozen very drunk young men boarded the southbound train for Chicago. They all headed to the crowded smoking car. There, an altercation broke out over a seat. Soon, a knock-down, drag-out fight was in full progress. The October 31, 1885, *Waukegan Gazette* reported, "It was a real Kilkenny scrimmage, every man for himself and the devil take the hindmost."[283] Everyone was getting punched out. About two dozen of Evanston's leading citizens were also in the smoking car. They were reluctant spectators and tried to stay out of the fight. It was impossible to leave the crowded car, so they stood on their seats and took cover.

The conductor and some of his fellow railroad workmen tried to break up the fight but to no avail. They were outnumbered by the fighters and needed a different plan. Finally, the conductor instructed the crew to uncouple the smoking car. After it rolled to a stop, the Evanston people made their escape. A few of them had minor injuries but were probably happy to get off the car.

Only the fighters were left in the car, and everyone else stood outside watching the brawl, claiming it was a sight to see. The fight continued for only a short time longer and then petered out; three brawlers were badly injured, and the rest nursed a variety of wounds. The newspaper blamed the police of Rose Hill for allowing so many drunken youths on the train.[284]

A memorable train riot took place in 1914. The smoking car of the northbound Chicago and Northwestern train was packed. It was a Sunday night, and the train had just left Evanston, destined for Waukegan. This almost sounds like the previous story. A high-stakes poker game was in progress and was the focus of most passengers in the car. Two of the participants were from Highland Park, one from Glencoe and the other from Lakeside. I'm not sure where Lakeside was. All the players' friends were standing around, watching the game.

Suddenly, one of the players charged a Highland Park man with cheating. The accused took offense and punched out his accuser. Next, a twenty-man free-for-all broke out. Those bystanders not taking part in the fight, all of them from Waukegan, stood on their seats to steer clear of the action. The railroad workers tried to stop the fight but didn't have the manpower. A burly Italian was cleaning everyone's clock, knocking people out with one punch. The fighting was so furious that the skirmishers from Lakeside and Glencoe missed their stops. The Highland Parkers did exit the train, leaving the others to fight it out. Neither side would give in, so the battle raged on until they got to the Waukegan city limits. Fighters disembarked from the train with fat lips, black eyes, and assorted bruises. They must have looked like hell after being in a brawl of this length. The only way home for those from Lakeside and Glencoe was the next southbound train.[285]

Drunks always seemed to cause trouble on trains, and this 1904 fight had an interesting ending. A party of six drunken men and two drunken women boarded the train and began making trouble. The conductor tried to quiet them down, but they only got worse. It was decided to kick them all off at the Lake Bluff Station. The conductor and some railroad employees told them all to leave, but the drunks attacked them. The conductor and his crew were getting the worst of it until Railroad Superintendent Downs showed up. Downs took the whole bunch on by himself and mopped the floors with the whole lot. The June 17, 1904, Lake County independent newspaper remarked that "the next time they want to start trouble they might want to first find out if Superintendent Downs is on the train."[286] According to the March 22, 1907, Lake County independent newspaper, the most troublesome drunks on the trains that year were from Lake Forest.

This riot took place in 1900 at Wember's Dance Hall on Tenth Street in North Chicago. The dance hall's clientele were all recent immigrants. For weeks, a gang of about twenty young toughs from Waukegan had been showing up on Saturday nights, bothering the dancers. The toughs finally went too far one night, and the police kicked them all out of the dance hall.

The Waukegan toughs slowly left but did not go far. Before long, they were trying to get back in but found the door locked. One of the toughs got even by breaking the front door window. Then another one shot through the broken window at Wember himself. The bullet missed, but a shard of glass hit Wember's forehead. To show how crazy the toughs were, the two police officers who had just kicked them out were still in the dance hall.

The officers ran out, and the crowd retreated to the Waukegan side of Tenth Street. The police crossed the street, but the toughs armed themselves with whatever they could find and warned the police to stay back. The police weren't intimidated and rushed the crowd. One member of the crowd charged at the police with a brick, but he was dropped with a billy club and then arrested.

The arrest really set the toughs off, and shots rang out. They rushed at the dance hall with renewed energy and pelted the front of the building with rocks, breaking all the windows and then leaving. Two of the hoodlums ended up in the hospital, one with a gunshot wound to the leg. The police maintained that they only shot their weapons in the air. Another tough was in jail, and warrants were sworn out for fifteen others.[287]

Here's another dance hall story. This riot occurred in 1922 at the Lincoln Dance Hall at Ninth and Lincoln streets. A new group of dancers from Fourteenth Street began attending the dances there. Previously, they had all gone to Phil Lewandowsky's Dance Hall. Lewandowsky's Dance Hall was going to close down, though, and all his regular customers had to find another dance hall. They decided to go to the Lincoln Dance Hall. Two weeks before Lewandowsky's closed down, a rumor spread that the Fourteenth Street crowd was planning to kick out the Lincoln Dance Hall regulars.[288] Cleaning out a rival tavern seems to have been one of the favorite pastimes of the time.

The Fourteenth Street gang made their first appearance at the Lincoln Dance Hall on a Sunday night. The arrival of the new dancers brought the total number of customers in the dance hall to about one hundred people. An unruly group of Fourteenth Street dancers had decided to hog the dance floor. The owners asked them to get off the floor, but the dancers ignored them. The police were called, and Officers Mihic and McMahon were sent to take control of the situation.

The police ordered all dancers off the dance floor. All but one complied. He told Officer McMahon to make him leave. Officer McMahon didn't waste any time and hauled off and punched the belligerent fellow twice in the face. McMahon's second punch landed on the man's chin, decking

63

him. Then someone attacked McMahon but succeeded only in knocking off the officer's hat. Officer Mihic went to the aid of McMahon but was almost knocked down by a punch to his neck.

The mob of dancers was now lusting for blood and went for the two officers. Both officers pulled out their billy clubs and met the charge. After the troublesome dancers tired of getting their heads busted, they fell back.

Next, the two officers went looking for the two hooligans who had started everything. One suspect ran out the door with Officer Mihic close behind. Mihic ordered him to stop but was ignored. Mihic then drew his weapon and fired once in the air. Still, the man would not stop, so Mihic shot him in the arm. He still managed to get away but was later found on a porch on Tenth Street. The other suspect went peacefully.[289]

In 1895, the only way to reach Fox Lake was by taking a boat on the Fox River. O. L. Stanley operated a steamboat from McHenry to Fox Lake at this time. At some point, the town of McHenry decided to build a dam across the river. The dam was supposed to make it easier to board the steamboat. This book is supposed to be about Lake County stories, but the town of McHenry is close enough.

Not everyone was OK with the dam. The residents of Wilmot, Wisconsin, had a flooding problem, which they blamed on the new dam. About fifty of Wilmot's citizens decided to do something about it and went to McHenry to tear down the dam. Mr. Stanley saw the mob trying to demolish the dam and had to think of something fast to save it. He knew there was an old cannon in town and ran over to get it. The cannon was placed on the town bridge over the Fox River and aimed directly at the mob. Stanley pretended to load the cannon and managed to trick the mob into believing he was ready to fire on them. The mob stopped their work in a hurry but later found out that the cannon was too old to fire. Besides, there was no ammunition for the cannon anyway. All the excitement must have been too much for the folks from Wilmot, and they decided to just go home.[290]

This brawl occurred in 1899 at the corner of Sheridan Road and Washington Street. A group of men had come up from Peoria to work at the sugar refinery. For whatever reason, they could not get along with anyone from Waukegan. Every now and then, a fistfight would break out between a man from Peoria and a citizen of Waukegan.

One day the men from Peoria took a train to Kenosha. They came back stinking drunk and were soon quarreling among themselves. One thing led to another, and half a dozen of the Peoria men came to blows. More men joined in, some from Waukegan. Some of the onlookers were attacked too, and they also joined the fight. The number of fighters kept increasing. The June 3, 1899, *Waukegan Daily Sun* mentioned that a Waukegan resident watching from across the street claimed that "men were lined up fighting from Neeley's saloon to the alley beyond the laundry. 'Why' remarked the person in question' it was the biggest and worst scrap I ever saw. First one man would go down and then another."[291]

In 1910, the Young Buffalo Circus came to town. During the show, a strong wind picked up and blew over the circus's sideshow, dining tent, and dressing rooms. The crowd in the big top panicked, and everyone ran to the center of the tent. In all the confusion, a girl bareback rider fell off her horse but was not seriously injured. Then a fight broke out between the circus workers and some residents of Waukegan. One of the circus workers had attacked a man from Waukegan, and a bad brawl was soon in progress. Many of the fighters from both sides suffered busted heads and had to be carried away.[292]

According to the May 17, 1923, Lake County independent newspaper, Waukegan High School had a bad hazing problem that year. The freshmen class was having a party when a mob of sophomores and a few upper classmen tried to crash the party. Their goal was to kidnap the class president and its top students. The high school superintendent had been notified earlier that the sophomores were planning something. The Waukegan police were notified, and two officers were sent over to stand guard in case there was any trouble. It wasn't long before the mob invaded the high school, coming in through doors, windows, and even the fire escape. The police ordered them all to leave the school, but the situation only got worse. It was time to get control of the mob, and the two officers drew their billy clubs and started cracking heads.

The mob was driven back, but the determined sophomores resorted to a different tactic. They formed up in smaller groups and resumed the attack. Some managed to get past the police and kidnapped a handful of freshmen. The freshmen were then driven out into the countryside and left there to walk home. The kidnappers were in the process of stealing the shoes and socks from a boy and girl when they were saved by the police. The class president was still their ultimate goal, however, and they found him walking home with a friend after the party. The kidnappers came after the president, but he was too quick for them and got away. His friend wasn't so lucky and had to spend the night walking home from the country. The May 17, 1923, Lake County independent newspaper wrote the next day that a number of sophomores had their first experience with a billy club and hurting from busted heads.

# CHAPTER 5

## Ethnic Waukegan/North Chicago

Originally, I wanted to write about the complete ethnic makeup of the entire county. After researching the large number of ethnic groups living in the Waukegan/North Chicago area, I realized that doing the whole county was not feasible. The Waukegan/North Chicago area would provide more than enough to write about.

### First Settlers in the Area

According to the *Waukegan News Sun*, the first settlers in the Waukegan/North Chicago area were mainly Yankees from New England as well as immigrants from England, Scotland, and Ireland—pretty much what I expected. A good number of the Irish immigrants were Catholics. Waukegan, founded in 1835, was first known as Little Fort. The *Waukegan News Sun* claimed that for the first dozen years of Waukegan's existence, most of the population was made up of these Yankees and people from the British Isles.[293] Three exiled Polish soldiers lived in Waukegan by 1840. The 1850 census shows that 137 Canadians lived in Waukegan.

North Chicago was incorporated on May 7, 1895, and became a city on April 12, 1909. North Chicago's ethnic makeup mirrored Waukegan's at first but soon became home to mainly emigrants. Profiles of the following ethnic groups are in alphabetical order.

## Albanians

Finding Albanians living in Waukegan in the early 1900s was a big surprise. Most Albanians that I have met are recent arrivals. Waukegan was thought to be one of only two cities in the United States that had any Albanian emigrants, Cleveland, Ohio, being the other city. About one hundred Albanians lived on Market Street in 1911.[294] The Rand McNally book *The World, Afghanistan to Zimbabwe* claimed that 70 percent of Albanians are Muslim, 20 percent Orthodox Christian, and 10 percent Roman Catholic. Many Albanians converted to Islam during the Turkish occupation of their country. My Albanian friends tell me that more than 20 percent of the population is Orthodox Christian.

Like the Greeks, Armenians, and Macedonians, the Albanians lived through periods of oppression by their Turkish masters. Albania was fighting for its freedom in 1911, and Waukegan's Albanian community frequently received news of the war and atrocities committed by the Turks. Many were worried about their wives and children still in Albania. They had to have someone read everything to them because most were illiterate in English and Albanian.[295] Albania won its independence from Turkey in 1912.

The first Albanian in Waukegan was Youssan Mustapha, who immigrated to Waukegan in 1909. He was the only Albanian living in Waukegan at the time. Youssan was famous for his novel way of relieving toothaches. He had a bad toothache on March 19, 1909, while living in a boardinghouse on Marian Street. Then he showed everyone how they treat toothaches in the mountains of Albania.

According to the *Waukegan Daily Sun*, Youssan "took a revolver cartridge, bored a hole in the end of the bullet, inserted a silk thread, loaded his revolver with the cartridge thus prepared, tied the thread to his offending molar, and fired in the air."[296] He never saw the tooth leave his mouth. Who needs a dentist?

## Armenians

The first Armenians came to Waukegan in the fall of 1891, the year the Washburn and Moen Manufacturing Company opened.[297] Washburn and Moen was purchased by "the American Steel and Wire Company" in

1899 and was known as the wire mill after that. One source I have claims Armenians were living in Waukegan by 1888.[298]

According to Ed Link, the Armenians established a church in 1895. The reverend G. M. Manavian was pastor. They had no building but conducted services at the First Congregational Church at Grand and Utica streets.[299]

According to the *Waukegan Daily Sun*, most Armenians in Waukegan came from the region around Adana.[300] The Armenians were Orthodox Christians, but their homeland was ruled by Muslim Turks. Armenia is the oldest Christian country in the world.

A total of nine Armenians are listed on the 1900 federal census for Waukegan. One is J. Onan, thirty-five years old. He and his wife of German descent and from Wisconsin were the parents of three children, the eldest four years old. The remaining eight Armenians are Manovg Toorian, forty years old; Charles Toorian, twenty-five; Dan Toorian, eighteen; Paul Sahagian, thirty-seven; Giragos Sahagian, thirty-five; M. Sahagian, twenty-five; Sarkis Kashoogian, twenty-eight; and John Hugasian, forty-four. All were born in Turkey.

Except for J. Onan, all the Armenians on the 1900 census were single men. The *Waukegan Daily Sun* claimed that three hundred Armenians lived in Waukegan by 1903, all single men. The first Armenian family to immigrate to Waukegan was the Magarians, arriving in 1903. Mr. Magarian would soon become the most influential Armenian in Waukegan. He convinced nine Armenian families to move to Waukegan in 1905.[301] By 1909, close to seven hundred Armenians called Waukegan home.[302] In 1930, six hundred Armenians showed up to hear ex-Armenian president Vratzian speak at Workers' Hall on Helmholz Avenue.[303]

The Armenian Educational Society used to put on an annual picnic at Waukegan's Electric Park. The 1906 picnic featured the first baseball game in town between two exclusively Armenian teams. A mock wedding was held, and a wrestling match between two of the best Armenian wrestlers in town was put on. Many attendees wore ethnic Armenian costumes. An expert swordsman named Zakar gave an exhibition of his skill and challenged anyone to a swordfight.[304]

I mentioned above that Dr. Magarian and his wife settled in Waukegan about the middle of 1903. Dr. Magarian attended the Congregational Schools in Beirut, Lebanon (then part of Turkey), and the University of Chicago. He was a dentist by trade.

Most Armenian immigrants in Waukegan were single men. Dr. Magarian thought so many single men in the Armenian community was not good and that the companionship of women would help keep them home and out of trouble. He established a night school in Waukegan to teach his fellow countrymen how to read and write in English and Armenian. After only one year, he gave up on the school, but his wife would still tutor anyone wishing to read or write English.[305] Dr. Magarian raised money to help Armenians in Turkey by giving talks in Waukegan and Chicago. Some of the topics included the history, geography, and political situation in Armenia.[306]

The August 23, 1910, *Waukegan Daily Sun* wrote that the Armenians in Waukegan were law abiding and orderly. The *Daily Sun* went on to say that the Armenian "record is one of fair dealing and honesty with all business people, land lords, and citizens generally. No one can complain that a full blooded Armenian ever beat them out of a penny."[307] There were twenty-five Armenian families living in Waukegan by this time. One thing that really ticked them off was when the Armenian residents of Waukegan were mistaken for Turks.[308]

Many of Waukegan's Armenians had lived through some horrific times in Turkey. The Armenian genocide in Turkey took place from 1915 to 1918. I've found stories in the newspapers about atrocities committed against Armenians as early as 1894.[309] An article in the April 29, 1908, *Waukegan Daily Sun* claimed that the Kurds massacred two thousand Armenians in Iran that year.

Mrs. Mary Sevanian witnessed the murders of fifteen members of her immediate family. Only Mary and her brother, Gregor Perzigian, survived. They were eyewitnesses to many massacres. Once, they were forced on a death march by the Turks. Anyone who could not keep up was killed on the spot. Mary thought the Turks were trying to starve them all to death on the march. She and her brother survived because they had hidden some money away and were able to buy some food from the Kurds.[310]

Mrs. Goelege Harion and her three daughters were also forced into a death march. First, the Turks stole all their food and then forced them to leave their homes. Only her eldest daughter, Eva, survived the march; her two youngest daughters didn't make it. They had been compelled to walk for thirteen days and lived on grass and herbs until they arrived in Aleppo. Mrs. Harion claimed the Turks had already cut down every fruit tree along their route so the marchers would have no fruit available to them. Mrs.

The Forgotten History of Lake County, Illinois

Harion's husband had immigrated to Waukegan at an earlier date and was able to save enough money to bring his wife and daughter to Waukegan. He sent money to the American consulate in Aleppo with directions to help his family if they made it there and find them passage to America.[311]

Fourteen-year-old Lavon Boghosian came to Waukegan in 1923. His father was an American citizen and Waukegan resident when he returned to Turkey to get his family. While in Turkey, Lavon's father was killed in a massacre. Lavon's mother lived for only a short time after the massacre. After his mother died, Lavon was kidnapped and sold into slavery. He was only seven years old at the time and sold to an Arab. J. Pedrosian of Waukegan found out about it and paid Lavon's master $100 for his freedom. Lavon's uncle, Avedias Kahazarian of Waukegan, then sent for Lavon and took him in.[312] The League of Nations estimated that thirty thousand Armenians were enslaved in Syria in 1927, the majority women.[313]

Waukegan resident Arthur Toomajanian escaped from the Turks in 1916 and hid in a cave for months. He had little clothing and almost starved to death. He was only able to survive because the Russian Army was able to wrest control of the area from the Turks. He claimed to have witnessed massacres of men, women, and children.[314]

Nishan Pilibosian was nine years old when his family was evicted from their home by the Turks and forced to march through the desert to Syria. Many people died or were murdered along the way, including Nishan's father and a brother. Nishan managed to escape the death march by lying next to a dead body and playing dead. After many different experiences, "most of them bad," he was sent to an orphanage. Later, he was reunited with his mother and sisters who had survived the march. Eventually, the Pilibosian family settled in Waukegan.[315]

A number of times, American charities asked citizens for aid to help Armenians. In 1909, the National Red Cross asked for contributions to assist Armenian refugees.[316] In 1916, the good citizens of Waukegan raised $11,000 in contributions for the relief of Armenia.[317] Waukegan and North Chicago set a goal of collecting $6,000 to donate to Armenia in 1919.[318] Waukegan's American Legion, churches, businesses, and women's clubs were all raising money to help Armenian orphans in 1920.[319]

Despite the *Daily Sun*'s glowing account in 1910, the Armenians weren't all saints. They got into trouble every now and then just like every other ethnic group. They were divided by political differences and had some serious interethnic conflicts.[320] They also engaged in a long-lasting

71

feud with Waukegan's Turkish residents and occasionally other ethnic groups as well.

## Austrians

Waukegan's Austrians were not of the German persuasion but four different ethnic groups whose homelands were ruled by Austria-Hungary. The Slovenians and Croatians were the two largest groups. After World War I, these two groups became a part of Yugoslavia. The Slovaks and Czechs were the other two ethnic groups. After World War I, they were joined together to form the country of Czechoslovakia.

## Slovenians

A small number of Austrians worked at the wire mill when it first opened in fall 1891. Some were definitely Slovenians, but it is not possible to figure out if any members of the other three groups of Austrians were among them. Frank Petkovsek was one of the first Slovenians in Waukegan, possibly by 1890.[321] The Slovenian National Home Society wrote that most of Waukegan's Slovenians worked at the wire mill. Some also worked at the sugar refinery until it closed in 1912. Many of Waukegan's Slovenians came from the Vrhnika region of Slovenia.

More Slovenians came in 1893. Their names are John Podboj, John Sctnikar, John Hamovc, John Mrlak, Frank Jereb, Frank Zdesar, Matic Surca, John Kocar, Frank Grom (Lukovc), and Miha, Frank, and John Jerina (Kocjan). The Slovenians must have liked the names John and Frank. Six of the names I just listed are John and four Frank.[322] Soon, they were joined by Frank Svete, Jacob Japel, and Joseph Smole.

According to Joze Zavertnick, a Slovenian society was formed in 1894. Joe Mihelic played a big part in organizing the society and was elected its first president. Mihelic was from the Belokraign region of Slovenia.[323]

The Slovenian National Society claimed that fifty Slovenians lived in Waukegan by 1899. The first Slovenians immigrants were all single men, but seven Slovenian families immigrated to town in 1899. The head of households were Frank Jereb, Anton Jereb (Bancar), F. Remzgar, Matevz Zitka, John Mrlak, Jacob Japelj, and F. Mrlak.

A few Slovenians managed to open their own businesses by the early 1900s. Frank Petovsek opened a grocery store in 1902 and later a tavern. John Umek was in the tavern business by 1901. Joseph Polansek and Joseph Root each got into the tavern business by 1902. From 1903 to 1905, Kosicek and Stefanic ran a clothing store. John Straziser sold cigars until he got into the tavern business in 1903. J. Root, Frank Marinsek, and Jacob and John Kukar established a meat market in 1904.

Few, if any, of these first Slovenians spoke English. Many had spent time in the Austrian Army and spoke German. A German saloon owner named Holstein was a great help to them, interpreting documents and newspapers for them. The Slovenians, in turn, patronized Holstein's saloon. Mr. Holstein also helped them become American citizens.[324]

So many Austrians lived on Market Street in 1906 that the March 16, 1906, Lake County independent newspaper referred to the place as "A Miniature Austria."[325] Market Street was the wildest part of town then. It was the place to go for illegal gambling, saloons, and dance halls. Fights were common, and the sound of accordion and violin music was the norm.[326] Waukegan's citizens constantly complained about Market Street. One man wrote a letter to the editor, stating that he had repeatedly talked to the police about Market Street but to no avail.[327]

The Slovenian National Society stated that the first Slovenians attended St. Joseph's German Church on Oak Street in Waukegan.[328] St. Joe's was established in 1863. The Slovenians built their own church, Mother of God, in 1903.

The 1900 census for Waukegan Township counted 144 Austrians in the township. A total of 500 Austrians lived in Waukegan and North Chicago in 1909.[329] By 1913, 897 Austrians lived in Waukegan and a grand total of 1,752 in Lake County.[330] The number of Austrians in Waukegan shot up to 1,030 by 1914.[331] There is no way to know exactly how many of these Austrians were actually Slovenians.

The Slovenian National Society wrote that Fr. John Plevnik arrived in Waukegan in 1903 and established Mother of God Church on Tenth Street. The church was consecrated on Thanksgiving Day 1903.[332]

Mother of God Church experienced some problems in 1911. Some of the parishioners began to question Father Plevnik about the church's finances. The dissatisfaction with Father Plevnik continued to grow, and in 1912, a representative was sent to Archbishop Quigley to ask for a different priest. Quigley temporarily replaced Father Plevnik with Father

Kalan. Father Kalan had just come over from Slovenia and right away became very popular with most of the parish. A minority of the parish still favored Father Plevnik, though, and wasn't too happy about his removal. At a church meeting in June 1912, one of the church trustees who favored Father Plevnik insulted Father Kalan. Father Kalan had him thrown out.[333]

The Slovenian National Society claimed that Father Kalan was only supposed to minister at Mother of God until a permanent replacement for Father Plevnik could be found. The replacement was Fr. Joseph Stukelj. By then, Father Kalan had become so well liked that a majority of the parishioners refused to accept Father Stukelj and asked the archbishop to reconsider keeping Father Kalan. The archbishop, however, was unwilling to reverse his decision.

The archbishop's decision didn't go over very well, and on July 21, 1912, a majority of the parishioners left the church. They, along with Father Kalan, started holding Mass at J. Root's store. Father Kalan tried to convince his new parishioners to build a new church, but they soon realized that the effort would be fruitless. They did not think the archbishop or the pope would accept a new church.

Many people did not want to go back to Mother of God Church and instead decided to build a benefit lodge to help one another out.[334] The new building took four years to build and was located at 424 Tenth Street, right down the street from Mother of God Church. It was completed in December 1918 and named the Slovenic National Home.[335]

In 1917, the Slovenians, along with some of the Croatian, Polish, Slovak, and Lithuanian residents of Waukegan and North Chicago, held a parade to demonstrate their loyalty to the United States. Fr. Francis J. Azbe, pastor of Mother of God Church, organized the parade. A total of eight different societies marched in the parade: St. Joseph's Society, St. George Society, Maria Pomagej Society, Holy Family Society, Croatian Society, and three different Slovak societies. School children from Holy Rosary, St. Bart's, and Mother of God also marched in the parade. A total of 1,200 men, women, and children participated in the parade.

The parade started on McAllister Avenue and snaked its way through the south side of Waukegan and North Chicago, finally stopping at Mother of God Church. The United States flag was raised to a great amount of cheering. A number of prominent men from Waukegan and North Chicago gave speeches, and school children sang patriotic songs. Next, some of the men pledged to stop using hyphenated names like Polish-American and

Lithuanian-American. From then on, they would only be Americans. The event ended with everyone singing the national anthem.[336]

## Croatians

The Croatian experience in Waukegan and North Chicago closely mirrors the Slovenian one. Frances Burkich Vetrone and Frances Matijevich Van Dyke, writing in Osling's book, *Historical Highlights of the Waukegan Area*, stated that the first Croatians arrived by at least 1895 and possibly sooner. They, like the Slovenians, went to St. Joseph's Catholic Church at first and later to Mother of God. I noticed in my research that Mother of God's basketball team was champion of the parochial league in Waukegan/North Chicago many times. A total of 90 percent of the Croatian immigrants worked at the wire mill. The first Croatians lived around St. Joseph's Church or on Market Street. Later, they moved to the area around Tenth Street. Like the Slovenians, a number of Croatians started businesses at an early date. Richard Pucin established a travel agency in Highwood. Andro Pucin had a beer distributing company. John Katalinich was a co-owner of a bowling alley in North Chicago. John Simcic was a contractor. Steve Krpan ran a gas station. George Pavelich owned Masterbuilt Fence Company. Michael Blazevich had the Nimco Company, and Frank Blazevich was associated with Lake Shore Harley-Davidson. George Jurkovac owned A B Tax Service.

Michael Pucin was North Chicago city attorney for twenty years and a Waukegan township attorney for twenty-eight years. He was also an assistant for the state of Illinois attorney general. Michael was responsible for obtaining land in Lake County for the construction of the tollway. He would have dealt with my uncle Dan Lodesky, whose farm was in the path of the tollway.

The Croatians were known for a dance group called the Kolo. Even better known was the Waukegan Tamburitzans, an orchestra organized in 1972. Your author was in a wedding at Slovenic Hall where the Tamburitzans played. The American-Croatian Cultural Center located on Sheridan Road in North Chicago was formed in 1975. It moved to a new building on the west side of Waukegan but is no longer at that location.[337] The Croatians and Slovenians always seem to have had baseball teams competing in the Waukegan baseball leagues.

## Slovaks and Czechs

There doesn't seem to be a great number of Czecho-Slovaks living in North Chicago and Waukegan. I can't find much about either of these groups. Most of what I have found is about the Slovaks. I heard by word of mouth that a couple neighborhoods of Slovaks lived near the Polish section in North Chicago. Joseph Potocky was one of the earliest Czecho-Slovak settlers in North Chicago. I'm not sure if he was Czech or Slovak. He arrived by at least 1896 and lived in North Chicago for forty years. Joe was a member of the North Chicago Police Department for thirty years.[338]

The Czecho-Slovaks had some trouble becoming citizens. They were considered citizens of Austria and listed as alien enemies. Their applications for citizenship kept getting turned down. The Slovenians and Croatians were both a part of Austria-Hungry too, but there is no evidence that they had any problems becoming citizens.

In 1919, the Czecho-Slovaks appointed John Simmons to petition Waukegan judge Edwards for help. Edwards took up their cause with the Federal Naturalization Bureau in Chicago. Simmons, along with a circuit court employee named Brockway, went to Chicago to argue their case. The naturalization bureau agreed to allow some of them to become naturalized. The rest would have to wait until the next naturalization day six months later. The names of some of the earliest Czecho-Slovak immigrants naturalized are George W. Bauman, Czeslaw Pecak, Stefan Drinka, George Pavlovic, Josef Sisolak, Jacob Sliva, and Andresj Ornatek.[339]

The Slovaks took their new citizenship seriously. They were known to turn out in large numbers for city, township, and county elections. The Slovak Political Society was one of the most notable clubs in North Chicago. They named their meeting hall after John Simmons, the man who had helped them get their citizenship.[340]

## Blacks

Amos Bennett, a free black, was one of the first settlers in the county, coming here in1835. Lake County was still Indian territory then, but the Indians were supposed to leave the county by February 23, 1835. White settlers started entering Lake County in large numbers in 1835 and 1836.

Amos was born in Connecticut in 1797. The Bennetts moved to Delhi,

New York, in 1799. Bennett settled in the future Warren Township with his wife Clara, son Henry, and daughter Emily. They settled near Gurnee at Washington Street and Route 21, next to the Des Plaines River.

Amos divorced Clara in 1840 and married Ann Frances six years later. Ann was born in Virginia in 1817. They were the parents of four children—Josephine, Lilly, and a set of twin boys. There is no record of the twins' names.[341]

The June 26, 1935, *Waukegan News Sun* wrote that Amos was remembered most for claiming he was "the first white man to ever plant corn in Lake County."[342] Supposedly, he made the declaration while in a tavern with some of the local farmers. They were debating about who was the first white settler in the county.[343]

Amos was supposed to have been a pretty fair doctor who knew many cures using only herbs. Once, he was sent for to save the life of a woman struck by lightning. Mrs. Blanchard had gone outside during a storm to check on a water barrel when she was struck by lightning. She looked dead, but Bennett took her arm and cut open a blood vein. The bleeding restarted her circulation, and she was soon awake.[344] The February 23, 1867, *Waukegan Gazette* wrote that Amos "was an industrious, peaceable man, and was much respected by all his white neighbors."[345]

Bennett lived in the Gurnee area until 1852. That year, he sold 40 acres to Philip Blanchard and moved to Wisconsin. At one time, he owned at least 140 acres and was known to buy and sell land on a regular basis.[346]

The 1840 federal census records two other free blacks living somewhere in the county in 1840. Their names were never recorded. One lived and worked on the John Flood Farm. The other lived and worked on the Abel Keys Farm.

James Dorsey, writing in *The Underground Railroad: Northeastern Illinois and Southwestern Wisconsin*, claimed that James Cory had a free black maid named Marina working for him before the Civil War. Cory was the editor of the *Waukegan Daily Gazette* newspaper and operated a grain business as well. He was also involved in the Underground Railroad and used Marina to help smuggle escaped slaves out of town. Everyone knew that Marina was free and worked for Cory. The escaped slaves would accompany Marina to the lakefront, and everyone thought that they, too, worked for Cory. Once at the lakefront, they would board ships for Canada.[347]

More blacks immigrated to Lake County in the 1840s and are listed on the 1850 federal census. Waukegan Township was home to four black families with a combined total of twenty-three people. Two single black men and three single black women also lived in Waukegan, making a total of twenty-eight blacks living in Waukegan in 1850. Three of the black men on the 1850 census were barbers. The February 28, 2003, *Lake County Journal* listed thirty-one blacks living in Waukegan in 1850.

By 1860, the population of blacks living in Waukegan had dropped considerably. James Dorsey thought that the passage of the Fugitive Slave Act in 1850 could have been the reason for the drop. They might have all gone to Canada. Dorsey also claimed that thirteen blacks lived in Waukegan in 1860.[348] I can only find six blacks living in two families and two single black men living in Waukegan on the 1860 federal census, for a total of eight blacks. Three of them were recorded on the 1850 census: W. H. Medlin, Henderson Medlin, and Warren Medlin. Henderson Medlin worked at Michael Dalanty's hotel. W. H. Medlin worked for a banker named C. D. Bickford, and Warren Medlin lived with the Walter Brown family. Warren's occupation was servant.

By 1870, the black population of Waukegan had turned over again. Not one black person listed on the 1860 federal census was still living in Waukegan on the 1870 federal census. Living in Waukegan Township in 1870 was John Dennison, eighteen years old and a laborer. He lived and worked for the Elisha S. Wadsworth family. Wadsworth was very wealthy and owned a large farm.

Living in the city of Waukegan was Charles Western, thirty-seven years old. His occupation was whitewasher, which must have meant a house painter. Charles's wife, Mary, was twenty-two years old and kept house. They had a three-year-old daughter named Nellie.

Living nine houses away from the Westerns was Joseph R. Hallston, age forty-three and occupation whitewasher. Hallston's wife, Elizabeth, was fifty years old.

James Brooks, age twenty, lived with the John Swansbrow family. Swansbrow worked at a livery stable. Brooks must have been a boarder; he listed his occupation as hotel worker.

Living and working at Jane Murry's boardinghouse was Julius Keyser, nineteen. Mrs. Murry had a good-size boardinghouse with a total of twenty-seven people living there, including herself.

Waukegan's third ward recorded Lewis Johnson, eighteen, occupation laborer. He lived with the Dennis Marr family. Also in ward 3 was Reuben

Lee, an eighteen-year-old laborer. He lived and worked at the Mariden Merchant Farm. This makes a grand total of ten blacks residing in Waukegan in 1870.

The April 29, 1876, *Waukegan Gazette* reported about two of our subjects recorded in the 1870 census. Julius Keyser planned to rent Phoenix Hall to host a fifty-mile walking match between himself and Reuben Lee. The winner would take home $50.

Reuben Lee escaped slavery and came to Waukegan during the Civil War. He never knew his age but figured that he was about fifteen years old when he first arrived. Reuben lost all contact with his relatives after escaping and never saw them again. His first job was clerking at the Sherman House. Later, he worked as a porter at the Washburn Hotel. Reuben died on June 21, 1917.[349]

By 1880, the black population of Waukegan had doubled. There were nineteen blacks living in three separate families. In addition, there were two single black men and one woman. The total number was twenty-two people. Once again, the whole black population of Waukegan had turned over. Reuben Lee must still have been living in Waukegan, but he was not on the census and appears to be the only one left over from the 1870 census.

Blacks living in Waukegan on the 1880 census were as follows:

Julia Crawford, a seventy-three-year-old widow. Her occupation was washerwoman.

Joseph H. Turner, twenty-eight years old, married, occupation laborer. Elizabeth, his wife, was thirty-eight years old and kept house. Elizabeth was the mother of Edward, twenty years old, occupation laborer. Joe and Elizabeth had a daughter, Adna, age nine.

Morris Robbins, a twenty-nine-year-old laborer. Morris lived at Nelson Landon's house and worked for him as well.

Samuel Daniels was a forty-year-old night watchman and was married. Caldonie, his wife, was thirty-three and kept house. They were the parents of three daughters: Martie, eight; Dora, ten; and Mary M., one month.

John Smith was a sixteen-year-old servant. He lived at the Patrick Gavigan home.

Tillman Smith, age fifty-three, was married and a farmer. Emeline, his wife, was forty-two and kept house. The Smiths had eight children: Joseph, nineteen; John, sixteen; Alexander, fourteen; Eddie, ten; Nellie, eight; Lillie B., six; Mary, four; and Lafayette, one. Tillman either owned or rented his farm. He was the first black since Amos Bennett to manage his own farm. All the others were hired men. Smith was born in Kentucky and had spent about ten years in Wisconsin before coming to Waukegan.

Two of Tillman Smith's sons, Joseph and Alexander, were arrested for stealing sheep in the winter of 1886. They stole six sheep from Charles Barnstable and put them all in a sled. The police followed the sled's tracks all the way to Smith's home on Grand Avenue. The same two were in trouble at the same time for stealing three sheep from Mr. Morrison.[350]

The *Waukegan Gazette* wrote about another black on the 1880 census. Joe "Harry" Turner's house caught on fire in 1879. Turner, with help from his neighbors, was able to put the fire out in time.[351]

I cannot find an 1890 census. The Waukegan city directories record only two blacks living in Waukegan at this time: Green Tarver and George Bell. Green Tarver was considered Waukegan's first permanent black resident. The first permanent black residents were probably Reuben Hill and Reuben Lee. According to the *Waukegan Daily Sun*, Reuben Hill was born a slave but during the Civil War became the servant of Dr. Evans of the Ninety-Sixth Illinois Infantry Regiment. He came to Waukegan with the Ninety-Sixth at the end of the war and was still living in Waukegan in 1910.[352] I can't find any record of Reuben Hill in census records, but Reuben was definitely living here. (I previously wrote about Reuben Lee.) He participated in a walking race against Julius Keyser in 1876.

The 1900 Waukegan census documents a substantial increase in the black population of Waukegan. There are now too many to list all their names. Ten black families then lived in Waukegan for a total of thirty-eight people. In addition, five single men and three single women lived in Waukegan. One man named Charles Downer was a fireman, making him the first black fireman in Waukegan.

Large numbers of blacks settled in Waukegan in 1903. Waukegan's factories needed workers and started recruiting blacks.[353] Some Waukegan factories provided company boardinghouses for their black workers. The Wilder Tannery planned to spend $125,000 to build fifty cottages for its black workers in 1918 and then make it possible for them to buy their cottage with a low-interest mortage.[354]By 1910, Lake County's black population reached a total of 491. They made up .9 percent of the county's population. A total of 339 of them considered themselves black while 152 registered as mulatto. There were 261 females as compared with 230 males. A total of 52 were going to school, and 2 blacks owned their farms, but the combined total of acreage for both was only fourteen acres.[355]

The Forgotten History of Lake County, Illinois

James Dorsey wrote in his master's thesis that an unknown black man was living in North Chicago by at least 1889. Richmond Duncan lived in North Chicago sometime before 1900. The Barretts, Bobos, Montgomerys, and Thompsons were some of the first black families to live in North Chicago. Other early black settlers in North Chicago were L. Evans, Fannie Evans, O. W. Evans, and Charles Edwards.[356]

North Chicago's black settlers had a much different beginning as compared with Waukegan's blacks. There was no segregation in Waukegan until about 1920. North Chicago seems to have been segregated almost from the beginning. The May 10, 1920, *Waukegan Daily Sun* claimed that in 1897, lots located west of the North Shore railroad tracks were sold to blacks to keep them from settling in the rest of town.[357] The April 26, 1907, Lake County independent newspaper published an interesting story about another black settlement in North Chicago. In 1907, a wealthy farmer living about two miles west of Twenty-Second Street tried to buy a neighboring farm. The wealthy farmer already owned most of the land around the farm, but the owner still refused to sell his land. The wealthy farmer fixed him. He divided the part of his farm surrounding his neighbor's farm into lots and sold them to blacks.[358]

North Chicago had an interesting beginning. *Historical Highlights of the Waukegan Area* by Osling wrote that it was all farmland until 1891, and it was considered the south side of Waukegan. That year, a group of investors from Chicago and Detroit came in and bought almost all the land that makes up the current North Chicago. They paid exorbitant prices for much of it. The future town was divided up into 1,500 lots. The government took some of the best land to build Great Lakes Naval Base on, but the investors still kept the rest. The investors promoted the town as a future manufacturing hub. It would also be a dry town with no taverns allowed. That didn't last long, and North Chicago soon had twenty-seven taverns. In 1892, a "Women's Land Syndicate" got involved and promoted the town as a "Dry Utopia." As I just wrote, the new town didn't stay dry for long.[359] The Women's Land Syndicate sold land to people from around the world. The investors thought they were buying property near Chicago. The women knew some people thought they were buying real estate on the north side of Chicago but never bothered to tell them.[360]

Cyrenius A. Newcomb was one of the main land investors in the future North Chicago. He joined the other investors in 1892. Newcomb ran into financial trouble in 1893, but two friends from Detroit came to his rescue

81

and loaned him money until he was back on his feet. On his death in 1915, Newcomb owned about fifty houses in North Chicago plus a good amount of vacant lots.[361]

North Chicago had a population of 733 blacks in 1926, 340 in the southern district of town, and 393 in the northern part of town. They lived mainly west of the Commonwealth School and on Eighteenth Street at the North Chicago city limits.[362]

The December 16, 1925, *Waukegan Daily Sun* wrote that the Black Lake County Political Club spent two months recording the number of black voters in the county.

The results were as follows:

| | |
|---|---|
| Waukegan | 1,568 |
| North Chicago | 481 |
| Highland Park | 81 |
| Lake Forest | 49 |
| Zion | 35 |

It was also found that two-thirds of the qualified black voters in the county never voted. The total number of black voters in the county in 1925 was 2,284.[363]

Curtis L. Dorsey wrote in *Historical Highlights of the Waukegan Area* by Osling that before 1905, blacks went to white churches. Blacks, however, longed for their own church. The reverend Harry E. Johnson came to Waukegan that year and began conducting church services in parishioners' homes. In 1911, he presided over building the Trinity African Methodist Episcopal Church on Oak Street.[364]

Waukegan's and North Chicago's black churches pooled their resources in 1922 to form the Christian Moral Protective League. According to the July 29, 1922, *Waukegan Daily Sun*, "The purpose of the league is to provide clean amusement, look after the civic and religious welfare of the Colored people of the community, and in this way lessen law violation and educate the young."[365]

White churches and organizations, like the Rotary and Kiwanis clubs, thought it was a great idea and were eager to help in any way. Many whites offered their assistance and support to the league.[366]

The county's black World War I military veterans decided to form a "Blacks Only" American Legion Post in 1927. At the time, there were 1,000 black veterans in Lake County. Many American Legion posts in

The Forgotten History of Lake County, Illinois

Lake County had black members, and black veterans had always been welcome there. Many blacks, though, did not feel comfortable in the white legion posts and wanted their own post.[367]

Waukegan's recreation board established a private playground for black children on south Genesee Street in 1928. Black children could use any park or playground at the time, but it was thought that it would be a great help to the black community.[368]

Waukegan had a community garden plot exclusively for blacks in 1932. Thomas McCann, the local alderman, assigned them the plot.[369]

Blacks living in the Oakland Subdivision, also called Frog Island, encountered some problems in 1926. The subdivision had a bad flooding problem, and its residents did not think the city was doing enough to fix it. The city of Waukegan claimed that seventy lots out of the three hundred in the subdivision were delinquent on their taxes, so Waukegan could not pay for all the needed improvements.[370]

Abraham Davis, author of the *History of the Negro in Lake County*, claimed that blacks had the run of the town before 1917. They could live anywhere in town and went to the same schools, theaters, and churches as whites.[371] White people also patronized black businesses. Ed Link stated that Waukegan High School's first basketball team in 1896 had a black on it.[372]

A large number of blacks immigrated to Waukegan during World War I. Abraham Davis thought that this emigration brought on segregation.[373] Curtis L. Dorsey, writing in *Historical Highlights of the Waukegan Area*, wrote that Waukegan was segregated by 1920.[374]

Some whites were getting nervous about the large increase of blacks and demanded the city create a black district in 1917.[375] In 1916, some kind of commotion in the black part of North Chicago caused the whites to react in the same way.[376] In 1920, two hundred North Chicago property owners demanded the city pass a law to prevent blacks from moving into majority white areas. Real estate agents had started selling houses to blacks in the majority white district. The whites might have also been afraid that black emigration to white areas might result in declining property values and increased crime. The whites held what turned into a raucous meeting at Parish Hall on Fourteenth Street. A resolution was passed by an almost unanimous decision to stop selling real estate to blacks in the white area between Tenth and Sixteenth streets.[377] There is no evidence that the blacks who had already purchased real estate in the white district were

83

forced to move. Old-timers tell me they remember black families living in all white neighborhoods in the 1930s.

## Some Incidents That Led to Segregation

An incident in 1900 raised the ire of Waukegan's white community. The thirty-fifth anniversary of emancipation from slavery took place at George's Grove on September 20, 1900. Ellen Williams Staben, author of the manuscript *As I Remember the Southeast Side of Waukegan in the Early 1900s* claimed that George's Grove, the site of the picnic, was located west of McAlister Avenue. Bands of gypsies used to camp there during the summer months. George's Grove was also used as a horse traders' market.[378] A total of ten thousand blacks from Illinois and Wisconsin were expected to attend the two-day event. Waukegan welcomed them all.

A number of contests and events were planned, but the whole affair proved to be a complete bomb.[379] Waukegan's welcome soon turned to disgust after a number of blacks tried to turn the event into a gambling casino on the first day.[380] Besides that, few people showed up the first day. The low turnout was not the problem but gambling was. Gambling was illegal, and most people took a very dim view of it. Gambling did take place but was always conducted in secret. It's amazing the police did not arrest anyone. Only about one hundred people came out on the second day, and half of those were white.[381]

Speakers from the Republican and Democratic parties were scheduled to speak. The top black speakers from Illinois and Wisconsin were also in attendance. The speakers, though, were appalled at the gambling and stormed out of the festival.[382]

The *Waukegan Daily Sun* newspaper was upset as well and wrote on September 22, 1900:

> *Colored people's picnic past and city glad of it. No more are desired. The affair as a whole has greatly disgraced the city. They'll never come here again.*[383]

Two articles published in the *Waukegan Daily Sun* in 1902 and 1906 shed more light on reasons for segregation.

Here's an excerpt from the October 19, 1902, *Waukegan Daily Sun*:

> *Justice Weiss explained that there had been numerous Negro cutting affrays lately, that they must stop, especially when the men branch out and begin cutting White people. So long as you keep to yourselves, it isn't so annoying, said the judge.*[384]

The *Waukegan Daily Sun* wrote on January 3, 1906:

> *The times in Waukegan are certainly getting strenuous as far as Negro troubles are concerned. The colored gentry here have been given lots of lee way and it is to be regretted that they have lately shown a disposition to create disturbances through cutting and shooting affrays.*
>
> *From certain quarters in the city word is sent out that the residents of the neighborhood are fearful that some night there will be a big riot among the colored men and that one, or more, of them will be killed.*
>
> *Reference is made to a particular hang-out of the Negroes which has lately come into disrepute because of frequent noisy rows, resulting in calls for police by neighbors. The authorities perhaps maintain the ideas advanced by the great emancipator, Lincoln, but the colored men should do their part in keeping quietude and peace in a community. Our sympathies are naturally with the still down-trodden colored men, but there is no getting around the fact that some Whites of the north are acquiring the feeling of their southern brethren, to a certain degree, hence it is up to the Negroes to avoid arousing those unkind feelings whenever they can.*[385]

The white immigrants living in "Little Europe" acted in pretty much the same way. The difference between the blacks and the new European immigrants was that the immigrants lived mainly in their own neighborhoods on Waukegan's south side and North Chicago. Waukegan's residents might read about trouble in "Little Europe," but they usually stayed away from the area. Blacks were not segregated, so whites witnessed black crime. Integration worked against blacks in this regard.

According to the January 1, 1907, Lake County independent newspaper, Mrs. Sadie Watkins, black, remarked in 1907, "Never have I been among such low down colored people as I seem to have found here."[386] A well-known Waukegan doctor remarked in the September 21, 1923, *Waukegan Daily Sun* that the recently arrived black immigrants living on Market Street were "Southern Cabin Negroes."[387]

The situation was much improved by 1908. The *Waukegan Daily Sun* reported in August that there had not been any Negro crime for almost a year. None had been arrested for months. Blacks in other cities had been forming societies to stop black crime and vice, but Waukegan did not need one. Blacks in Chicago formed a society in 1907 to stop black crime and demanded that black lawbreakers spend more time in prison.[388]

The reverend H. E. Johnson, black pastor of the First Methodist church in Waukegan, knew how to get along with the white population. An article in the July 2, 1909, *Waukegan Daily Sun* mentioned that many black emigrants to Waukegan in the early 1900s were no strangers to the police. Reverend Johnson knew that black troublemakers had to go if Waukegan's blacks ever wanted to be on the good side of whites and encouraged his congregation to run them out of town. His efforts paid off, and Waukegan's black citizens were soon considered some of the best citizens in town.[389]

In 1910, a large conference was held in Lake Forest to urge blacks to lead better lives. Blacks from most towns between Chicago and Milwaukee attended the conference. Quite a few whites were also present. The goal of the conference, according to the August 18, 1910, *Waukegan Daily Sun*, "seeks to induce colored citizens of both sexes to live sober, industrious, orderly lives that will earn the respect of their white brethren."[390]

The improvement in the black community was only temporary. A new problem was soon on the scene: vice! Black crime was bad enough, but vice seems to be the last straw for Waukegan's white population, and Waukegan was segregated by 1920.

In 1920, Waukegan's law-abiding blacks volunteered to help the police run the worst black offenders out of town. Blacks from Waukegan and North Chicago formed "the Negro Uplift Association" in 1923. They also worked with the police to bring black criminals to justice, but it was already too late to stop segregation.

I only partially agree with Abraham Davis that the large amount of black immigration caused segregation. Some whites no doubt thought it was an invasion. In 1921, Waukegan's chief of police thought that blacks were trying to segregate Market Street.[391] Eventually, they did take over

Market Street. My own opinion is that segregation was caused by three factors—the large black immigration, vice, and violent crime.

Some segregation was of the blacks' own making. Blacks segregated themselves in all black churches and American Legion posts, even though they were welcomed by whites. Some blacks believed in segregation. According to the December 8, 1906, *Waukegan Daily Sun*, a black preacher named Hubert Grant believed in the separation of the races. He lived in Zion but sometimes preached at the African Methodist Church in Waukegan.

## The Ku Klux Klan

Waukegan had 450 Klansmen in 1922.[392] Waukegan's Klan was probably one of the tamest Klans anywhere. Unless I missed something, I can't find anything bad the Klan did in Waukegan or Lake County besides burning a few crosses. In 1924, they donated $50 to the Black Sinai Baptist Church in North Chicago, claiming that they "wished to help the race, rather than antagonize it."[393] The same thing happened in Galesburg, Illinois, in 1924. There, the Klan donated $65 to a black church, but the board of directors gave the money back.[394] In 1922, the Waukegan Klan donated $100 to the Salvation Army.[395] In 1925, the Klan built a four-bedroom house for the widow of a Waukegan motorcycle policeman killed because of a Halloween prank. On Halloween night, someone had put a log across a Waukegan Street, and the policeman ran into it and was killed. A picture in the *Daily Sun* shows a number of Klansmen dressed in full Klan garb, building the house.[396]

The Waukegan Klan seems to have caused more trouble to Waukegan's white citizens than its black ones. In 1922, someone produced a list of the names of supposed Klan members in town and gave it to the mayor. The mayor shared the list with many others with the result that he almost started a feud with the *Waukegan Daily Sun* newspaper. One man on the list was a member of the newspaper staff. The newspaper wrote that the mayor was an idiot (among other descriptions of the mayor) and disputed the allegation. The paper pointed out that it had always treated every race, nationality, and religion with the highest regard.[397]

The following month, a Waukegan attorney tried to sue the *Waukegan Daily Sun* newspaper and eight suspected Klansmen. The attorney was upset that the newspaper had printed a story claiming that the attorney had drawn a gun on a man in his office and ordered him out. The man had asked the attorney if he knew who was circulating the list of names of suspected Klansmen. The attorney was suing the eight men for acting like Klansmen. The eight men were very well-known around town, and all denied the charges. Some of the men were known to have campaigned against the Klan and considered it all a joke. By this time, it looked like the list of suspected Klansmen was just a fraud, and the attorney was trying to make a name for himself.[398]

In 1923, the Ben L. Jones Camp number 50 United Spanish-American War Veterans of Waukegan came out against the Klan. They thought the Klan was un-American and promoted division between the races and religions. They also called on law enforcement to break up the organization.[399]

In 1924, the Klan burned ten crosses on the same night in the county. The cross burnings took place in Antioch, Deerfield, Grayslake, Highland Park, Lake Forest, Lake Villa, Lake Zurich, Wadsworth, Wauconda, and Zion.[400]

The Klan had a bad day in 1924. A total of ten thousand Klansmen from all over Northern Illinois showed up for a grand meeting at an unknown location on Grange Hall Road. Grange Hall Road started at Route 21 and continued west at least as far as Route 45. It's part of Washington Street now. The Lodesky farm was situated on Grange Hall Road, and I have to wonder what my relatives must have thought about the meeting since we are Catholics. The Klan was anti-Catholic for a time but eventually admitted Catholics.

It rained the morning of the festivities, but it didn't stop anyone from attending. Thousands of cars were parked along the road and in nearby fields. Then a drenching rain started at noon, and everyone ran to their cars and tried to leave. Unfortunately, the fields were so muddy by then that hundreds of cars were stuck and had to be pushed out. The *Waukegan Daily Sun* reported that many of the cars and their passengers made it back to Waukegan all covered in mud.[401]

A strange incident took place in 1924. A white man was found in a Winthrop Harbor cabin barely alive. He was tied up, starving, dehydrated, and branded with the letters KKK on his breast. He was also gagged with a cloth and had a towel covering his eyes.

The man claimed that he left Cudahy, Wisconsin, a week earlier

The Forgotten History of Lake County, Illinois

to visit his father-in-law in Detroit, Michigan. He planned to discuss a business deal with his father-in-law and carried $360 with him. After arriving in Detroit, he was captured by half-a-dozen blacks and taken to a shack. He claimed that about thirty blacks were hanging around the place. They tortured him until he pleaded for them to just kill him. Next, he thought his captors drove him through Michigan City and Gary, Indiana, but didn't remember anything else until Officer Jensen revived him in Winthrop Harbor.[402]

Another strange incident occurred in 1925. A white Chicago man rented an eighty-acre farm east of Wauconda with the intension of starting a chicken farm. No one had lived on the farm for some time. The Chicago man was accompanied by his wife and three daughters. The man and his wife went to visit her cousin in Mundelein and left their eldest daughter, a twelve-year-old, in charge. When the man, his wife, and her cousin returned, they found their daughters scared and terrified.

The eldest daughter explained that a group of men had carried a twelve-foot-high oil-soaked cross onto the front lawn and leaned it on a fence about sixty feet from the house. Next, a man crept up to the cross and lit it on fire while another man stood by with a shotgun. A notice was later found in the yard with the letters KKK printed on it and a message to "Get Out."

The cousin decided to stay for the night in case there was any more trouble. He didn't have long to wait, for trouble was about to begin. About eleven o'clock, he was awakened by his cousin's husband, who immediately gave him a rifle. The house was being strafed with gunfire by a group of local farmers. The two returned fire, and the battle was on. The Chicago man was a veteran of WWI and later claimed that he had been in worse predicaments in the war. A long firefight took place before the locals withdrew. No one on either side was shot. The police came out the next night and hid around the house, hoping the troublemakers would mount another attack. The police didn't fool the farmers, and nothing happened the next night.

The police investigated the assault and arrested three people for instigating the whole thing, all neighbors. Each one's bond was set at $5,000. More people were expected to be arrested.

The police investigation turned up two different stories. One story found that neighboring farmers were trying to scare the newcomers away. It turns out that the neighbors had been helping themselves to the produce from the orchards and fields of the farm and were mad that the newcomers ruined their sweet deal.

The other story is altogether different. They claimed that the Chicago man didn't do any farming at all. Instead, he was training his daughters to sing and dance and having them perform at a resort on Davis Lake. The eldest daughter was supposed to be very talented and was soon noticed by a singing group named the "Duncan Sisters," who wanted to take her under their wing.[403]

## Some Profiles of Early Black Settlers

James Joice of Fremont Township came to Lake County in 1863. He was born a slave in Kentucky but ran away from the plantation during the Civil War and became the cook for First Lt. Addison Partridge. Partridge served in the Ninety-Sixth Illinois Infantry but was forced to resign his commission in 1863 because of "camp disease." Partridge took James along with him when he went back home to Ivanhoe. After the war ended, James brought his wife Jemima, son Asa, and daughter Sarah up to Ivanhoe from Kentucky.

James was known as Darky Jim to everyone. After the Civil War, he took up the occupation of farm laborer. His wife, Jemima, became a servant and daughter, Sarah, a housekeeper. The Joice family always lived in the Ivanhoe/Mundelein area. James died in 1872, leaving his family in poor financial condition. Jemima died from the flu in 1920 during the worldwide flu epidemic. She caught the flu while nursing sick flu patients. Daughter Sarah died in 1941.

Son Asa started out as a farm laborer too but was elected town constable in 1889, being Lake County's first black elected official.[404] Partridge had made sure that Asa got a good education. During his lifetime, Asa was a tax collector, road commissioner, assessor, and constable in Fremont Township. The August 1, 1924, *Waukegan Daily Sun* wrote that Asa was "the only Negro politician Lake County ever had."[405] Asa died in 1924 and was supposed to have lost his mind. His wife claimed his mind was confused; he probably had Alzheimer's. Mrs. Joice was in bad health herself. She said they were still in touch with the Partridge family and that Charles Partridge, Jr. watched out for them.[406]

Curtis L. Dorsey writes in *Historical Highlights of the Waukegan Area* by

Osling that George Washington Bell was one of the first permanent black residents in Waukegan—Reuben Hill and Reuben Lee are probably the earliest black residents. George was a mortar maker who lived on North Spring Street in 1892.[407] George's obituary states that he was born on a plantation outside Nashville, Tennessee, in 1816. During the Civil War, George had to accompany his master when he brought food and supplies to the Confederate Army. They were captured by some Union troops on one of their supply runs. At the Union camp, they were told that nothing bad would happen to them if they joined the Union Army. George and his master then enlisted.

George was consigned to the Tenth Tennessee Cavalry and rose to the rank of sergeant by the end of the war. He met his future wife while in the army. She was a slave on a plantation near the Union camp and would frequently come to camp to trade vegetables for meat. They soon married.

President Lincoln once stopped into the Union camp where George was stationed. George was ordered to cook for the president. President Lincoln liked the food so much that he complimented George on the great meal. From then on, President Lincoln looked up George to shake his hand whenever he visited the camp.[408]

The Bells moved to the town of Fairbury in Southern Illinois after the war and lived there for ten years. George then decided to move to Waukegan. He left his wife and family in Fairbury until he found work in Waukegan and then brought them all here. If they lived in Fairbury for only ten years, it means that the Bells were living in Waukegan by 1875.

George hated trains and rode on them only twice in his life. He never let anyone take a picture of him either. His family had no pictures of him when he died. The 1892 Waukegan directory records George's occupation as mortar maker. According to George's obituary, he was a stonemason. He was supposed to have had a real talent for predicting the weather. George died at ninety-four years of age, leaving six children. One of his daughters was married to Green Tarver. Tarver was another early black settler, immigrating to Waukegan in 1889. George Bell might have been the oldest person in town when he died in 1910.[409]

The November 8, 1910, *Waukegan Daily Sun* claimed that George Bell was one of the healthiest men in town. The paper added that George was sick and bedridden for the first time in his life at the age of ninety-three.

Edward Bailey is number 4 on the list of permanent black residents in Waukegan. Ed's obituary states that he came to Waukegan when he was eight years old in 1876 and lived in Waukegan for fifty-eight years. He died in 1934 and was sixty-eight years old. Edward was a highly regarded coachman in Waukegan.[410]

Curtis L. Dorsey wrote in *Historical Highlights of the Waukegan Area* by Osling that Green Tarver came to Waukegan with Dr. Vincent Price in 1889.[411] Dr. Price is the grandfather of actor Vincent Price. On the 1900 federal census, Tarver's occupation is coachman.

Ed McGee started and owned the first shoe-shining parlor in Waukegan and was supposed to have shined more shoes than anyone else in the county. He claimed to have shined one hundred thousand pairs of shoes in a twelve-year period. This figure includes the work done by his employees. In 1900, he rented a room in the Moran Building to start his business. Most people thought he would never make a go of it, but he proved them all wrong. His shoe-shine parlor became known throughout Waukegan.[412]

Scott Ricks opened Waukegan's first black hotel in 1917. The hotel was located in a residential area on the west side of Waukegan. Some people objected to the hotel being in a residential neighborhood, but it was the only site he could find. Large numbers of blacks were coming to Waukegan, and there was a need for more rooms. It was a segregated hotel; only blacks were admitted.[413]

Frank Childs worked as a porter at the Brand Barber Shop and was an ex-boxer who had fought Jack Johnson three times. Johnson had been heavyweight boxing champ of the world at one time. Frank said he knocked down Johnson in one of those bouts. Frank also conducted boxing lessens in Waukegan.[414] He retired from boxing in 1902 after fighting in 218 bouts. One of his fights with Johnson ended in a draw. Frank always claimed that some of Jackson's people had gotten him drunk before another match with Johnson, and he lost the decision.[415]

Frank had an interesting experience in 1922. He was working at the Brand Barber Shop and went to the basement to add coal to the water heater. While in the coal bin, he heard a noise but thought it was just a rat. Then he saw a creature poke its head up from behind a pile of coal. At first, he thought it was a snake, but a closer look revealed it was a real live alligator. No one had any idea where it came from, but they figured it must have gotten in through a hole in the basement wall. Frank called Mr. Brand down to the basement to take a look and then remarked to Brand that there was nothing for an alligator to eat down here. The October 5, 1922, Lake County independent newspaper claimed that Brand turned to him and said, "I've heard they are mighty fond of dark meat."[416]

Zara Randall claimed to have been a runner for the Jesse James gang and loved to tell stories about his time with the gang. Up until Randall's death in 1907, he kept in touch with Frank James. Randall made his living as a rag picker (junkman?) in Waukegan. The definition of a rag picker in the dictionary is a person who collects rags, refuse, and rubbish. He was so well liked around Waukegan that when his workhorse died, the whole town chipped in to buy him another one.[417]

Waukegan was also home to an old black woman who tried to join the army in 1918. The newspaper article does not give her name or age, but she was old enough to have buried bodies during Sherman's March to the Sea. She said that she did not particularly want to bury dead bodies again but would if needed.[418]

## Bulgarians/Macedonians

I put these two ethnic groups together because it's almost impossible to tell them apart. Sometimes the newspaper calls them Macedonians and at other times Bulgarians. The country of Macedonia is divided between two ethnic groups. About one-third of the country is populated by Albanians. Two-thirds of the country is populated by Slavic people related to the Bulgarians. Modern Macedonia is located north of Greece and in the southern part of the former Yugoslavia. Many of Waukegan's Macedonians might have been from the town of Bansko, located in the Slavic area of Macedonia. The town was known as Little America because so many of its residents had worked in America at one time or another.[419]

Macedonia was still under Turkish rule when the first Macedonians came to Waukegan in the early 1900s. Bulgaria had already thrown off the Turkish yoke in 1878. Many of Waukegan's Macedonian immigrants had the same types of bad experiences that Waukegan's Albanians and Armenians had undergone with the Turks.[420]

Bulgaria is located east of Macedonia and the country of Serbia. The first Bulgarians were a Turkic people from Asia who conquered the Slavic people living in the present Bulgaria around AD 700. Over time, they assimilated with the Slavs, so the present Bulgarian people are considered

Slavic. Both the Bulgarians and Slavic Macedonians are Orthodox Christians.

There were never a great number of these people in the Waukegan/North Chicago area, but the *Waukegan Daily Sun* liked to write about them. According to the October 6, 1908, *Waukegan Daily Sun*, the Macedonians "are so peaceable and quiet that they have rarely been heard from."[421] Don't worry, readers, the Macedonians weren't perfect and managed to get themselves in trouble on occasion.

To keep things simple, I will just use the word "Bulgarian" from now on because it's easier than spelling Macedonians. A total of 250 Bulgarians lived in Waukegan in 1908, all men. Most of them lived in boardinghouses on Waukegan's south side.[422] A total of 40 of them alone lived above a pool room and cigar store on Marian Street.[423] I remember reading an article in the newspaper about the Bulgarians taking turns sleeping in the same beds. Night shift workers slept in the beds during the day, while day shift workers slept in the same beds at night. Unfortunately, I gave away some of my research to a Bulgarian friend long before I ever thought I'd be writing about them. You'll have to take my word for it.

Waukegan was the winter headquarters for Bulgarian immigrants living in the Middle and Western parts of the country. In the spring, they went West, looking for work. A lot of them found temporary employment as laborers on railroads. Of the 250 Bulgarians in Waukegan, all but 20 left for jobs in the West by the end of April 1908. The 20 Bulgarians who stayed all had steady jobs in Waukegan and saw no reason to leave.[424]

About 70 to 100 Bulgarian laborers were back in Waukegan in early October. Many found jobs right away at the sugar refinery, naval base, and a north side sewer and cement plant. These Bulgarians got some good news when they came back to Waukegan. Macedonian prince Ferdinand had declared independence from Turkey. An Armenian translated the news for them since none of them could read English. Their Armenian translator spoke seven languages, including Bulgarian.[425]

The police almost got involved in an incident in the Bulgarian community in spring 1909. Anywhere from 10 to 30 Bulgarians had begun arriving in Waukegan daily. They came from Chicago and Granite City, Illinois, as well as Indianapolis, Indiana.[426] A total of 40 Bulgarians just off the boat also showed up.[427] None of them had jobs and most had spent all their money getting here. It was feared that before long, Waukegan would be overrun by 500 broke, unemployed Bulgarians, and the city would have to support them all.

The police started interviewing the new arrivals. They had all been told that a new railroad was under construction in Waukegan and were lured here for railroad jobs. There was only one problem: there was no new railroad being built in town and no jobs either.

The police found out that some Bulgarian employment agency on the south side of Waukegan was advertising for workers in Bulgarian papers in Chicago, Granite City, Indianapolis, and other nearby towns. It was thought that the employment agency was charging a fee to each Bulgarian who arrived in town, but the Bulgarians all declared it untrue. There was plenty of evidence to dispute their claim however.[428] Many of the newly arrived Bulgarians found out that they had been had and were in ill humor. The boardinghouse owners on the south side had no complaints. They were cramming 30 to 40 Bulgarians at a time into small rooms.[429]

To make matters worse, 60 Bulgarians who had recently left to work on a railroad in Montana returned, reason being they were too short. The railroad refused to hire them because of their height.[430] The Bulgarians must have really been short. The Western railroads used Chinese laborers for years. Most Chinese don't seem to be giants to me, but they were hired by the railroads.

I have met a few Bulgarians, and they did not seem all that small. This tells me one thing: the Bulgarians living in Europe suffered from poor diets, probably not enough protein.

Waukegan's Bulgarian community saw another event in 1909. Some of the earliest Bulgarian settlers with steady jobs were starting to prosper. They had saved enough money to send for their wives and for Bulgarian women looking for husbands. A total of 30 Bulgarian women came en masse to Waukegan on April 4. Up to that time, most Bulgarians were single. A few did manage to marry Austrian (Slovenian or Croatian) women."[431]

There were 300 Bulgarians in town in 1910.[432] In 1911, 300 Bulgarians left in the spring to work as railroad laborers in the West. They weren't too short this time; the railroad needed strike breakers (scabs).[433]

In 1912, Waukegan's Balkan immigrants (Greeks, Bulgarians, and Serbs) were all fired up over the First Balkan War.[434] The First Balkan War lasted from October 1912 to May 1913. It pitted Greece, Serbia, and Bulgaria against Turkey.

An unknown number of Bulgarians left Waukegan in 1913 to fight in the Bulgarian Army. Only 30 made it back. Turkey had been defeated, but the king of Bulgaria refused to let the soldiers leave the country. Bulgaria had lost a large number of men in the war, and the country needed every able-bodied man to help rebuild it. Waukegan's Bulgarians had other ideas, and the 30 managed to escape from Bulgaria. Most of them made it to Athens, Greece, and from there by ship to America.[435]

The *Waukegan Daily Sun* did not write much about the Bulgarians after 1914. I know for a fact that some did stay permanently in Waukegan. There is something else to add to their story.

The Bulgarians had a benefactor in Waukegan. A man named Brother Francis had established a monastery mission on the south side to minister to Waukegan's Balkan residents, the Bulgarians in particular. Brother Francis was not a Bulgarian or even an immigrant. In November 1909, he established the St. Gregory Mission in a rented house located at 767 Marion Street on the south side of Waukegan.

Brother Francis moved to Waukegan in 1903. He was only fourteen years old but soon became highly involved with "the Christ Church." Later, he switched Christian churches and became affiliated with the Franciscan Order of Friars Minor.[436] Next, he moved to Fond du Lac, Wisconsin, and became the right-hand man to Bishop Grafton. When Bishop Grafton died, he left his chalice and robes to Brother Francis. Brother Francis was so enamored by his gift from Bishop Grafton that the chalice always occupied a prominent place in his mission.[437]

Brother Francis lived in Waukegan at 808 North Avenue and owned a workshop on Julian Street. He was only twenty years old when he established the St. Gregory Mission. He knew a little Greek and Arabic when he first started his mission and learned more languages over time. Besides Bulgarians, his mission ministered to Armenians, Albanians, and Turks. Serbs and Assyrians were also known to stop in. Incredibly, he was able to keep the peace between Turks and everyone else. Outside the mission, it was a different story. Brother Francis had a lot of guts for a twenty-year-old, ministering to people at such a young age.

According to the *Waukegan Daily Sun*, Brother Francis originally wanted to start a monastery instead of a mission. The idea for the mission came later. He was worried that the Franciscan Order was dying out. Brother Francis was aware of the Franciscan's history and wanted to revive

The Forgotten History of Lake County, Illinois

the order. His monastery was supposed to be the only Franciscan Order of the Episcopal Church in the world.[438]

Brother Francis told the *Daily Sun* that he had gotten the idea to start the mission while working at a factory in Waukegan. He saw a foreman treat a Bulgarian worker like a dog. Brother Francis could see that the man was disturbed by the incident, asking the foreman why he treated him like that. Then he pointed out that the man might be a good worker if he was treated better. The December 18, 1909, *Waukegan Daily Sun* printed the foreman's response: "No, the dogs don't know anything."[439]

Later on, Brother Francis asked the Bulgarian if he knew anything about America. The man replied that there was no place to learn. Brother Francis decided that he would teach the man about America himself and invited him to move into his home. At night, he taught the man English. Brother Francis believed in charitable acts and, according to the December 18, 1909, *Waukegan Daily Sun*, told the newspaper, "Wrap a mantle of charity around a man and you not only make him your friend but you also help him to lead a better life and to become a better citizen."[440]

His mission on Marian Street must have been a good-size house. Each ethnic group had its own club. The mission was a place to worship, learn English, provide ethnic comradeship, and read newspapers from one's native country. It also served as a post office. All mail from Bulgaria and Macedonia was delivered there and then sent West to the railroad workers.

Within the first year of its existence, Brother Francis's monastery/mission was getting popular with other priests. Brothers Paul (Louis Keorian), Gregory, and Peter took up residence at the mission. They seemed to do as they pleased and spent a lot of their time away from the mission.[441] A Turkish Iman (Islamic) also came to the mission in 1910.[442] Father Alexandrief of the Holy Trinity Russian Orthodox Church in Chicago also stopped by on occasion. (Your author has visited the Holy Trinity Russian Orthodox Church in Chicago.)

At some point, Brother Francis started a second mission on the southwest side of Waukegan. By this time, his mission had become well-known, and he was able to obtain donations from wealthy North Shore residents.[443]

In May 1910, a prosperous man from Chicago (name unknown) offered Brother Francis a great deal: a monastery on a 180-acre tract of land in Southern Illinois. It would be his to do with as he pleased, but his benefactor's name was not to be disclosed.[444] Brother Francis might have regretted not accepting the deal. He could have been long gone from Waukegan before the police showed up at his mission on the southwest side.

Up until this time, I thought Brother Francis was a saint for establishing his mission. Then in 1917, five young boys walked into the police station and complained that they had all been sexually molested by Brother Francis. Four of them recanted after questioning, but a seven-year-old boy steadfastly stuck to his story.

The police raided his mission on July 12, 1917, and arrested Brother Francis, Brother Placid, and Father Cyprian. Brother Placid was released two days later because there was no evidence that he had done anything wrong. Brother Francis spent the next three weeks in jail. His lawyer managed to get his bond reduced from $5,000 to $3,000, allowing Brother Francis to get out of jail. Father Cyprian remained in jail despite a bond of only $30. Before leaving, Brother Francis told him not to worry because he would get him out within a couple of days.

Father Placid, along with Brother Francis's father, worked tirelessly to refute the charges against Brother Francis and thought the whole thing was a setup by the police. He wasn't the only one thinking it was a setup either.[445]

After his release from jail, Brother Francis stayed around the mission. His trial was supposed to start on November 5, but a grand jury decided to put him on trial in October instead. He was indicted on four counts and bail set at $2,500 on each count for a grand total of $10,000. Brother Francis wasn't ready for trial just yet and took off after he was indicted. He went into hiding at his sister's home in Chicago, becoming a fugitive from the law. The police couldn't find him, but his friends knew where he was at. Brother Francis told his friends that he would not pay the new bail and would stay in Chicago until his original trial date of November 5.[446]

Brother Francis, however, did not always stay in Chicago. All this time, he had been sneaking back to Waukegan and Lake Forest at night. He took the train back and forth from Chicago and had gotten away with this ruse for weeks. The police had been watching for him all along and finally caught up with him one night, three days after his original trial date of November 5.

Brother Francis told the police that he had the $10,000 bail and was going to turn himself in the next day. The police thought it was all bull and threw him back in jail. Looks like bull to me too.[447]

The trial started the following week. Anyone under eighteen years of age was not allowed to attend the trial because of the nature of the case. The newspaper did not print any details of the testimony either.[448]

The jury went out at five o'clock on a Friday evening. They soon came back with a hung jury. Seven jurors favored acquittal, and five thought he was guilty. They went back again and again, trying to reach a decision, but no one would change their mind. Four of the jurors favoring acquittal were from Zion, and one in particular tried to sway the jury toward acquittal. The jurors for a guilty verdict felt just as strongly for their position, and tempers flared up. A policeman was sent in to keep order. By three o'clock in the morning, it was decided to throw in the towel. The jurors told the judge that it was impossible for them to all agree. The judge declared a mistrial and dismissed the hung jury.[449]

Assistant States Attorney J. W. Welch was very disappointed by the outcome of the trial. There were three more cases to try, and Welch was confident the state could still convict Brother Francis. Rumors soon started to fly, claiming that there was not enough evidence to ever convict Father Francis and that the three cases would soon be dropped. Welch said he was determined to try the cases, but it looks like the three remaining cases were, in fact, dropped. At least I cannot find a record of any more trials.[450]

Brother Francis surprised everyone the following year. He married a woman from Wisconsin, who had moved to Waukegan the previous year. Brother Francis was still operating a mission on the southwest side of Waukegan, but the newlyweds made their home on the north side of Waukegan.[451]

## Danes

The Danish immigration to Waukegan was never large. The first Dane in Waukegan was George Peterson. On the 1860 federal census, he was forty-nine years old, and his occupation was ship's captain. His wife, Mary, was thirty-nine years old and born in England. They were the parents of Caroline, eighteen, and George, fifteen, both born in Illinois.

Six Danes lived in Waukegan in 1870. John C. Johnson was forty-five years old, and his occupation was shoemaker. His wife, Catherine, was thirty-nine years old and born in Pennsylvania. They had six children, all born in America. In addition, Catherine Johnson, seventy-two years old, lived with the family.

Also on the 1870 census is Mary Hanson, twenty years old, occupation servant, and Nelson Jacobson, twenty-two years old. No occupation is recorded. They were living in the Ebenezer Warner household. Ebenezer was a wooden ware merchant.

Mrs. Elizabeth Borom was born in Denmark. She was fifty-four years old and kept house.

The last Dane is George Hillfrick, twenty-four years old, occupation shoemaker. George was living at the Dave Hopkinson home. Dave Hopkinson was also a shoemaker.

John C. Johnson is the only Dane recorded on the 1880 federal census. His wife and three children also lived in the household. All these people I just mentioned claimed to be Danish, but most of their names look Swedish.

The 1900 federal census of Waukegan lists 96 Danes living in Waukegan, city and township. By 1907, the Danish population of Waukegan had grown to 133. There was a total of 23 families, 31 men, 31 women, and 69 children.[452] By 1913, Waukegan had 150 Danes in the city. The total number of Danes in the rest of Lake County was 470.[453]

The Danish Congregational Church was established in Waukegan in 1892–1893. Waukegan also had a chapter of the Danish Brotherhood. In 1909, 3,000 members of the Danish Brotherhood held a large picnic at Waukegan's Electric Park. Chapters from Chicago, Kenosha, Racine, and Milwaukee all came. A small number of Danes from Lake Forest and Libertyville also showed up. More were expected, but a morning rain kept some away. The Chicago chapter chartered two trains, each one pulling six cars to haul their members to Waukegan. The combined weight of the passengers on one of the trains was so heavy that the train could not make it around a curve at Belvidere Street.

A parade was planned, and the different chapters all assembled in Downtown Waukegan. From there, they marched through town led by a marching band with everyone waving flags. A large number of Waukegan residents turned out to watch the parade, which ended up at Electric Park.

After the parade, a picnic took place. The picnic began with a song. Then L. B. Larsen gave a speech, greeting all the guests. Other songs and speeches followed. Mayor Buck of Waukegan also addressed the crowd.

Activities included singing, foot races, and dancing. The *Waukegan Daily Sun* reported that it was the biggest picnic in Waukegan that year.[454]

A chapter of the Danish Brotherhood was organized in Wadsworth in 1906. In 1931, 156 Danes came out to Wadsworth for the twenty-fifth anniversary of the society. Danes from Chicago, Racine, and Waukegan attended the event.[455]

## Finns

Mrs. Irene Haapanen wrote in *Historical Highlights of the Waukegan Area* by Osling that the first Finns came to Waukegan in 1892 and were employees of the Washburn and Moen Manufacturing Company. The American Steel and Wire Company bought the plant in 1899, and from then on, it was known as the wire mill. These Finns first worked in the Washburn and Moen plant in Worchester, Massachusetts, but relocated to the new plant in Waukegan in 1892.

The Finns settled first on Market, Browning, and Spring streets on the south side of Waukegan. Later, they moved a few neighborhoods to the West when new immigrant groups began moving into the area.[456]

According to Esa Arra, author of *The Finns in Illinois*, the first Finns to come out to the new plant in Waukegan (and their region of origin in Finland) were Peter Anderson (Sakkijarvi), John Carlson (Sievi), Matti Mattson (Munso), Jacob Kyndberg (Ylistaro), and (no first name) Erickson and William Jacobson (Viipuri). They all brought their families with them. Most Finns who came after them were single men who came mainly from the South Northlander and Savo regions of Finland. The greatest number of Finns in Waukegan came from the South Northlander region of Finland.

Over 100 Finns lived in Waukegan by 1893, most working at the Washburn and Moen Company. Finnish women began to immigrate to Waukegan at the turn of the century. They worked as servants or maids for the well-to-do families in Waukegan.[457] The 1900 federal census records 167 Finns living in Waukegan. Esa Arra claimed that about 500 Finns lived in the Waukegan/North Chicago area in 1900 and made up 10 percent of Waukegan's population that year.[458] These other Finns must have come after the census was taken.

Waukegan's Finns joined an exodus from the city in 1908. At least 200

Hungarians and an unknown number of Austrians had had enough of the wire mill. They were working only three or four days a week and were not making enough money to make ends meet. At least 50 Finns went back to Finland that year.[459]

About 100 Finns and possibly more left Waukegan and returned to Finland in 1911. They were certain a recession would occur after the presidential election and thought they would be better off in Finland. Times were not that great in Finland either, but it was much cheaper to live there as compared with Waukegan. Most doubted they would return to America.[460]

The Young People's Finnish Temperance Society picnic in 1905 drew 1,500 people. The picnic was held to observe the seventh anniversary of the temperance society. The temperance society had only 175 members but was one of the most successful temperance societies in town.[461]

Mrs. Irene Haapanen stated that Waukegan's Finnish population in 1916 was estimated to be 1,500.[462] Esa Arra claimed that by the 1920s and '30s, 2,000 Finns lived in Waukegan, most on the south side. They lived throughout Waukegan by the 1940s.[463]

Finns established the Finnish Evangelical Lutheran Church in 1893.[464] In 1912, a night school was established in Waukegan to teach Finns the English language and help them become good citizens.[465]

Andrew Sund was supposed to have been one of the most prominent Finns in Waukegan. He came to Waukegan from Finland in 1897 and found employment as a carpenter. Soon after that, he started his own construction company, building many houses on the south side of town.[466]

One of Finland's greatest athletes settled in Waukegan in 1909. Uno Railo was the decathlon champion of Finland and known throughout the world. In 1910, he was working as a millwright at the wire mill.

Railo entered the Irish-American Athletic Club track meet in 1910. The event took place at White Sox Park in Chicago. It was the first year the track meet was held, and top athletes from around the country were present. Most athletes at the track meet belonged to athletic clubs, but Railo ran as an independent.

Railo won the three-hundred-yard race and was third in the one-hundred-yard dash. The *Daily Sun* said Railo had run the one-hundred-yard dash despite some unnamed handicap. Spectators at the track meet thought Railo could have been as good an athlete as anyone in the country if he had the right coach. Various athletic clubs tried to recruit him, but he was not interested. Maybe Railo figured his athletic career was about over. At any rate, he kept his millwright job at the wire mill.

The *Daily Sun* wrote that Railo was also a great shot putter, could high-jump five feet eleven inches and broad-jump over twenty feet. He was a great runner and sometimes put on demonstrations at Finnish picnics.[467]

## Germans

Thomas Buck, author of *Waukegan, A Mini-History*, claimed that most of Waukegan's first settlers were Yankees from New England as well as some Scottish, English, and Irish immigrants. According to Buck, the Germans began immigrating to Waukegan in the mid-1840s.[468]

The 1850 federal census records 80 Germans living in Waukegan. According to the 1860 census, 183 Germans lived in Waukegan, city and township. Those German settlers came from all over Germany, but the largest number was from Prussia, located in Eastern Germany. Germany was not a united country then but was divided into independent states. The 1870 census shows Waukegan's German population doubling to 345. The 1880 census shows that the number of Germans in town actually dropped to 323. There is no 1890 census, but the 1900 federal census records 596 Germans in town. Herbert Ehnert, writing in *Historical Highlights of the Waukegan Area* by Osling, stated that many of the Germans on the 1900 Waukegan census came out from Worcester, Massachusetts, with the Washburn and Moen Company.[469] In 1913, Waukegan had 572 people of German descent, and the rest of the county contained a total of 2,713 people of German descent.[470]

The first Germans settled mainly on Market Street, which soon became almost exclusively German.[471] At one time, Market Street was home to Waukegan's most affluent families. Market Street was located on the south side of Waukegan, below the bluff and on the flats. There are now only two houses left on Market Street. What used to be the rest of Market Street is now a landfill.

The German Workman's Club was founded at some point. There is no date for when it was first established. According to Herbert Ehnert, meetings were held at Turner Hall on Spring Street. The workman's club provided accident insurance and a place to socialize. It organized picnics along the Des Plaines River in the summer. The German Musikverein, a singing club, also met at Turner Hall.[472]

St. Joseph's Catholic Church on Oak Street was built by Germans. Early church records go all the way back to July 1863. In 1872, the congregation bought a school building and converted it into a church. The first church had 125 parishioners and 50 students in its school.

German Protestants established St. John's Reformed Church in the 1860s. Only German was spoken in church services and in the school. At first, they held church services in members' homes, schools, and even the courthouse. A church was built in 1872. To help finance the construction of the church, they sold ownership of the pews to church members.[473]

The Germans in Waukegan and Lake County found themselves in a bad position in 1917. America was just entering World War I. German residents thought it might be a good idea to show their patriotism for the United States, so German aliens turned out in force to become American citizens.[474]

The German-American Club was organized in 1926. It was estimated that about 600 people of German descent were living in Waukegan at the time. The club planned to get involved in local, state, and national government, the goal being honest government. The club also enjoyed listening to public speakers and politicians.[475]

There is not much information in the early newspapers about the German settlers in Waukegan. The newspapers did not record much local news at the time. In fact, there is not much information at all about any group in Waukegan from the years 1886 to 1897. All the *Waukegan Gazette* newspapers were destroyed by fire during those years.

# Greeks

According to Peggy Moraitis, only a few Greeks were living in Waukegan in 1890. The main Greek immigration didn't take place until 1900. These early Greek settlers came from all over Greece. A few lived in Downtown Waukegan, but most lived in the southwestern part of North Chicago near Twenty-Second Street. Some of the first Greeks to settle in town were Peter Canelakes, Sam Damos, Christ Conteas, Gust Loulentis, and Pater Helis. Many of the earliest Greek immigrants worked at the wire mill, tannery and foundry, and of course, in restaurants.[476]

An article from the 1910 *Waukegan Daily Sun* stated that from four hundred to five hundred Greeks were in town to take part in a war with the Polish residents of North Chicago.[477] I wrote about the war in chapter 3. Only seventeen Greeks lived in Waukegan on the 1910 federal census. A total of ninety-one Greeks lived in the rest of the county, probably in North Chicago.[478] The rest of the Greeks in town taking part in the war must have been recruited from other parts, possibly Chicago. The *Waukegan Daily Sun* reported in 1926 that around three hundred Greek families lived in the Waukegan/North Chicago area.[479]

The *Waukegan Daily Sun* published an interesting story about the Greek government. A large number of Waukegan's Greeks went back to Greece in 1912. The First Balkan War was just starting, and the Greek government required them to come back and fight in the war. Most of those who went back to Greece did so more out of concern for their parents than for patriotic reasons. It seems the government of Greece kept a tight rein on its citizens no matter what country they lived in. It was against the law for a Greek citizen to become a citizen of any other country. It was very difficult to leave Greece, and if you were able to get out, the government considered it only temporary. Greeks were obliged to return within five years. They also had to pay the Greek government $50/year for each year they were gone. The family homes of any Greek not returning after five years risked being looted by the Greek government.[480] The *Daily Sun* also wrote that many of Waukegan's factories lost their Greek employees in 1912.[481]

The Greeks engaged in a bad blood feud among themselves in 1917. They were divided by political factions, similar to the Armenians.

In 1917, a Greek candy store on State and Twenty-Second streets in North Chicago was the scene of a murder. Two different Greek political factions from North Chicago were fighting with each other. A number of shootings and stabbings had recently taken place at the candy store, but this was the first murder.

A Greek shot and killed another Greek but maintained it was in self-defense. The shooter and his wife were arrested. They also shut down the candy store and arrested the store's owner, Chris Gekes. Gekes was soon released when it was determined that he had nothing to do with the crime. The shooter's wife was arrested because she was supposed to have instigated the fight.

The Greek community in the Waukegan/North Chicago area was up in arms. They were split between two factions, and a war was about to break out. One faction thought it was self-defense. The other faction thought the victim was shot in cold blood.

The *Daily Sun* declared that each faction started to arm themselves with weapons. One Greek bought twelve pistols in Chicago and brought them back to North Chicago. A number of Greeks tried to buy weapons in Waukegan.[482] Within two days, hundreds of Greeks began pouring into North Chicago. One faction intended to break into the jail and lynch the shooter. The other was determined to stop them.[483]

Fortunately, the Greek Orthodox Church in Chicago caught wind of all the commotion and sent two priests to North Chicago to find out what all the excitement was about. The priests were able to calm things down and talk some sense into everyone.[484]

In 1926, the Greek residents of Waukegan/North Chicago decided to build their own church. A meeting was held at the Broadway Confectionary Plant. At least fifty Greek families were making the trip to Racine, Wisconsin, to attend church every Sunday. It was thought that at least three hundred Greek families lived in the Waukegan/North Chicago area, and a church was sorely needed. They planned on spending from $20,000 to $25,000 to build the church.[485] The church was built and located on Glen Flora Avenue near Victory Memorial Hospital.

# Irish

The Irish were the first big foreign immigration to Waukegan. Lake Country was first opened to white settlement in 1835–1836. Most of the early immigrants to Lake County were New England Yankees with roots from the British Isles. The first Irish settlers were Catholics. They settled in a number of locations around the Waukegan/North Chicago area when Lake County first opened for settlement.

The 1850 federal census records 327 Irish immigrants living in Waukegan. The 1860 federal census shows that the number of Irish living in the city had jumped to 520. Their numbers dropped to 472 on the 1870 federal census and 382 on the 1880 federal census. Despite the drop in numbers, they were still the largest group of foreign born in the city. Their numbers continued to drop, and by 1900, the census records just 254 Irish living in Waukegan. In 1913, only 168 people in Waukegan were born in Ireland. The rest of the county had a total of 789 people born in Ireland.[486]

A large group of Irish settled on the west side of Waukegan.[487] In those days, the west side was only a few blocks west of Genesee Street. The west side Irish were a little better off than the North Chicago Irish. An article written by Barbara Apple and printed in the March 15, 1980, *Waukegan News Sun* called the west side Irish Lace Curtain Irish.[488] Irene McCann wrote in *Historical Highlights of the Waukegan Area* by Osling that North Chicago had three different Irish settlements. One was Meehan's Settlement at Green Bay and Buckley roads. Another was Dwyer's Crossing located across from the entrance to Great Lakes Naval Hospital. The third settlement was St. Ann's Mission at the corner of Green Bay Road and Illinois Route 176.[489]

According to Adele Kweder, the earliest Irish settlers on the west side established "St. Mary's Catholic Church" around 1835–1836. The church was first located in a log cabin and was the first Catholic Church in Waukegan. Father St. Cyr was the first pastor. While the log church was under construction, a rotting large old wooden cross was discovered nearby and erected near the church. The Indians claimed it was left over from an earlier French mission.

They soon realized that a bigger and better church was needed, and construction of a new church began in 1844.[490] Barbara Apple wrote that three of St. Mary's parishioners—Michael Dulanty, J. McCanna, and Thomas Tiernan—get the credit for finding a site to build the new church on. Located at the northwest corner of Water and County streets, construction was completed in 1847. The first Mass was celebrated on Easter Sunday 1847. The church was renamed St. Bernard's in 1851.[491] The Irish families living along Illinois Route 120 west of town also went to church at St. Mary's. My relatives came out from Wilson and Gurnee to attend Mass at both St. Mary's and St. Bernard's. The church was renamed Immaculate Conception in 1864. The south side Irish in North Chicago built their own church, "Holy Family," in 1902.

Barbara Apple, writing in the March 15, 1980, *Waukegan News Sun*, listed the last names of some of the first Irish settlers in Lake County: "Tiernan, Tyrell, McDermott, Kelly, Moran, Rudd, Meehan, Flood, Kehoe, Jenkins, Dorsey, McLaughlin, Mullery, Dwyer, Murphy, Dady,

McCann, Collins, Reardon, Burke, O'Shea, Donnelly, Grady, Tobin, Durkin, O'Meara, Kilbane and Kennedy."[492] Irene E. McCann Murphy recorded a few more names of early Irish settlers: Carroll, Cochran, Dulanty, Dwelly, Foster, Hinckley, Matthews, McCanna, McGovern, McGuire, Ragan, Strong, Sunderlin, and Sullivan.[493]

I have not found much evidence for any type of discrimination against the Irish in Lake County. No "Irish need apply" signs or anything like it in the newspaper. It is possible discrimination occurred, but early newspapers did not cover much local news. A fire destroyed the *Waukegan Gazette* newspaper from 1886 until 1897, so possible information about the Irish was lost. A nativist organization called the Know Nothings was supposed to be in the area, but I haven't read about any trouble from them.

I did manage to find a couple of complaints in the *Waukegan Gazette* newspaper about the Irish. Numerous Irish saloons were located along Washington Street near Genesee Street and were stinking up the place. It seems the saloons were located in cellars, which the July 25, 1857, *Waukegan Gazette* referred to as cesspools.[494] The *Waukegan Gazette* also wanted the health department to look into the matter and wrote on July 25, 1857, that the saloons should be moved "down to some sewer or back in some hog pen where they belong."[495]

A group of Irish engaged in a brawl in Waukegan on the Fourth of July 1873. Baseball games, horse races, and firecrackers were all part of the Fourth of July celebrations in Waukegan. The other entertainment occurred when two groups of Irish men, women, and children fought a knock-down, drag-out fight in front of everyone. The newspaper was not sure of the cause of the fight, but too much whiskey was the leading suspect. According to the July 12, 1873, *Waukegan Gazette*, "[M]en, women and children were pounded, kicked and cuffed."[496] There was supposed to be a police presence at the celebration, but they were all watching the baseball game and pretended not to notice the brawl. Onlookers had to break up the fight.[497] Some of my Irish ancestors happened to live in Waukegan at this time and might have seen the event or even participated in it.

The Chicago newspapers published numerous articles about Irish immigrants in the 1850s, most of them bad. Since there's not much information about the Irish in Waukegan or North Chicago, I'll write about the Irish in Chicago. The Irish were accused of being pawns of the Democratic Party. The Democratic Party was the proslavery party, and many people could not understand given Ireland's history why the

Irish would do their bidding. The Irish were frequently accused of illegal voting (vote early and vote often). Voter intimidation was another charge.[498] The November 4, 1857, *Chicago Daily Tribune* wrote about one of the rare instances when the Irish behaved themselves at the polls. "The Irish entirely refrained from their favorite pastime of breaking skulls and creating rows. Citizens voted without the fear of bruises or bludgeons."[499] The Democratic Party was also known to supply the Irish with whiskey to persuade them to vote.[500] Irish immigrants were roused out of the poor house by the Democrats to vote as well. There was not much good written about Irish priests either. The priests were said to check voting ballots to make sure all votes were for the Democratic Party.[501] Not all Irish were Democrats, and a few did vote Republican.

In the 1850s and '60s, many of Chicago's Irish immigrants lived in squatter shanty towns spread out all over Chicago. It was thought that at least fifteen thousand people lived in these towns. The biggest and worst one was named Kilgubbin and was forty to fifty acres in size. The landowners were supposedly Eastern capitalists who didn't care what took place on their property. Some of the shanties were small three-room buildings. The family lived in one room and their animals and poultry in the other two. Others were described as seven-foot-by-nine-foot shacks. Kilgubbin was packed with hundreds of shanties. Flocks of geese, pigs, dogs, cats, and cows wandered about. The residents grew potatoes and cabbages in their gardens. The residents of Kilgubbin didn't trust strangers or anyone who looked like they might be the real landowner, for obvious reasons. It was a wild, ungovernable place that not even the police wanted to go into. The residents feuded and fought among themselves as well. It was not just the men either. The women were described as always carrying their brooms.[502]

After reading the above story in the newspaper, I detected some bias by the author against the Irish. He could have sensationalized the story too.

Lake County was the last part of Illinois to be settled and was a frontier when the first Irish Catholic immigrants appeared. Lake County's first settlers appear to have welcomed anyone who wished to settle there. Waukegan, in particular, was grateful for new immigrants.

# Jews

Much of the information I have about the Jewish immigration to the Waukegan/North Chicago area comes from the book *Historical Highlights of the Waukegan Area* by Osling. Rose J. Lidschin is the author of the story. According to Rose, Jonas Ziv is regarded as the first permanent Jewish settler in Waukegan. Other Jews had lived in Waukegan for short periods before Ziv, but none stayed for long. He came to town by at least 1880 and operated the Chicago Bee Hive Clothing Store on Genesee Street.[503]

Ziv was a colorful character, and the *Waukegan Gazette* frequently wrote about him. He was described as short, fat, and always happy. The November 25, 1882, *Waukegan Gazette* wrote, "Ziv the smiling, irrepressible, and rapid salesman who impresses all his customers that he wants to give away his goods and feels that money is a burden to him."[504] Ziv was real big into advertising and always used plenty of it. The *Gazette* claimed he always paid the newspaper in advance for advertising. He also enjoyed telling tall tales (BS) to anyone who would listen.

Ziv started his business in a small front room on Genesee Street. Ziv's store was named the Chicago Bee Hive, but everyone just called it Ziv's cheap shop. Ziv's business expanded rapidly. By 1882, his business had expanded four times and occupied two stores. It still wasn't enough room, and he was in the process of building two more rooms in the back of his store the same year.[505]

Ziv's Chicago Bee Hive was supposed to be a clothing store, but the *Waukegan Gazette* claimed he sold almost anything. The September 9, 1882, *Waukegan Gazette* wrote that he sold "ladies' and gents' furnishing goods, tin ware, crockery, hardware, in fact, as said before, from a pin to a threshing machine."[506] I like his innovative method of supplying merchandise to his store. He used hot-air balloons. Ziv owned two balloons and flew one himself.[507] The *Gazette* wrote that he came back from New York in his balloon in September 1882 and was loaded with merchandise. He was afraid he might have to expand again. Ziv made it known to all that he closed for Jewish holidays and had the *Gazette* publish the dates. Some of his customers came from as far away as fifty miles, and he did not want them to make the trip to his store only to find it closed.[508]

Rose J. Lidschin wrote that Abraham Simon bought Ziv out sometime in the 1880s. Ziv moved to Chicago after selling his business.[509]

Rose listed some of the names of Waukegan's early Jewish settlers mentioned in *Historical Highlights of the Waukegan Area* by Osling. The Rosenblum family came to Waukegan in 1887. They operated a clothing store on Washington Street.

Samuel Schwartz and family came to Waukegan in 1889. They were Romanian immigrants who ran a boardinghouse at first but later started a soft drink and beer distributorship. Sam built the Schwartz Theater at County and Water streets. The theater hosted plays and operas. Sam also helped establish the Am Echod Synagogue and was its first president. Before the synagogue was built around 1896, they worshipped in one another's basements.

Max Rosenblum came to Waukegan in 1890. He was not related to the Rosenblums who came in 1887. Max only stayed around for ten years and then moved to Kenosha, Wisconsin. Max was a good friend of Meyer Kubelsky, Jack Benny's father. In Kenosha, Max was affiliated with the Northwestern Iron & Metal Company for thirteen years. He came down with tuberculosis in 1913 and moved to Phoenix, Arizona, hoping the change would improve his health. The move didn't work out, and Max died the same year. He was only forty-eight. Max wrote a letter to Meyer right before he died, claiming his health was much better. He died before Meyer could respond to his letter.[510]

Meyer and Jacob Kubelsky came to Waukegan in 1890. Meyer was the father of Waukegan's favorite son, Jack Benny. They were partners in a store named Illinois Clothing Boot and Shoe Store. By 1892, the store was named the Clothing & Gents Furnishing Goods on Genesee Street. Meyer was one of the founders of the Am Echod Synagogue. He later operated a saloon in Waukegan with his brother-in-law Louis Sachs. I'll write more about that later. Louis Sachs brother Max was also an early Jewish settler in Waukegan.

Moses Cohn arrived in 1892. His daughter and her husband, Barney Janowitz, settled here in 1893.

Abraham Diamond came in 1892. Abe and Max Rosenblum formed a partnership operating a scrapyard. I remember Diamond Scrapyard. It was located below the bluff on the flats. Mrs. Diamond's brother, Abraham Morris Gordon, arrived in Waukegan in 1897 or 1898.

In 1894, the Alschuler family came to town. They operated a clothing factory named Morning Glory Garments. Mrs. Alschuler was also a well-known artist in town.

Charles Morrison immigrated to Waukegan in 1896. His first job was working at Harry Rosenblum's store. He started his own store in 1899. Charles established the "Globe Department Store" in 1903.

Jacob Blumberg and family came to Waukegan in 1900. They created the "Chicago Furniture Company." Later, they established a large store called Blumberg's located on Genesee Street near the bridge.[511]

I could list more Jewish businesses, but I have to stop somewhere. The Jewish community was never large in Waukegan/North Chicago. I checked the 1900 federal census and counted names that could be Jewish and found 126 men, women, and children living in Waukegan.

The November 12, 1908, *Waukegan Daily Sun* reported that a "Jewish Negro" had just showed up in Waukegan. He claimed to be from Arabia and could speak only the Hebrew language and some German. Nothing like it had ever occurred in Waukegan.[512]

Jack Benny is Waukegan's favorite son but not so with his father Meyer. Meyer was more like Waukegan's least favorite son. Meyer and his brother Jacob immigrated to America from Russian Poland about 1884.[513] The area is now located in Ukraine. The Kubelskys grew up in the town of Patrench[514] near the Nieman River.[515] Meyer's sister was a very successful businesswoman and chose to stay in Patrench. A large battle between the German and Russian armies took place near Patrench in World War I, and Meyer didn't hear from his sister until three years later.[516] Two of his sister's letters finally made it to Waukegan that year; both had been mailed three years earlier. Meyer tried to find out what happened to her, but it is not known if he ever did.[517]

Meyer operated a saloon at Genesee and Water streets that was considered one of the two worst saloons in town,[518] the Schwartz saloon being the other one. Schwartz owned both saloons. Waukegan had fifty-nine saloons in 1907.[519] Meyer also operated a liquor store for a time.[520]

The *Waukegan Daily Sun* wrote on January 19, 1899, that the Kubelsky and Schwartz saloons were a "Disgrace to Waukegan."[521] The newspaper blamed half the crime in Waukegan on the two saloons.[522] The January 19, 1899, *Waukegan Daily Sun* had some other interesting comments about these two saloons.

*The licenses of the Schwartz and Kubelsky saloons must be revoked. Where are the police? There are nightly rows in these disgraceful resorts. On June 24th, two people were nearly killed there. The whole section of the city lying about the Genesee Street Bridge has been aroused and intimidated by these beastly law breakers. The proper place for these two scoundrels is the county jail.*[523]

Meyer and an employee of the Schwartz saloon named Corn got into it in 1898. The two did not like each other very much to begin with, and an argument between them turned violent. Corn blamed Meyer for some missing beer bottles. Meyer lost his temper and broke a beer bottle over Corn's head. The bottle caused a severe wound to Corn's right temple, and a doctor had to treat the wound. Meyer entered a plea of guilty to assault and battery and was fined $3 and costs.[524]

Another night, Meyer hit a customer named Anton Kromeli over the head with a billiard ball, seriously injuring him. Meyer was arrested, but his lawyer got him out of it.[525] Meyer's brother-in-law Louis Sachs got in trouble at the saloon in 1899. He was tending bar for Meyer when he attacked a patron named John McGlaughlin. Sachs pled guilty and was fined $5 and costs, which amounted to a total of $25.[526]

In 1901, a new police chief took over in Waukegan. Chief Green wanted to clean up gambling in town and the Kubelsky saloon was first on his list. Two policemen raided Kubelsky's at ten thirty. They walked in as if making their rounds and noticed the door to the back room closed. They burst through the door and caught four men gambling. The police found a draft for $1,500 and $40 in cash on the table. Each man had large amounts of cash on him. All four men were arrested and taken before a judge at midnight and fined $10 and costs, which added up to $15 apiece.[527]

Meyer had a long-running feud with another Waukegan Jew. Waukegan's Jewish community seems to have been split into two camps at this time. This man was on one side of the split and Meyer on the other. Unfortunately, the man was elected constable in 1905 and immediately started issuing threats to Meyer.[528]

First, he tried to get a warrant for Meyer's arrest but was denied the warrant.[529] A week later, the man, along with four friends, walked into Meyer's saloon and ordered drinks. Meyer refused to serve them and ordered them all to leave. The outraged man sued Meyer for $200, claiming it was against the law for a business to refuse to sell to anyone.[530]

The case went to court on July 18, and Meyer won. The judge ruled that a saloonkeeper was not required to sell to anyone who entered his business.[531] The local Jews followed the case closely. The same man also tried to file charges against Meyer for selling liquor on Sundays, but the charges didn't stick.[532]

Abe Diamond, another Waukegan Jew, had trouble with the same man in 1907. The man was sent to collect a $20 payment for an insurance policy taken out by Diamond for his son Heinie. Diamond claimed the insurance company cheated him, and he never got the policy. He therefore refused to pay for it.

Our newly elected constable didn't care if Abe was cheated or not. When Abe wasn't looking, the man jumped on Abe's junk wagon and drove off. Abe picked up a gas pipe and ran after him but could not catch him. Diamond had to pay the $20 at the police station to get his junk wagon back. The whole episode took place in Downtown Waukegan and was seen by a large number of people, many of them Jews.[533]

Jack Benny claimed that his mother urged Meyer to get out of the saloon business after he was hit over the head with a pool cue.[534]

In 1907, Meyer went back to selling clothes with his brother Jacob and Charles Gordon. The new partnership with Jacob didn't last long. Jacob sold his share of the business to Meyer the same year and moved to Dalhart, Texas.[535] Meyer's partnership with Gordon lasted only three years. Meyer took complete control of the store on Genesee Street, and Mr. Gordon took control of their other store on Tenth Street.[536]

Meyer lost his cool in September 1913. He stopped into the Star Theater to watch a movie named the *Fire Bug*. The movie featured Jews burning down their shops to collect insurance money. Meyer went ballistic and chewed out the theater's manager, Mr. Luedtke, for showing the movie. The confrontation almost ended in a fistfight. Meyer threatened to destroy Luedtke's projector. Luedtke ran out of his ticket booth and grabbed Meyer by the coat and told him to watch himself.[537]

Meyer filed a charge of assault and battery against Luedtke. Meyer, however, never showed up to court, and the case was dismissed.[538] An unexpected event occurred after the *Daily Sun* published the story. The Jewish Independent newspaper of Cleveland, Ohio, found out about the story and published it. A boyhood friend of Meyer's named I. B. Cohen happened to read the story and contacted Meyer. Cohen had attended the same school in Russian Poland as Meyer, and the two had been best friends but had not seen each other in twenty-nine years. They lost touch after they immigrated to America. Both had tried to find out what happened to the other over the years but had always failed.[539]

Meyer served as secretary of the Am Echod Synagogue for seventeen years. When he quit in 1913, the synagogue gave him a silver and gold loving cup in appreciation of his work.[540]

I found a little information about Jack Benny's mother. She was born in Saice, Kovno, Russia, in 1869 and came to America in 1891. Her maiden name was Emma Sachs. She was the founder of the Waukegan Jewish Ladies' Aid Society and was always involved with the synagogue. She died when she was only forty-eight years old after being sick for two years. Mrs. Kubelsky left behind her husband Meyer, son Jack, and daughter Florence. The November 20, 1917, *Waukegan Daily Sun* wrote, "The Jewish folks of Waukegan lose one of the most enthusiastic women in their various church and society work that ever lived here."[541]

## Lithuanians

With the exception of Dominis Norkus, Waukegan's first Lithuanians arrived with the Washburn and Moen Company in 1890. The Washburn and Moen Company later became the wire mill. The company's home office was located in Worcester, Massachusetts, but the company decided to expand and built a plant in Waukegan in 1890. Some of Waukegan's first Lithuanian settlers had worked at the Worcester plant before transferring to the new Waukegan plant.

Many of Waukegan's first Lithuanians lived on Market Street. Others lived in company housing at Eighth Street and Prescott Avenue. This area later became known as Washburn Springs. After establishing themselves in Waukegan, most Lithuanians moved west to the area around Lincoln and Eighth streets. A few were still living on Market Street in 1910, however.

Dr. R. Giniotis, writing in *Historical Highlights of the Waukegan Area* by Osling, claimed the Lithuanians first established St. Bartholomew's Church in 1896.[542] The church was first located on Ninth Street, but a new church was built at Eighth and Lincoln streets.[543] A total of one thousand men supposedly marched in a column to the future church when the cornerstone was laid on October 4, 1906. A number of Poles and Slovenians marched along with the Lithuanians.[544] The church was dedicated on July 15, 1907.[545] Lithuanian Auditorium, or what everyone called Lougin Hall, was built a block away at Ninth and Lincoln streets in 1929.

According to Dr. Giniotis, Dominis Norkus is the first Lithuanian settler in Waukegan. He walked all the way to Waukegan from Chicago. Mike and Matthew Ruta and Anthony Jesiukevicius were next on the scene, coming in 1890, all were transfers from the Washburn and Moen plant in Worcester, Massachusetts. Other early Lithuanian settlers were John Visockis, Charles Gust, Vincent Zupus, and Charles Vaitekunas. The Jocius family was also early Lithuanian settlers. I personally know some of the Jocius, and they have an interesting story. One of the Jocius girls married a Nugent. Their son Patrick married the daughter of Pres. Lyndon Johnson.[546]

The *Waukegan News Sun* published the obituary of Joseph Selenak in 1934. Joe was also here about 1890. He worked for the Chicago North Shore and Milwaukee Railroad for a number of years. He was also one of the founders of St. Bartholomew's Church.[547]

John A. Ashmus immigrated to Waukegan about 1894. He operated one of the first grocery stores on the south side located on Tenth Street. John was also an alderman for North Chicago's first ward.[548]

One ex-Waukegan Lithuanian named Charles Wember died a hero. Wember operated a tavern in Waukegan during the early years of Lithuanian immigration to Waukegan and was one of the foremost Lithuanians in town. He moved to Hammond, Indiana, in 1909 after his tavern business failed. There, Charles found a job at the American Maize Company near Hammond in Roby, Indiana. He was employed there for only a few months when he tried to stop some starch dust from exploding. The attempt failed, and he got himself blown up instead. Charles left a wife to grieve for his demise.[549]

In 1905, there were 250 Lithuanian families living in Waukegan. A total of 37 families owned their homes. The total number of Lithuanians living in Waukegan and North Chicago in 1905 was 1,500.[550] Waukegan and North Chicago had a combined population of 4,000 Lithuanians in 1930.[551] The Lithuanians were one of the largest ethnic groups in town.

What really stands out to me about the Lithuanians is their church wars. These church wars were a riot—literally.

The first one occurred in 1904. Father Ambozatis, pastor of St. Bartholomew's Church, thought he could treat his congregation like they were still living in Russia. Lithuania was ruled by Russia at the time. He tried to control their lives, but they rebelled. According to the December 16, 1904, *Waukegan Daily Sun*, the Lithuanians "think they are in a free country and that 'Free' means that they are their own bosses in everything, church, as well as ordinary life."[552]

The problems started almost as soon as Father Ambozatis arrived. The situation had become so bad that the police had to guard Father Ambozatis's house after someone threw a brick through his picture window.[553]

Next, the church committee got involved. They refused to turn over the money from the collection baskets to Father Ambozatis for seven straight months. Father Ambozatis had to work without pay the whole seven months. Finally, Father Ambozatis complained to the archbishop who called for a new church committee. The new committee tried to take over the collection baskets, but the old committee stopped them. Father Ambozatis had to step in and calm everyone down and told everyone that the archbishop would handle the problem later. The archbishop did handle it later. He thought the money belonged to the church and threatened to hire a lawyer to get it back.

A spokesman for the Catholic Church said the Lithuanians had the wrong idea about living in a free country. Most were poor and uneducated in Europe. They thought that no one could lord it over them here and that they did not have to comply with our laws.[554]

Fighting over money broke out again in 1909, not only at St. Bartholomew's but also at Holy Rosary, the Polish church in North Chicago. Fr. Joseph Staszkiewicz was the pastor at St. Bartholomew's and Father Grudzinski the pastor of Holy Rosary. Both seem to have been as old school as Father Ambozatis (whom I wrote about in the previous story). Both wanted complete control of all the money collected at Mass. The parishioners at both churches had other ideas. The congregation at St. Bartholomew's thought Father Staszkiewicz was using the money for nonchurch purposes. They wanted a committee to oversee the funds collected at Mass. The parishioners at Holy Rosary hijacked the church fund and found it contained no money at all.

The collection plate was passed around at St. Bartholomew's one Sunday in July, and everyone got up and left. The week before at Holy Rosary, a mob of women chased away some painters working in the church. Later in the week, the same group of women refused to let Father

Grudzinski enter the church or say Mass. The police were called on both occasions.[555, 556]

The next Sunday at Mass, Father Staszkiewicz had to go out and pass the collection basket around himself. Only three nickels were collected. This was the last straw for Father Staszkiewicz, who completely lost it and started scolding the congregation. The congregation responded by laughing and clapping their hands. They also petitioned Archbishop Quigley to get rid of Father Staszkiewicz.[557]

But Father Staszkiewicz wasn't about to quit just yet and the following week stationed four lawyers from Chicago at the church entrance. Everyone entering the church was required to pay a fee of 10¢. This idea didn't go over very well either, and soon, a good-size mob started forming outside the church. The nervous Father Staszkiewicz called the police, who arrived just in time to prevent a riot.[558]

Both sides stubbornly refused to give in an inch, and the church war dragged on until September. Finally, Father Staszkiekicz threw in the towel. He had not collected any money in months and decided to go back to Russia.[559]

The year 1916 saw the next round of trouble. That year, the city of Waukegan put prohibition up for a vote in April. Father Zajkowski, St. Bart's parish priest, was a big supporter of prohibition. His influence with the women of the parish resulted in them voting for prohibition, and their support helped Waukegan become a dry town.

The male parishioners were outraged by the vote and let Father Zajkowski know it by throwing stones at his house. The next night, someone broke into Father Zajkowski's cellar and set fire to a stack of firewood. The fire then spread to the coal bin, and soon, the cellar was in flames.

A woman living near Father Zajkowski's house saw the fire and called the fire department. In the meantime, someone ran into the house and woke up the housekeeper, who was able to run out of the house. It was later thought that she might have died if no one had awoken her. The fire department was able to put the fire out and save Father Zajkowski's house. Father Zajkowski was not in the house that night but in Chicago. Supporters of Father Zajkowski decided it might be best to watch over his house until a guard could be hired.[560]

Father Zajkowski also started getting death threats by phone and letter. The Waukegan police got involved and sent an armed policeman to guard Father Zajkowski day and night, along with the church property. The parish, however, had to pay the guard's salary.[561]

I could actually write more about other church wars but am getting writer's cramp.

Waukegan's Lithuanian population showed their unwavering support for their adopted country in 1918. World War I was going on at the time.

*Whereas, we, the Lithuanians of Waukegan, are wholeheartedly in sympathy with our adopted fatherland, whose cause, we believe, is just and therefore supported with all our means, especially with the blood of our countrymen in the ranks.*[562]

## Polish

Polish immigrants were some of the earliest pioneers in Lake County. Stanislaus Lisiecki, an exiled Polish soldier, was Waukegan's first Polish settler. His name is recorded on the 1840 Waukegan census. His son, Philip, was born in Waukegan in 1839. Stanislaus might have been in Lake County as early as July 1838. Another Polish immigrant named Theodore Domski settled in Hainesville in July 1838, and it's possible Stanislaus came here with him. There is no way to prove it though. Stanislaus bought 80 wooded acres in Waukegan in 1841 and eighty more acres in 1842.[563] His occupation was carpenter, but he was also clearing his land and turning it into a farm.

He had some help clearing the land in the 1840s. Another Polish exile named Stefan Gasiorowski was listed on the 1850 census as living and working on the Lisiecki farm.

Alexander Belinski, another exiled Polish soldier, arrived in Waukegan in 1840. He bought 80 wooded acres in Waukegan in 1842.[564] His occupation was joiner (carpenter). He sold all his land by 1850 and moved into town. He didn't stay for long and bought 40 acres on the shores of Diamond Lake in 1851. In 1852, Alexander left his family with his brother-in-law in Waukegan and went gold mining in California. After a short stay in California, his health took a turn for the worst, and he had to return to Illinois. Still, he had found enough gold to expand his farm in Diamond Lake to 155 acres. Alexander still has descendants living in Lake County.

Two more Polish exiles made Lake County their home at this time. My ancestor Franciszek Wlodecki settled in Warren Township in 1843, and Basil Jaroshinski settled in Newport Township in 1845. Two men of Polish descent settled in Benton Township when Lake County first opened for settlement. Hanson Minskey was here by 1836 and his brother, Robert, by 1837.[565]

Polish emigration to Lake County pretty much dried up after these first early settlers. Ludwig Muschewske was probably the next Polish settler to the area. A man named Joslin settled near Green Bay Road in 1865 and wrote that Muschewske was one of his neighbors.[566] I could not find Muschewske in the 1870 census, but the 1880 census records him as living in Warren Township. His daughter, Lena, was born in Illinois in 1874. Ludwig's occupation was brickmaker, and he listed Prussia as his home country. The western part of Poland was a part of Prussia at the time. The 1900 census shows Ludwig still living in Warren Township, but his occupation then was farmer.

Here's a delightful story about a Polish immigrant printed in the April 4, 1885, *Waukegan Gazette* titled "A Bloody Quarrel."

In 1885, Richard Kotzinsky rented a house in Lake Forest from an Irishman named William Baldwin. Kotzinsky was three months behind on his rent when Baldwin told him to move out. What happened after that is up for debate as both sides told completely different stories.

William Baldwin claimed he went to collect the rent when Kotzinsky started swearing at him and came after him with an ax. Baldwin decided to let Kotzinsky cool down a bit before kicking him out of the house. He waited a couple of days and told Kotzinsky once again to move out. The result was the same, and Kotzinsky came after him with an ax again. This time Baldwin was able to wrestle the ax away from Kotzinsky. Kotzinsky then ran into the house and locked the door. Next, Baldwin chopped his way through the door with the ax and chased Kotzinsky away. Baldwin was afraid Kotzinsky would return and asked his nephew, son-in-law, and two black neighbors to hang around for protection. Baldwin also armed himself with an old pistol. Kotzinsky did come back. He was riding shotgun on a wagon driven by a man named Horenbustle. As soon as the wagon got close, Kotzinsky jumped out and hit Baldwin over the head with an ax, severely wounding him. Somehow Kotzinsky was shot in the thigh, but no one could remember hearing or seeing a shot. Baldwin had to tell his side of the story from a hospital bed.

Kotzinsky's version of what happened was much different. He says Baldwin came for the rent money cursing and swearing at him and told him to leave. Kotzinsky claimed the reason Baldwin got mad at him was because he reported that Baldwin was an eyewitness to some type of crime having to do with alcohol. Kotzinsky had filed a lawsuit over the crime, and Baldwin was so enraged about it that he told him to leave.

Kotzinsky said he would leave soon but was waiting for someone to come and buy his chickens. When the man showed up Baldwin chased him away. Kotzinsky told Baldwin to mind his own business and proceeded to lock himself in the house. Next, Baldwin grabbed an ax and chopped his way through two doors. Kotzinsky ran out of the house and headed for the train station with Baldwin in hot pursuit. According to Kotzinsky, Baldwin pulled out his pistol and swore he'd kill him on the way to the train station. Kotzinsky took the train to Waukegan and took out a warrant for Baldwin's arrest. He missed the last train back to Lake Forest so had to pay Mr. Horenbustle to take him back.

When they arrived in Lake Forest, Baldwin and his friends were waiting for them. Once again, Baldwin took out his pistol and threatened to kill him. Kotzinsky then grabbed the ax and hit Baldwin over the head, knocking him to the ground. Next, Baldwin's friends jumped him and beat him to within an inch of his life. He was able to escape but without his coat. Kotzinsky passed out not far from the beating and did not come to until the following morning. Then he was arrested and taken to jail.

The newspaper reported that too much whiskey was the cause of the whole thing. Kotzinsky came back from Waukegan drunk, and Baldwin was thought to have been drinking too. Baldwin was well liked around town and not known to have caused any trouble before. Kotzinsky had a bad reputation as a violent drunk and wifebeater. Kotzinsky was treated for his wounds in jail by two doctors but never recovered from the beating he received from Baldwin's friends and soon died.[567]

The *Waukegan Daily Sun* wrote about a Polish wedding in the Polish settlement of Washburn Springs in November 1897. The newspaper liked to write about Polish weddings and wrote about them a number of times over the years.[568]

Writing about Polish brawls seems to have been another favorite of the newspaper, and they had plenty of them to write about. These brawls could take place anywhere, and Polish weddings were not off-limits. To be fair, many of the other ethnic groups engaged in the same type of behavior. The earliest newspaper mention of Poles in Waukegan occurred in August 1897, when a number of Poles battled it out with one another on Market Street.[569] Four Poles caused more excitement on Market Street in 1898 when a feud broke out between two Polish families. Both parties pelted each other's doors and windows with bricks, bottles, and rocks. Three of the participants were fined $5 and costs.[570] Poles were probably here earlier than 1897, but a fire destroyed issues of the *Waukegan Gazette* newspaper from 1886 until 1897.

I wrote quite a bit about church wars in my stories about Lithuanian and Slovenian residents of Waukegan. These church wars seem to have been quite common. The Finns had one in 1919 when the congregation threatened to tar and feather Pastor John Wargelin.[571] Eight people were roughed up in a church war in Zion in 1906.[572] I have already written about the troubles at the Holy Rosary Polish Catholic Church in the Lithuanian story so will not go into it again.

The 1900 Lake County census lists forty Poles living in the Waukegan/North Chicago area. There were probably many more, but it's impossible to say how many. Most listed their place of birth as Russia, Prussia, or Austria. Poland was divided up among these three countries at the time.

The Polish population of North Chicago really took off in 1901. In 1903, Poles purchased six lots to build a Catholic church and school on.[573] Construction was completed in 1904, and the church was given the name Holy Rosary.[574] More Poles continued to immigrate to the Waukegan/North Chicago area. By 1905, there were fifty Polish families living in the area.[575]

The year 1907 was a memorable year for Polish immigration to North Chicago. That year, the E. A. Cummings Company purchased 150 lots in North Chicago. They needed buyers and, after researching the subject, decided to target the Polish residents of Chicago. The Cummings Company stated in the April 30, 1907, *Waukegan Daily Sun*, "The Polish people are honest, industrious, saving, and property acquiring and are welcome additions to any community."[576] The *Waukegan Daily Sun* thought the same about the Polish people already living here and considered them some of the most successful immigrants in town. They already owned 700 properties in North Chicago by 1907.[577]

## The Forgotten History of Lake County, Illinois

On June 1, 1907, the A. E. Cummings Company started bringing prospective buyers from Chicago to North Chicago. The company chartered a steamship on the weekends and sailed from Chicago to North Chicago and then back to Chicago all summer until the lots were all sold.

The Cummings Company started advertising in Polish newspapers in Chicago at the same time. Their marketing campaign emphasized country living, where it was possible to have lawns, gardens, poultry, and animals, something that was not possible in Chicago.[578]

A Polish prince named Arthur J. Sobieski showed up in North Chicago in 1914. He was friends with the Neahaus family and came for a visit. Sobieski was in line for the Polish crown if Poland ever won its independence.[579] Poland became independent in 1918, but unfortunately, Sobieski never had his chance to become king. The nobility class was dissolved after only a few years of independence.

The January 26, 1939, *Independent-Register* newspaper wrote about a fundraiser for Holy Rosary Church. A giant six-foot-nine-inch, three-hundred-pound Polish professional wrestler named Wladyeslaw Talun put on a wrestling bout in Waukegan the first week of January 1939. Wladyeslaw was considered one of the best wrestlers in the world and a future world champion. He was trained by legendary Polish wrestler Stanislaw Zbyszko. *Wikipedia* wrote that Zbyszko was a three-time world champion in the1920s.

I have to write more about Zbyszko. His real name was Jan Stanislaw Cyganiewicz. Stanislaw was born in 1879 in Austria-Hungary but now part of Poland. His wrestling weight was 260 pounds, and he stood 5 feet 8 inches tall. A website named Muscles of Iron claims that Zbyszko grew up in Vienna and began his wrestling career there. He was a graduate of the University of Vienna, spoke eleven languages, and was a lawyer, musician, philosopher, and poet. He invented an exercise tilt-top table and held a patent on it. Stanislaw acted to two films: *Madison Square Garden* (1932) and *Night in the City* (1950). Stanislaw died in 1967 in St. Joseph, Missouri.

Now back to Talum. He had annihilated all his competition since coming to America eight months earlier, and his match in Waukegan was no different. He beat up on his opponent so bad the man had to be carried out of the ring after only six minutes.

North Chicago's Polish residents decided another fundraiser was in order, and there was talk about arranging a bout between Talun and a German wrestler named Friedrich von Schacht. Von Schacht was a

123

6-foot-5-inch, 250-pound wrestler and supposed to be the strongest wrestler in the world. The match would take place at the North Chicago Auditorium. I was not able to find out if a match did take place. Blame the coronavirus. The libraries have been closed for three months, so I can't check the micro films.

I googled wrestlingdata.com for the results of the match, but there is no record of it. There is no record of most of Talun's matches; however, Talun did meet Von Schacht eight times over his career. Talun won six matches, lost one, and no results for the other match. Wrestlingdata.com had some interesting data on it. Von Schacht's real name was Frank Altinger. He was not even born in Germany but Milwaukee, Wisconsin. He changed his wrestling name sixteen times over his career and wrestled in 901 bouts. Frank retired from wrestling in 1953 and died in 2001.

Talun also had an interesting career. He was born in Vilnius, Lithuania, in 1909. Vilnius was a mostly Polish city at the time. Wrestlingdata.com claimed that Talun wrestled in 774 bouts, winning 377 bouts and losing 245. He also had 152 draws. Talun retired from wrestling in 1960 and changed his name twelve times over his wrestling career. Talun's niece, Barbara Gross, wrote about her uncle in the "Find a Grave" website. Talun portrayed Goliath in the film *David and Bathsheba*. I saw the film years ago. Talun died in North Tonawonda, Niagara County, New York in 1980. His body was donated to science at the University of Buffalo.

In 1918, the Polish population of North Chicago organized a great going-away parade and dinner for nineteen of their countrymen. The nineteen had just enlisted in the Polish army in France. A total of twenty-one had tried to enlist, but two were turned down. One was fifty-four years old. Another man named Joe Harkut was turned down because he had a wife and seven kids. He made such a commotion that he was finally accepted.

First, the enlistees and their families sat down to a dinner at Holy Rosary Church. Speeches were given, and a twenty-five-man band from Great Lakes Naval Base entertained them.

Later, a parade escorted the men to the train station. At least 1,500 people took part in the parade. Many Polish school children dressed up in Polish costumes and joined the parade. It was thought that 3,000 people watched the parade. The procession was led by the North Chicago police department and North Chicago politicians.

The Forgotten History of Lake County, Illinois

At the train station, the enlistees boarded a specially chartered train car. As the train was pulling away, the navy band struck up "The Star-Spangled Banner." The train engineer immediately stopped the train until the song was over. He was rewarded with a big round of applause.

The train was headed for Canada. There, the recruits would receive four weeks of basic training. Then it was on to France for more training.[580]

## Swedes

Most Swedish residents of Waukegan transferred from the Washburn and Moen Company in Worcester, Massachusetts. They were the first employees to buy company lots in the Waukegan Highlands. The Waukegan Highlands was located between Tenth and Fourteenth streets on the west side of Sheridan Road. The Washburn and Moen Company had purchased the land and divided it up into lots, which were sold to their employees. Waukegan Highlands later became known as Washburn Springs.

I found an interesting short history about the Swedes in a folder at the Waukegan Historical Society titled "The Swedish Presence on the Waukegan Highlands." It was taken from a book titled *Ga Till Amerika* by Charles W. Estus, Sr. and John F. McClymer. The authors claimed that hundreds of Swedish employees at the Washburn and Moen Company came from the Varmland region of Sweden. These Swedish workers so impressed Philip W. Moen, the company's owner, that he personally went to Sweden to recruit more of them.[581]

An article published on July 18, 1907, in the *Waukegan Daily Sun* contains some information about the Swedish immigration to America. Titled "Sweden Wishes Her People Back from America," it states that there was a severe shortage of labor in Sweden. The shortage of skilled labor was especially acute. So many people had immigrated to America that formerly flourishing towns had become almost ghost towns. The Swedish government wanted to know why so many of their citizens had left and how they could get them back. They finally figured out that they had all left because there was more opportunity in America than Sweden.[582]

Fred Fortney and Elmer Anderson wrote in *Historical Highlights of the Waukegan Area* by Osling that Swedes not associated with the Washburn and Moen Company found employment at the Waukegan Sugar Refining

125

Plant. They settled on Market Street. After establishing themselves, most Swedes moved west of McAllister Street.[583]

A few Swedes were here at an early date. G. Larson and family came to Waukegan in the late 1850s. Larson was thirty-six years old on the 1860 census and worked for the railroad. His wife, Sofia, was twenty-eight. Son Charles was seven and born in Sweden. Daughters Mina, two years old, and Amanda, ten months old, were both born in Illinois.

A few more Swedes came in the 1860s. Charles Pepard, twenty-eight years old, occupation laborer, got here just in time to be recorded on the 1870 census. Pepard doesn't seem like much of a Swedish name to me. His wife, Ida, was also twenty-eight years old. They had three children: Richard, seven; Ida, three; and Mary, one. All were born in Sweden.

Other Swedes recorded on the 1870 census were the following:

Victor Joonpain, thirty-four, occupation musician. Victor was living at the house of a stone cutter named Mr. Zitts. (If I had a last name like that, I'd change it.)

Hilda Tenburg, twenty-two, occupation servant. Hilda was living at the home of merchant Thomas W. Jones.

Charlotte Anderson, forty, and Mary Burkhart, thirty-five, were both servants at Experience Parks boardinghouse.

Swedes recorded on the 1880 federal census were as follows:

Mrs. Augusta Pierson, twenty-four. Her husband Thomas, twenty-five, was of Norwegian descent. They had two daughters: Minnie, three, and Lilly, three months old.

Lawrence Johnson, twenty-three, occupation hotel worker.

Charles H. Johnson, forty-three, occupation express wagon driver. His wife, Margaret, was thirty-one and born in Prussia.

I counted over 900 Swedes living in Waukegan on the 1900 census. The numbers went down a little by 1913, when only 746 Swedes lived in Waukegan. Some, no doubt, moved out of Waukegan to other parts of the county. The total number of Swedes in all of Lake County in 1913 was 1,647.[584]

According to Fred Forney and Elmer Anderson, a Swedish building contactor named Oscar Sandstrom was supposed to have built a great many houses, schools, and churches on the south side of Waukegan.[585] Ed Link stated that the Swedish Methodist Church came into being on January 7, 1892. The Swedes had no church until then and had used the Women's Christian Temperance Union Hall located on Washington Street at first.

The Forgotten History of Lake County, Illinois

A Swedish Baptist Church was organized in 1895. It changed its name in 1950, becoming the Immanuel Baptist Church, which is located on Grand Avenue.[586] I attended the church one time with my cousins who were regular members. The Swedish Glee Club was formed in 1905.

Swedish strongmen visited Waukegan on occasion. Two Swedes named Lundin and Johnson gave an exhibition of their strength in 1898. The event took place at Magnusson Hall on Tenth Street. One of their feats was playing catch with sixty-pound dumbbells. The audience claimed they made it look no more difficult than throwing baseballs.[587] The Swedish population of Waukegan got to see one of their countrymen put on a good show in 1927. A Swedish strongman named Ricardo Nelson gave an exhibition at Slovenic Hall. Ricardo might have been the strongest man in the world. Some of his feats of strength seem impossible, but I'll let the readers decide for themselves. He could bend horseshoes, crowbars, and prison bars. He could pull apart a hemp rope that not even a team of horses could break and lift the team of horses as well. His first feat of strength took place at a brick factory when he was eighteen years old. A train car carrying bricks derailed. Ricardo was able to pick the car high enough to put it back on the track. Train cars must have been much smaller and lighter in those days.[588]

## Turks

According to the *Waukegan Daily Sun*, Waukegan had the largest population of Turks in the country. A total of 130 Turkish men were living in Waukegan in 1910.[589] They first showed up to town in the early 1900s.[590] Most were political exiles who had engaged in some type of anti-government activities and fled the country to avoid arrest.[591] Some of them had three or four wives back in Turkey who were counting on them for support.[592]

They were all members of the Islamic faith and fiercely clung to it. They lived mainly in boardinghouses on the south side of Waukegan. One boardinghouse supposedly had 50 Turks crammed into a single room like sardines. They all slept on mattresses on the floor with their heads toward the wall and their feet toward the middle, taking up all four walls of the room.

The Turks all ate around one large table. The main course was always

127

put in the middle of the table, and each man served himself with his own large spoon. The main course usually consisted of black bread and either beef or mutton stew.

Like all Muslims, they wouldn't go near pork. (Your author is an ex-pig farmer so would have made a bad Muslim.) The *Waukegan Daily Sun* wrote about an incident at a Turkish boardinghouse in 1910. Someone not familiar with Islam took some pork into one of the Turkish boardinghouses. Every Turk in the house panicked and ran out with all their possessions. One courageous Turk finally got up enough nerve to run back in and grab the pork and throw it away. The rest of the Turks came back in but would not eat off any of the dishes or from the pots and pans. The boardinghouse was forced to replace everything before they would eat. In addition, all the old pots, pans, and dishes had to be thrown out.[593]

The Turks had it tough in Waukegan. Every Armenian, Greek, Bulgarian, Albanian, Serb, and Romanian in town probably hated them. All these groups had been ruled by Turkey at one time or another and had endured bad treatment by the Turkish government or army. Asst. Police Chief Thomas Tyrrell told the newspaper that for the most part, the Turks behaved themselves. He also mentioned that they would not take any guff from the other ethnic groups.[594] Another problem for the Turks was their support for Germany in World War I. Turkey was allied with Germany in World War I. A good number of brawls between Turks and Armenians or Greeks took place. The Turks and Armenians clashed repeatedly over the years. One particularly bad scrap occurred sometime in the early 1900s, and a large number from each side were badly cut or stabbed.[595]

The Turks loved their coffeehouses, and there were two in town. One coffeehouse was run by a woman who could speak twelve languages.[596] Joe Abdula was operating a coffeehouse for the Turks in 1929.[597]

The Turks also hung out at the St. Gregory Mission on the south side of Waukegan. The St. Gregory Mission was founded by Brother Francis in 1909. It was used by Waukegan's Turks, Armenians, Albanians, Bulgarians, Macedonians, Serbs, and Assyrians; it's a miracle that Brother Francis was able to keep them away from one another's throats. Outside the mission, it was a different story. (I will write more about Brother Francis in my story about Waukegan's Bulgarian and Macedonian immigrants.) A Turkish mullah also lived at the mission. He taught his countrymen English and called them to prayer every day.

The mullah's name was Hoja Abraham, and he was a political exile

The Forgotten History of Lake County, Illinois

like many of Waukegan's other Turkish immigrants. He arrived at St. Gregory's Mission in 1909. The first time he met Brother Francis, he refused to shake his hand because he was a Christian. Hoja Abraham couldn't speak English, and despite the bad impression, Brother Francis told him he would teach him English and also invited him to stay at the mission. Hoja Abraham lightened up a little after living in the mission for a short time and became friendlier.[598]

Hoja Abraham had had to escape from Turkey. Hoja, along with three other mullahs, had spoken out at one of Istanbul's greatest mosques against the Armenian massacres of 1893. The four thought it was beneath any Muslim to commit those kinds of atrocities. The Turkish government was not too happy with their statements, and two of the mullahs were arrested and beheaded. Hoja and the other mullah evaded arrest and escaped the country.[599]

One Turkish emigrant in Waukegan named Alli Hassen was supposedly the world lightweight wrestling champ. He was a veteran of World War I, surviving a gas attack and shell shock. He had been seriously injured and sent to Great Lakes Naval Hospital to recover. He made Waukegan his home after recovering and lived in the city until 1928.

In 1928, a friend from his old wrestling days named Yussof Mammouth contacted him. Mammouth offered him a job, coaching the wrestling team at a YMCA in Istanbul, Turkey. Hassen accepted and left for Turkey. Too bad for Hassen, he was already too Americanized and used to having freedom of speech. He immediately started criticizing the Turkish government, business, and culture, all the while praising everything American. Not a good idea in a country with no freedom of speech. He was arrested by the government and tried for his crimes and then hanged.[600] (I read someplace that he managed to avoid the hangman's noose.)

In 1910, a Turkish immigrant named John Iglihasson arrived at his new home in Waukegan in grand style. Instead of waiting for the train to stop at the station, he exited early by stepping off the train backward. He hit the station platform upside down, making a sensational landing on his head. Exiting passengers said it was a miracle he did not kill himself. A doctor was sent for, but the only injury he could find was a knot the size of an egg on the Turk's head. The November 16, 1910, *Waukegan Daily Sun* claimed, "Many foreigners have come to the city in rather unconventional manners, but John was the first who made his appearance here on his head."[601]

129

That was not the first time something like that happened. In 1909, some drunk thought he missed his stop in North Chicago. He panicked and jumped off the train when it was still going forty miles an hour. He was supposedly highly intoxicated. He would have had to be highly intoxicated to jump off a train at forty miles an hour. It was eleven o'clock at night, and when he hit the ground, the passengers heard a loud groan. He got up right away, though, and the passengers could see him sitting on the railroad tracks as the train was moving away.[602]

Only fifty Turks called Waukegan home by November 1915. All the rest had left.[603] Some of those fifty Turks did settle permanently in Waukegan, and I know for a fact that some of their descendants were still living in Waukegan in the late 1960s.

## Other Ethnic Groups

Some ethnic groups were here but never had much written about them. I put Russians in this category because I only had one story about them but found more about them later.

## Belgians

The 1900 Waukegan census records 55 Belgians living here. Some names of these first Belgians immigrants were Van Haecke, DeMeyer, Landit, Shark, Opel, Christeona, Van Hunder, Strobe, and DeLoof. The number went down a little by the 1910 census when only 42 Belgians lived in Waukegan. The rest of the county contained 127 Belgians.

More Belgians came to Lake County in 1906. They were contract workers for the Rock County Sugar Company, which was looking for farmers to grow sugar beets for them. Sugar beets were a new crop in the county, and none of the farmers knew how to grow them. All the farmers had to do was supply the land, and the Belgians would do all the work.

They already had experience growing the crop in Europe and had been recruited in Belgium by the company. The *Daily Sun* wrote that the Belgians started work at daybreak and only stopped at dusk. All had been poor peasants in Belgium and had lived a tough life there. Their usual meal

The Forgotten History of Lake County, Illinois

in Belgium consisted of bread and a pint of beer. They were lucky to get meat once a month.[604]

The Lake County independent newspaper wrote that just thirty acres of sugar beets were planted in the county in 1906. Sugar beets proved to be a very profitable crop for most of the growers that first year when they made from $75 to $125 an acre. The next year, eighty-seven acres were contracted out to the Rock County Sugar Company, and more farmers showed an interest in the crop. The Belgians, however, didn't work for the company again the next year. Many stuck around the county and found other work. The company was planning to bring in German peasants to take their place.[605]

# Chinese

A Chinese immigrant named Sam Sing was living and operating a laundry in Waukegan by mid-1890. His brother, also named Sam, joined him in 1898.[606] One of these two must be the same person who had to put up with an irate customer in 1898. One day a Waukegan businessman came into the laundry and asked for his garments. The laundry worker told him he had not left any clothes there. The man insisted that the clothes were there and called the police. The episode soon ended when the man realized he had left his garments at a different laundry.[607] The Sings must have left town because the 1902 *Waukegan Daily Sun* claimed that Ying Lee was the only Chinese man living in Waukegan. Lee also operated a laundry.

Lee had a bad experience coming back from Chicago one Sunday in 1902. He had gone to Chicago to visit his girlfriend and was returning home by train. Lee fell asleep on the train and woke up to a disturbing experience. He was wearing some special shoes made in China. A Waukegan man riding on the same train decided to play a joke on Lee and stole his shoes while he was sound asleep. Then the man hid the shoes in a different car and hurried back to see Lee's reaction.

Lee exploded when he woke up and found out he had no shoes. He jumped up and began running through the car screaming "Shoe! Shoe!"[608] In the meantime, the Waukegan man decided to keep the shoes as a souvenir. Later, he went back to pick up Lee's shoes, but they were gone. Someone else had stolen them. Poor Lee had to walk back to his laundry without shoes.

## Hungarians

I can sum up in one paragraph all I know about the Hungarians in Waukegan. The June 25, 1908, *Waukegan Daily Sun*, wrote that two hundred Hungarians had been working in Waukegan, but they all went back to Europe. There were still some Hungarians working at the wire mill in 1917, however.[609] There is no more information about them.

## Italians

Only one Italian is recorded on the 1900 Waukegan township census. More came after 1900, but there is no way to tell how many. Articles in local newspapers show that quite a few Italians were in the county at the time. Some came up from Chicago for temporary jobs.[610] Others found employment on railroads. The railroad provided boxcars for their workers to live in, and sometimes this led to trouble. In 1906, seven Italians working on the railroad in Somers, Wisconsin, fought a gun battle with two tramps over ownership of a boxcar.[611] A fight among Italians living in a boxcar left two people dead and two others almost dead in 1922.[612] The Italians got in their share of brawls with other ethnic groups as well.

A quarter of Waukegan's Italians went back to Italy in 1908, reason being not enough jobs in town. Most were back in 1909, when the economy got better. Waukegan was supposedly one of the favored destinations for Italian emigrants.[613]

Vivian Merlo wrote in *Historical Highlights of the Waukegan Area* by Osling that the year 1910 saw a large increase of Italian emigrants to Waukegan. Most of them lived on Market Street and worked at the tannery. Vivian listed some of the early Italian families: Serrentino, Carr, Sposito, and Ingoglio.[614]

The *Waukegan Daily Sun* claimed that in 1910, 100 Italians worked as section hands building a sidetrack for the Fels-Morrow Sand and Gravel Plant in Waukegan. The food provided by the company was so bad that they all quit en masse the same day.[615] By 1913, there were 116 Italians living in Waukegan and 535 living in the rest of the county. Most were probably living in Highwood.[616] I will write more about the Italians in my story about Fort Sheridan in chapter 4.

# Mexicans

I was surprised to find Mexicans living in Lake County by 1917. That year, 12 Mexicans went on strike at the American Fence Plant in Libertyville. They could not stand an American Indian working there and went on strike rather than work alongside him. The Indian claimed to be Mexican, but the Mexicans said he was full of it. It was thought that he was afraid of being drafted into the army and was pretending to be a Mexican. Some of the Mexicans complained about him to the federal authorities in Chicago, and he was soon arrested.[617]

In 1919, 15 Mexicans were brought in as scabs during a strike at the Vulcan-Louisville Smelting Company in North Chicago. The strikers were not too happy about it, but no one caused the Mexicans any trouble.[618]

Almost 700 Mexicans were living on the south side of Waukegan by 1926. On April 24, 1926, they organized a fundraiser to build a Mexican church in Waukegan. There was also a carnival and fiesta. All Waukegan residents were invited. The affair took place at St. Joseph's auditorium on Oak Street.[619]

Mexican Independence Day was celebrated in Waukegan for the first time in 1926. Over 450 Mexicans showed up.[620]

# Norwegians

Mary Jenson was the first Norwegian to settle in Waukegan, arriving sometime in the 1850s. She was also the only Norwegian living in Waukegan at the time. On the 1860 census, Mary was seventeen years old, occupation servant, and lived at the home of Dr. Jerod Bassett.

Mary Jenson was not on the 1870 census, but a different Norwegian woman was living in Waukegan's third ward. Anna Denishler was twenty-eight years old, occupation servant. She lived at the home of Thomas W. Jones, a Waukegan merchant. Anna Denishler's name is missing from the 1880 census. Thomas Pierson and family were the next and the only Norwegians in town. Thomas was twenty-five years old, occupation cabinet maker. His wife, Augusta, was twenty-four and born in Sweden. Their daughter Minnie was three years old and daughter Lilly three months old.

According to the Waukegan Historical Society, Waukegan was home to 35 Norwegians in 1900.[621] Waukegan's Norwegian population increased to 84 in 1907.[622] By 1910, Waukegan had a population of 98 Norwegians while the rest of the county had 319 Norwegians.[623]

I would have liked to write some stories about the Norwegians, but nothing was ever written about them in the paper. They never seem to get into any trouble.

# Romanians

Six Romanians called Waukegan home according to the 1900 Waukegan census. In 1907, a Romanian was caught stealing fifty pounds of coal from a train car. Arresting police officer Wells said the man was from a mountainous region of Romania and towered over him, being at least six-foot tall. Officer Wells also mentioned that the man had brute strength and was living with a group of Romanians on Market Street.[624]

A total of twenty-three Romanians were living somewhere in the county in 1910, possibly Lake Forest; none of them lived in Waukegan.[625]

Romanians were back on Market Street in 1911. Three Romanian families were living there, none with kids. Their wives were all close friends, but none of them were happy with their lives. They cooked up a plot to rob their husbands and then go back to Romania. Each one stole half the furniture in their homes and every penny they could lay their hands on and went back to Romania. Their husbands were devastated.[626]

Lake Forest had a total of eighty Romanians living there in 1915, wives and children included. They all lived in one house and were employed constructing the Harold F. McCormick summer home. The house was located in one of Lake Forest's best neighborhoods. The Romanians were hired to take the place of forty Italian workers who were fired. The Italians had gone on strike for more pay.[627] After the project was finished, the Romanian workers were all let go. They must have liked living in Lake Forest and decided to stay for a while. With nothing to do, the Romanians started hanging out at the post office, train station, and Downtown Lake Forest. Their presence suddenly became more noticeable around town. They were heavy smokers, and a cloud of smoke always seemed to be hanging around them. To make matters worse, they all smelled like garlic. This reminds me of all the commotion in Lake Forest when Mr. T cut down all his trees.

One neighbor living next door to the Romanians' home had had

The Forgotten History of Lake County, Illinois

enough and started complaining to the town's sanitary inspector. It was decided that the Romanians had to go, and they were all kicked out en masse. The Romanians loudly protested the eviction but to no avail and surged out of the house with all their possessions. By this time, more Lake Forest residents showed up to watch them get the boot and were amazed at how many Romanians came out of the house. After their expulsion from Lake Forest, the Romanians were all sent to Chicago.[628]

## Russians

North Chicago had a community of Russian immigrants, but it does not seem to have been very large. Census records are useless because most Lithuanians and Polish list Russia as their home country. The names of a few Russians are recorded.

I wrote about a Russian wedding, "Exciting Time at Wedding Celebration," in my chapter on Lake County mobs and riots so will only touch on the story here. A Russian wedding took place in North Chicago in 1903. Most of the guests had been drinking all day. The more they drank, the louder it got until most of North Chicago could hear them. The band tried to quit playing at midnight, but the enraged Russians would not hear of it and beat the sense out of the band.[629] You can read the whole story in chapter 4.

A man named Mike Usrkarovitch was supposed to be one of the most prominent Russians in town. He lived on Kennard Avenue in Waukegan. Usrkarovitch supposedly had worked as a bodyguard for the little Russian czar before immigrating to America. I'm not sure if this was the czar or his son. Mike came to Waukegan sometime in the early 1900s and worked at the Corn Products plant.

The American economy went through a bad period in 1911, and many immigrants went back to Europe, returning after the economy recovered. That same year, Usrkarovitch received a letter from a friend in St. Petersburg, Russia. The friend claimed that a new cannon and gun factory was opening up there, and the plant needed skilled workers. Usrkarovitch, along with ten other Russians, left town for St. Petersburg.[630] I am not sure if they ever returned.

Krum Volkoff was also living on Kennard Avenue in Waukegan in

1911. He was held up by a bandit on Adams Street in Chicago that year. The bandit got away with $220.[631]

A few members of the Russian nobility made appearances in Lake County in the early 1900s.

A Russian named Shapnowsky lived for a time in Waukegan in the early 1900s. He was supposed to have been a count but didn't go around town broadcasting it. The other Russian immigrants were sure of it though. Shapnowsky worked as a draftsman in town but got into some financial trouble. He hobnobbed with Waukegan's upper crust and probably spent more money than he made. Shapnowsky rented an expensive penthouse in the Larsen building and was known as a ladies' man. He had to flee town for financial reasons in 1910 and went to Des Moines, Iowa. There, he married a local woman and was never heard from again.[632]

A Count Orloff hung around St. Gregory's Mission on the south side of Waukegan in 1909. He did not talk much about his past life but was thought to be nobility. His full name was John Deschovitch Orloff. The Orloffs were supposedly one of Russia's wealthiest families. In Russia, he was a Cossack captain but had run afoul of the Russian government because of his socialist views. He arrived in America about 1905 and spent four years in Texas. He spoke a dozen languages but had to learn English when he got to America. Next, he moved to Waukegan and became a good friend of Brother Francis. Brother Francis founded and operated the St. Gregory Mission. Orloff ran out of money in Waukegan and, while in a state of depression, joined the army at Fort Sheridan. He deserted eighteen months later and was being court-martialed in 1911.[633]

Count Theodore (Feodorovitch) Tsalekoff was living in Waukegan in 1909. He was twenty-four years old and born in Kasson, Russia. Theodore was sent to a school in Paris when he was seventeen years old. He was not into school at the time and wanted some adventure. He took all the money meant for his schooling and bought a ticket to South Africa and joined the Boer army fighting against Great Britain. He was wounded in his third battle. After his recovery, Theodore went back to Paris. As soon as he got back, his family in Russia had him arrested for stealing his college funds. The Russian consul held Theodore until his brothers could make the trip to Paris. Theodore acted happy to see his brothers and was let go by the Russian consul. The Russian consul still held on to his passport, however. Theodore had no intention of going back to Russia and took off the first chance he got. He went to the city of Le Havre, France, and bought himself another passport and left for America. Theodore didn't think he needed his passport when his ship sailed into New York's harbor and ripped it up. This mistake got him arrested and almost deported. Theodore was locked up in Ellis Island but was able to hire a lawyer to find his cousin. The cousin came to the rescue and told the authorities that Theodore had immigrated to America and was supposed to live with him.

Theodore stayed in New York for six months before going to Chicago. He was in America for seven years when the *Waukegan Daily Sun* interviewed him in 1909. During that time, he had finished grammar school, high school, veterinary college, and two years of medical school. Theodore told the newspaper that he would like to go back to Russia but not until he graduated from medical school. If he went back before graduating, he would have to serve seven years in the Russian military. The nobility was obliged to serve time in the military, and Theodore would have had to spend his time as an officer in the Cossacks.

Theodore was a landowner in Russia, but the government had confiscated all his property until he served his time in the military. He told the *Daily Sun* that he had a plan to get around serving in the military. Doctors did not have to serve in the military, and that exemption should also be enough to get his estates back. Too bad for Theodore, the Russian Revolution would take place in 1917, and the Bolsheviks would likely have taken all his property.[634]

If you think you have it tough, then read this story. Max Kriefzoff settled in Zion in 1898 and was a follower of Dr. John Alexander Dowie. He never talked much about his experiences in Russia but decided to write about his life in 1909.

Max was born in Kriefnoff, Russia, in 1850. He took his last name from the village he was born in. Max's family was very poor. His father owned two acres of land, but it was not enough to support his family. There was no work in town, so the family resorted to begging. Max was begging alongside his father by the age of ten. His pants were made out of sacks and his shoes out of basswood bark.

As Max got older, he was able to find work as a shepherd. Most of his earnings went to his father. Next, he found work with a tailor. His father still took most of his wages. Max, however, was able to buy himself some better clothes. Once, he asked his father for money to buy some real shoes, but his father said no. The family needed the money to buy a new religious icon; the old one was in bad shape.

Max got a little upset over the incident. He was doing all the work but couldn't even get a new pair of shoes. The sight of the new icon really started to bug him, and he became completely turned off by the Russian church and stopped going there.

One day a former resident of Kriefzoff returned to town for his family. He was also a tailor and offered Max a job. Max would have to move to the town of Taurien, but first, he had to get his father's approval. To his surprise, his father agreed to it but only for a period of one year.

Things were going well for Max in Taurien. He learned to read and spent his spare time reading the Bible. His employer was also dissatisfied with the Russian church and had converted to a different Christian faith.

A year later, a letter arrived from Kriefzoff. It was from his father, and it was time for Max to go home. Max wrote back that he was not going back to Kriefzoff. He also said he was no longer a member of the Russian church and could not be forced to attend the church.

His father wrote back and warned that he would have him arrested for being a "disobedient son." The law was on the father's side. His father also threatened to enlist him into the militia for fifteen years.

Next, Max did what any levelheaded person would do: he ran away. He crossed over into Romania and joined a religious commune. The commune was made up of ex-Russians known as the Malokaimen and Skopzen. The sect started getting under the skin of the Russian czar. The czar finally had had enough of the sect and told the Romanians to either run them out of the country or face the consequences. The commune was soon disbanded.

Max made his first mistake by going back to Russia. He decided to accompany a eunuch back to Russia. I won't explain what a eunuch is but will let the readers find out for themselves. Max was twenty-two years old and a religious zealot. The authorities soon arrested both of them, the charge being "missionaries." They had been preaching against the Russian church. Both were put in chains and sentenced to three years in jail. Max spent time in several different prisons over the next three years, all the time wearing chains on his ankles. He was separated from the eunuch when they were first arrested and never saw him again. Max claimed he suffered greatly from the chains.

After his three-year sentence was up, Max was exiled to Yakutsk, Siberia, for life. He left for Siberia with a large group of prisoners, the

The Forgotten History of Lake County, Illinois

whole group chained together. They left for Siberia on August 20, 1873, and arrived in Irkutsk, Siberia, on February 28, 1875. The trip took eighteen months. The first part of the trip was by either boat or wagon. The last 1,500 miles was by foot. Along the way, they spent time in some real squalid prisons. A great number of prisoners died along the way.

Max had some rare good luck in Irkutsk: his chains were removed. He was still 2,000 miles from Yakutsk but, after another long journey, made it to the town.

Max finally settled down to his new life in Yakutsk. He took on most any job he could find and landed a good job plastering at a monastery. Unfortunately, Max got into a disagreement with one of the monks over some plaster. The monk had him arrested. This time Max was sentenced to leave Yakutsk and told to move to the town of Uenkojansk, located 1,000 miles to the north.

Max was able to find employment in Uenkojansk. He even saved up enough money to build himself a small shack. The place was so cold that it was impossible to raise a garden. Max was able to buy two cows and lived mainly on milk, meat, and fish for the next three years. Wheat flour was available but unaffordable at 50¢ a pound.

After three years in Uenkojansk, Max's life changed directions again. A U.S. Navy ship commanded by Rear Admiral Melville and named the *Jeanette* was shipwrecked on the shore near Uenkojansk. The crew abandoned ship and made their way over the ice to Uenkojansk. Max and the other exiles took them all in and gave them all the food they could spare.

One of Max's guests was Rear Admiral Melville. Melville asked Max why he lived in such a desolate place. Max explained how he got there, and Melville suggested he escape. According to Melville, all he needed was a boat. He could sail down the Jana River to the ocean and then hug the coastline all the way to the town of Cape Techuktsich. Alaska was only seventy miles away from Cape Techuktsich and was visible on a clear day.

Max started work immediately and recruited eight other exiles to join him. The police came close to discovering the boat a number of times. When spring came, the exiles made their escape. They sailed down the Jana River to the sea coast but found the ocean still frozen. The exiles tried to hide until the ice melted but were discovered by a Cossack patrol.

The exiles were all sent away to different locations. Since Max was the ringleader, he got the worst treatment. First, he was flogged and then

139

sentenced to work in a salt mine near Lake Baikal, which is basically a death sentence. The salt mines at Lake Baikal had a notorious reputation, and few people survived the place. Max was beaten with a seven-pound whip with five knotted lashes, each one with three points. It could cause wounds anywhere from three to seven inches long and could penetrate all the way to the bone. Most people could not survive more than four or five lashes. The almighty must have been looking out for Max. He was hit only three times and not very hard at that. The beating was still hard enough to leave ridges on his back months later. Max carried the scars for the rest of his life.

Max was back in chains again for the two-thousand-mile trip to the salt mines. He was part of a group of prisoners being sent to the mines. They rode in wagons part of the way and walked the rest. A fortunate occurrence happened during the trip; a link on his chain snapped. The guard didn't bother to get it repaired but told Max to just put it in a sack. The final leg of the trip was by wagon. The driver was drunk most of the time and frequently sent Max on errands to buy vodka for him. Once, when the driver was three sheets to the wind, he passed out after drinking another bottle of vodka. Max's big chance to escape had finally arrived. He hijacked the wagon and left the driver in a drunken stupor. Next, he tore up his identity papers and buried them. He also used his real name. He had been using a fake name ever since his first arrest.

At the city of Irkutsk, he was confronted by the police. Max told them his real name, and they found it on a list of missing persons. He was allowed to go back to his original home in Kriefzoff. In fact, sometimes the authorities helped him on the journey back.

Max made it all the way home but got a cold welcome there. His parents were still mad at him for leaving the Russian church. Max said goodbye for good and left for the city of Taurien. Taurien was where he had worked as a tailor when he was younger. Once there, Max converted to the Baptist faith and became a preacher. Soon, the authorities began to notice his activities. Max thought it a good idea to leave Russia this time and fled the country.

Max then joined a group of Russians immigrating to America. Their ship docked in New York on June 1, 1893. In America, he became a kind of rolling stone and traveled around the country working at various jobs for the next five years.

During his travels, he discovered Zion City in 1898 and decided to

The Forgotten History of Lake County, Illinois

make it his permanent home. Dr. John Alexander Dowie was establishing Zion City, and Max found the religious atmosphere to his liking.

Max also got in touch with Rear Admiral Melville, and the two started writing to each other. He wrote to his family in Russia as well and found out both his parents were dead, but two of his brothers and a sister were still living in Kriefzoff. He also found out his sister had converted to the Baptist faith.[635] Max died on November 24, 1925.[636]

## Serbs

I can only find a small community of Serbs living in the Waukegan/North Chicago area in the early 1900s. Some were hanging out at St. Gregory's Mission on the south side of Waukegan.[637] The October 3, 1912, *Waukegan Daily Sun* mentioned that only a small number of Serbs and Montenegrins lived in Waukegan.[638]

A Serb named Kosta G. Mitrykeff immigrated to Waukegan in 1908. He found employment at the wire mill and worked there as a mason. Kosta returned to Serbia in 1919 for his wife and children, but the government would not issue his family passports. The government wanted him to stay in Serbia, but Kosta had other ideas. He went to the American consulate for help and was able to get passports for his family after a two-month wait.

Kosta's brother fought in the Serbian army in World War I. During the war, he was captured by the Turks and compelled to join their army. Later, he was captured by the British army and taken to a prisoner-of-war camp in India. Discussions were taking place for his freedom while Kosta was in Serbia.

Another Serb named Peter Atseff might have gone back to Serbia with Kosta. Unfortunately, Peter had never bothered to become an American citizen. The government refused to issue a passport not only for his wife but also for Peter. The American consulate couldn't help him, and Peter was stranded in Serbia.[639]

Even though there were not many Serbs in the county, they chose a spot in Lake County to build the St. Sava Serbian Orthodox Monastery. Located on Route 21 halfway between Gurnee and Libertyville, the monastery is the headquarters of the Serbian Orthodox Church in the United States and Canada. It sits on thirty-one acres and was built in

141

1925 with contributions by Serbian immigrants from the United States and Canada.

The monastery, built under the direction of Russian architect Alexander Zacharoff, is a blend of Russian and Byzantine architecture and has thirteen cupolas that represent the thirteen different regions of Serbia. An old folk's home was built in the back, overlooking the Des Plaines River.

Bishop Mardary Uskokovich came over from Serbia in 1917 to take over leadership of the Serbian Church in the United States and Canada. He bought the thirty-one acres of land in 1923 and oversaw construction of the monastery. The monastery was dedicated on September 1, 1931. The entry gate to the monastery is written in the Cyrillic alphabet and reads, "St. Sava's Monastery and Home for the aged."[640, 641, 642]

## Syrians/Middle Easterners

Waukegan had a few residents from the Middle East in the early 1900s, mainly Assyrians, Syrians, and one Arab. There were a few Syrians living in Waukegan in 1909.[643] Four Assyrians were arrested for peddling without a license in 1912.[644]

A Syrian named Hogar Homda was arrested for peddling without a license in 1914 and fined $9.40. The price of a peddling license was $50 a year. An amount of $50 a year seems pretty steep for 1914. Assistant Police Chief Tyrrell claimed that the peddlers had started renting out their licenses to one another to get around buying one. When Homda was arrested, he was using a rented license.[645]

Waukegan's lone Arab had an interesting story. In 1910, an Arab named Hussain Adji showed up at the St. Gregory Mission on the south side of Waukegan.

Hussain claimed he was an escaped slave from Turkish Arabia (Saudi Arabia). Arabia was ruled by the Turks at the time. Hussain was born into slavery in the city of Mecca. According to Hussain, he longed for death to free him from such a miserable life. But Hussain had one thing going for him; he was a tall, good-looking man.

One day Hussain was working in the garden when he noticed a young woman watching him. She was the daughter of his master's neighbor. The neighbor also owned a large number of slaves. It wasn't long before she made contact with him, and it became obvious she liked him. Hussain could have been punished severely if they were caught alone together.

Nevertheless, they kept seeing each other and, after a few encounters, decided to run away together. They could each have been sentenced to death if caught. Hussain had some friends living in a nearby village named Arafat some twelve miles east of Mecca. The couple made it safely to Hussain's friends, who hid them in their home. The friends also provided new clothes for Hussain, who was still wearing his slave clothes. Hussain had to do one more thing before he and his new wife left the country. He went back to Mecca dressed as a traveler to visit Mohammed's tomb.

Hussain and his wife were soon on the road. The trip was full of difficulties, but they finally made it to Beirut, Lebanon. There, Hussain and his wife led a happy life. Next, a child was born to the couple. Everything was going great for Hussain, but it wasn't to last. His wife and child died on the same day. Hussain never gave the reason for their deaths.

Hussain did not want to live in a city that gave him such bad memories and decided to immigrate to America. Somehow he knew to come to Waukegan, where he thought he would find friends. Once in Waukegan, Hussain found employment at the wire mill.[646]

# CHAPTER 6

## Self-Made Men in Early Lake County History

A number of Lake County men started life without many prospects. The honorable Elijah Haines is probably the most famous of the group. The village of Hainesville is named after him. Elijah was born on April 21, 1822, in Oneida County, New York. Elijah's father died when he was a young boy. His mother later remarried, and in 1835, the family moved to Chicago. They stayed in Chicago for a year and then moved on to Lake County in May 1836.

Once in Lake County, Elijah's stepfather filed a claim for land located at the present site of Hainesville. Elijah would have been about fifteen years old at the time. His stepfather died not long after arriving in Lake County, and Elijah became the man of the family. He ran the farm during the day and self-educated himself at night. Elijah had only a rudimentary education up to that time but was determined to continue his education.

His hard work paid off in the winter of 1841–1842 when he was hired as schoolmaster of the Little Fort School in Waukegan. Waukegan was still named Little Fort then. Elijah continued self-educating, teaching himself surveying. He platted the village of Hainesville in 1846 and surveyed other parts of the county as well.

Next, Elijah was elected Lake County school commissioner. Two years later, he was elected justice of the peace. All this time, Elijah continued to educate himself. He collected every law book he could get his hands on

144

and taught himself the legal profession, passing the bar in 1851. Elijah soon became one of the top attorneys in Lake County.

In 1859, Elijah was elected to the Illinois state legislature. He spent two terms in the state legislature and became Speaker of the House. He was supposed to have really known his law and had a big influence defining Illinois state law.

Elijah established two newspapers: the *Patriot*, a weekly paper, and the *Legal Adviser*, a legal newspaper. He also wrote three books: *The American Indian*, *The Red Man*, and *Historical and Statistical Sketches of Lake County*.

Elijah married Melinda Griswold on August 18, 1845. There was no mention of any children born to the marriage. Elijah died on April 25, 1889.[647]

Hiram Burritt of Wauconda is our next subject. He was born on November 16, 1817, in Harpersfield, Delaware County, New York. Hiram started working on a farm at the age of eight. He was able to attend school for only two or three months during the winter. Hiram arrived in the Wauconda area in 1837. He claimed that there was just one cabin in (what is now) the town of Wauconda and only two cabins between Wauconda and Wheeling. Hiram was a lifelong farmer and, after much hard work, acquired 234 acres in Wauconda Township.[648]

Antioch farmer William S. Westlake was born on September 22, 1844, in Midsomer Norton, Somersetshire, England. He started working in a coal mine at the age of eight. He spent four years in the mines and then immigrated to America. After a twenty-eight-day journey, William's ship landed at the port of New York. He made his way to Lake County and found employment as a farmhand six miles south of Waukegan.

William served in the Seventeenth Illinois Cavalry during the Civil War. He married Isabella E. Paul on March 5, 1867. They were the parents of four children. In time, William purchased his own farm and over the years expanded it to 400 acres.[649]

The reverend Samuel Breakwell was an early shop owner in Highwood. He was born on February 22, 1835, in Parish Hopton Wafers, Shropshire, England. He went to work at the age of ten and never went to school. Samuel studied in his spare time and was almost entirely self-educated. He was apprenticed to a shoemaker at sixteen years of age. Unfortunately, the shoemaker Samuel worked for couldn't make a go of it, and Samuel was laid off after eleven months. Samuel managed to pick up enough knowledge in those eleven months to go into business for himself. He became successful enough to open his own shop when he was twenty-five years old.

Samuel converted to the Methodist religion at some point and started preaching. He married Mary Ann Norris in July 1854. The couple had four children.

Samuel and his family immigrated to America in 1873, establishing themselves in Highwood. Once in Highwood, Samuel bought a grocery store. He also invested in real estate but lost most of it the same year because of a financial panic. He did manage to hold on to his grocery store.

Later, the Chicago and Northwestern Railroad selected Samuel to be its station agent. He also became Highwood's postmaster. He held both jobs for twelve years.

Samuel kept up his preaching in America, but it looks like he converted to a different religion again. He converted to the Baptist faith this time and was asked to preach in churches in Newport and Benton townships. He became pastor at the Newport church for two years. After leaving Newport, he seems to have traveled around the state preaching in different locations for short periods.

The whole time he was out preaching, Samuel's family continued to operate the grocery store, which became a very thriving business.[650]

Early Wauconda resident Emerson Jenckes Philips had a tough start in life. He was born on October 14, 1835, in Stamford, Bennington County, Vermont. His father died when he was eight years old, so Emerson had to go to work. He had very little education and spent most of his early years doing hard physical labor. He managed to save $303 by the age of twenty-two and headed West in 1857.

Emerson had some bad luck on the trip West. He was walking through the Green Mountains when he hit a patch of ice and fell about a hundred feet. He survived the fall and made it all the way to Aurora, Illinois. From there, he went to Wauconda Township and worked as a farm laborer for a year. Emerson decided to go into farming for himself but lost all his savings because of more bad luck. He didn't let it discourage him and went back to work as a farm laborer.

Emerson married Jane B. Rouse on January 2, 1862. They were the parents of three children. Jane was the daughter of John Rouse, one of Lake County's earliest settlers.

Despite little education, Emerson became the Wauconda school director for thirteen years. He was also road commissioner for six years.

Emerson succeeded in farming on his second try and eventually owned 387 acres.[651]

William Stewart Seals was on his own by the time he was nine years old. He never gave a reason for leaving at such an early age but claimed he didn't return home again for the next twenty-one years. He was born on August 17, 1820, in Washington County, New York. William might have been supporting himself but knew he should also get himself educated. He worked during the summer and was able to go to school during the winter session.

William continued his winter sessions and, by the age of eighteen, was educated enough to get hired as a schoolteacher. In 1838, he moved to Michigan, where he seems to have worked at a variety of jobs. He taught school again and worked on farms at harvest time. It took William a few years, but he was able to save up enough money to carry him over while he trained to be a lawyer. He was hired by a law firm in Ann Arbor, Michigan, and passed his bar there in 1846.

The following year, William quit the law firm and went to Chicago but didn't stay long. There were too many lawyers and not enough work. Next, he went to Waukegan and formed a partnership with C. P. Ferry. The partnership did not last long, however. Ferry left for the state of Washington and eventually became governor of the state.

William settled down for good in Waukegan and continued practicing law. He purchased some land and built his own house on it. William married Emily Cuthburt in November 1850. One daughter was born to the marriage. William became one of the foremost lawyers in Waukegan.[652]

Robert Clinton Green was born on November 27, 1831, in Franklin County, New York. He barely had any education at all and started working at a woolen factory at the age of ten. The normal workday was twelve hours. Robert immigrated to Lake County with his parents about 1846. He was fifteen years old and worked on his father's farm for the next six years. In 1852, he became apprenticed to a bricklayer named William Ladd. In 1855, Robert started his own bricklaying construction company. His company became the largest construction company in Waukegan, building both businesses and residences.

Robert married Christiana Miller in Detroit, Michigan, on November 30, 1854. Three children were born to the marriage.[653]

Capt. William Hammond was born on September 21, 1800, in Fair Haven, Massachusetts. Both of William's parents died when he was seven years of age. He went out to sea on a merchant ship the same year and made it his career for the next thirty years. He proved to be a good sailor and became captain at an early age. During his maritime career, William sailed in the Pacific and Atlantic oceans and the Mediterranean Sea.

William was married twice. His first marriage to Lucy Tallman bore seven children. Lucy died at some point, and William married Lucinda Bothwell. That marriage produced eight children. One of his sons from his first marriage spent time in the Andersonville prison camp during the Civil War. Another one of his sons from his second marriage died in the Civil War.

After William retired from the sea, he moved West to the town of Wayne, DuPage County, Illinois, and took up farming. He moved to Wauconda in 1870 and lived there for the rest of his life. William died on November 21, 1880.[654]

Martin Lux was born on January 16, 1856, in Newport Township. The town of Wadsworth was built on what used to be his father's farm. Martin barely had any education at all. He had to work on his father's farm and, by the age of seventeen, started self-educating in his spare time. Martin went to work at James Pollock's grain business when he was twenty-two years old. He worked at the grain business for thirteen years and then bought into the business, along with his father-in-law in 1885. Two of Martin's brothers bought them out in 1888. Martin had been planning a new business since 1886. His new business was up and running by 1888 and expanded rapidly. His store sold farm equipment, wagons, feed, grain, salt, wool, flour, and coal.

Martin married Clara Doerk in the spring of 1879. They were the parents of three children. Clara died when she was only thirty-three years old. She was so well liked by everyone in Wadsworth that the whole town turned out for her funeral.[655]

Robert Sneesby was born on August 11, 1816, in Graveley, Cambridgeshire, England. His father died when he was eleven years old, and Robert had to go to work. His first job paid 60¢ a week plus room and board. He was later fired for losing a pitchfork. His mother was not too happy about it since his family was poor and depended on his paycheck. A typical breakfast for Robert was salt on bread and warm water.

Robert immigrated to America in 1849. He came to Waukegan right away and found a job building the plank tollway. The road is now Route 120. He worked there for only three weeks, quitting after getting cheated on his paycheck. Robert next found a job at a mill in Waukegan. When the mill burned down, Robert went into business for himself, starting a landscaping business. His business became very successful, and it was thought that Robert did more to beautify Waukegan than anyone else in town. Those who knew Robert said he could do as much work as any two men.[656]

John Austin was born on April 18, 1819, in Devonshire, England. He was an only child and still a young boy when both his parents died. A neighboring family adopted him. They would later leave him some money.

John went to work in a mill when he was only seven years old. He didn't have much of an education. He worked at the mill until he was eleven years old and then took up farming.

John immigrated to America in 1849 and found a job as a farmhand near Libertyville. John saved what money he could and bought 37 acres. He worked on his land until 1854 and then moved to Chicago. There, he established a butchering business. John returned to Libertyville in 1860 and bought 84 acres of land and spent the rest of his life there.

John married Elizabeth Ann Dymond on September 16, 1843, in Devonshire, England. They were the parents of eight children.[657]

Tristram C. French was born on March 11, 1831, in Stuekly, Quebec, Canada. His father died when he was only six years old. His mother later married Edmund Bartlett. The family immigrated to Newport Township in 1846.

It doesn't look like Tristram stayed in Newport Township for long. He left home when fifteen years old and worked as a lumberjack in Michigan. In 1852, he went to California and spent two years mining for gold. After that, he operated some type of business for the next twelve years. Tristram moved back to Illinois in 1866 and bought a 355-acre farm in Warren Township.

Tristram married a widow, Mrs. Frank Palmateer, on Christmas Day 1866. They were the parents of three children. The former Mrs. Palmateer was the daughter of William McClure, an early settler of Warren Township.[658]

Robert S. Ferguson was born April 23, 1852, in Easton, Northampton County, Pennsylvania. He ran away from home when he was eleven years old. His first job was as a sailor on board the ship *Algiers*, and he spent sixteen months at sea. Robert went back home after his ship docked and was getting ready to go back out to sea when a contractor for the Western

Union Telegraph Company offered him a job. He worked as a "pole climber" during his first nine years with the company. Next, Robert went to work for the Atlantic and Pacific Telegraph Company. There, he rose through the ranks to become assistant superintendent of construction for the Western division of the company. At some point, the Atlantic and Pacific Telegraph Company was bought out by another company.

Robert was out of a job and decided to form his own company. His first job was reinstalling the fire alarm lines in Pittsburg, Pennsylvania. He first came to Chicago in 1878 when he was hired to install the Board of Trade telegraph line to Milwaukee. Robert worked on a number of projects in the Midwest before finally settling down in Benton Township.

He married Mary J. Cole in 1879. Mary was raised in Lake County. Robert and Mary were the parents of two daughters. Robert owned and operated a 110-acre farm in Benton Township and raised racehorses.[659]

William Briggs was born on February 13, 1811, in Rhode Island. His family was poor, and William left home at eleven years of age. He worked the next fifteen years as a farm laborer. A farm laborer's life was not an easy one. The normal hours were dawn to dusk. He married Lucinda Snow in 1837. They moved to Chicago the same year and spent the winter there. In the spring, they moved to Ela Township and bought land from the government. The Briggs were parents of eight children. William's farm grew to 260 acres in size.[660]

Dr. Aaron Lewis has an interesting story. He was born on February 12, 1818, in Loudoun County, Virginia. His family was not well off, but Aaron was able to get a normal education for the times. Aaron wanted more than a normal education and was able to get admitted to a Quaker high school when he was seventeen years old. Aaron made up his mind to become a doctor and spent the next three years undergoing training from two different doctors. Training must have paid little or nothing. To survive during his training, Aaron had to come up with a plan. He built himself a hovel in the woods out of scrap lumber. Then he built a chimney out of mud and subsisted on the cheapest food available. Aaron lived like a hermit for eighteen months, only coming out for doctor training every two weeks. He must have spent the rest of his time in the woods studying.

Aaron went on to pass the medical board exam and got his license. He first practiced medicine in McHenry, Illinois. Aaron later moved to Libertyville in 1843. In 1846, he moved again, this time to Little Fort, "Waukegan."[661]

# CHAPTER 7

## Famous Lake County Women

### All Stories Contributed by Diana Dretske, Curator of the Dunn Museum

Clara Colby was born in 1878 in Milwaukee, Wisconsin. She was a graduate of the Columbia School of Music and earned a degree in public debate. Clara later helped establish the Alpha Club. The club was a liberal institution where women could congregate and discuss women's issues of the day. The club also established a library.

In 1905, Clara married a well-known lawyer from Libertyville named Elhanan Wayne Colby, who later became mayor of Libertyville. One son, John, was born in 1909. Clara was involved in the women's suffrage movement. Women in Illinois were given the right to vote in any election on June 26, 1913. A week later on July 5, Clara voted in Libertyville for a new town hall, becoming the first woman voter in Illinois.[662]

Bess Bower Dunn definitely made her mark in Lake County history; the Lake County history museum is named after her. She was born in 1877. In 1896, she starred in a motion picture called *Morning Exercise*. That year, a Waukegan inventor named Edward Amet asked Bess and her friend Isabelle Spoor to put on a boxing match for his new invention, a movie camera. Bess and Isabelle happily obliged and became the first women to star in a motion picture.

Bess became Lake County assistant probate clerk in 1899. She might

151

have been Lake County's first genealogist as well. Being probate clerk gave her access to county records, and she was more than willing to help anyone researching their family history. Bess was even known to accompany family researchers to Lake County's cemeteries if need be.

Bess also helped establish the Lake County Historical Society, where she gave talks and lectures about county history. Bess interviewed some of the county's first settlers, recorded county history, and photographed notable locations of county history.

Bess married Ronald R. Dunn on November 21, 1918. Unfortunately, the marriage only lasted ten years. Ronald died after undergoing an appendicitis operation. She spent the rest of her life a widow. Bess worked for the county from 1899 to 1959, a period of sixty years. No one had ever worked for the county that long. Bess died in 1959.[663]

Jane Strang McAlister was born in Perthshire, Scotland, in 1817. She was the sixth child of John Strang and Margaret Clelland Strang. The family immigrated to Canada in 1835. Jane was eighteen years old at the time. In Canada, she met John McAlister, and the couple soon married. Jane's parents immigrated to Millburn in 1837 and would become some of its most influential citizens.

John and Jane McAlister left Canada in 1842. Jane's obituary states that all John owned was a team of horses and $25 when they first arrived in Millburn. Their first purchase was a cow, which cost them $23. The McAlisters settled down near Millburn on a 160-acre sheep farm at the corner of Kelly and Hunt Club roads. The McAlisters became very successful farmers. John was always ready to help his neighbors out and loaned many of them money over the years. He was supposed to have made a lot of money in this endeavor. Jane spent most of her time on the farm raising and shearing sheep and working in the fields.

After spending forty years in the sheep business, the McAlisters quit farming in 1882. They moved to Waukegan and bought a house on Clayton Street. Waukegan was the place to go for many of the county's farmers when they retired. John McAlister died in 1888. That same year, Jane sold the farm to her nephew.

The McAlisters always had good business sense and knew how to hang on to a dollar. After John's death, Jane was worth about $2 million in today's money. She didn't sit on her fortune, however, and was soon donating to good causes. She attended the First Presbyterian Church in Waukegan and helped them out a number of times. Her first act was to

The Forgotten History of Lake County, Illinois

buy a house for the preacher. She also purchased a new pipe organ for the church and paid off all its bills. Jane's obituary states that she got hundreds of letters from people asking her to help them out financially with one thing or another.[664]

The Lake County Hospital Association came into being in 1891 with the goal of establishing a hospital in the county. Lake County had no hospital at the time. They didn't have much money but managed to scrape up enough to rent a house on North Avenue and turn it into a six-bed hospital. Some local doctors helped the new hospital out by tending to the patients for no charge.

Jane donated $20,000 to the hospital association in 1903. The donation was used to construct a new four-story brick hospital building at the corner of Franklin Street and North Avenue, named the Jane McAlister Hospital. The Jane McAlister Hospital was the predecessor of Victory Memorial Hospital located on Sheridan Road and built in 1922. Jane never lived to see the good work done by her hospital. She died in 1903.

Shimer College used the old Jane McAlister Hospital building for a dormitory from 1979 to 2006.[665] The school rented out the dormitory rooms during the summer to anyone who could afford the $205 monthly rent. Your author lived there in the summer of 1987 and never had one good night's sleep the whole time. I was awoken every night by some type of commotion in the neighborhood. I don't know how the students could take it. There was a noisy bar nearby, and a number of fights took place in the street. Also, a guy everyone called Howling Larry lived next door. Larry was famous for standing out on his porch and screaming at the top of his lungs in the middle of the night. Rumor had it that Larry had volunteered to be a guinea pig in an army experiment and had blown his mind. During his nightly rants, there were always some choice, but unprintable, comments directed his way by dormitory residents.

Dr. Beatrice Dickinson was born in Waukegan in 1866. Her father was Dr. William S. Pearce, an English immigrant who left England in 1847. He moved to Waukegan in 1855 to get away from Chicago's mud. Both Beatrice and her brother became doctors.

Beatrice was a Waukegan High School graduate and the first woman doctor in Lake County. She went to the Woman's Hospital Medical College in Chicago from the years 1883 to 1887. Beatrice came back to Waukegan after graduating from medical school and started her own practice treating

153

mainly women and children. She was also active in the women's suffrage movement and became treasurer of the Waukegan suffragette chapter.

Beatrice married English immigrant Dr. George E. Dickinson in 1908. They met at a medical convention in Chicago. At the time, her future husband was working in the medical profession in Ketchikan, Alaska. After they married, Beatrice moved to Alaska. Both practiced medicine in Ketchikan for the next forty years. Ketchikan must have been somewhat of a shock to Beatrice when she first moved there. It had a population of only 1,600. Waukegan had 16,000 residents at the time. Nowadays, Ketchikan calls itself the salmon capital of the world. It's also popular with tourists.

Beatrice died on March 16, 1948. Her husband outlived her and died in 1956. They never had any children.[666]

Mother Rudd was the first woman innkeeper in the county, operating a temperance tavern in Gurnee. A temperance tavern does not serve alcohol. Gurnee used to be known as O'Plaine, and her tavern was called the O'Plaine House. She also rented out rooms to travelers.

Mother Rudd was born Wealthy Buell in 1793. She married Jonathan Harvey in 1813 in New London, Connecticut. They lived in the states of New York and Ohio before coming to Lake County about 1842. Both Jonathan and Wealthy were involved in the temperance movement. The Harveys had ten children ranging in age from six to twenty-nine years old when they first arrived in O'Plaine.

The O'Plaine house is still standing but is now called the Mother Rudd House. It is located on Kilbourne Road and Old Grand Avenue and is now the site of the Warren Township Historical Society. The historical society sits on three acres, but the original farm encompassed seventy-seven acres.

Jonathan Harvey died on January 22, 1845. Wealthy was in mourning for the next two years. In those days, women in mourning always wore black.

Wealthy married Erastus Rudd on November 14, 1856. After her marriage to Erastus, Wealthy became known as Mother Rudd for the rest of her life. Mother Rudd continued to run her temperance tavern while Erastus operated the farm. Mother Rudd's tavern soon became the community's gathering place. Elections, town hall meetings, and Christmas dinners were all held there. The Mother Rudd House was supposedly a stop on the Underground Railroad. I always heard there was a hiding place under the barn.

The Forgotten History of Lake County, Illinois

Erastus Rudd died from edema in June 1870. Mother Rudd never remarried and wore black the rest of her days. She did sometimes wear a white lace cap after her two-year obligatory mourning period. Mother Rudd retired from the inn business in her late seventies. She died on August 8, 1880.[667]

Edith F. Sherman was born in Lake County in 1876. She studied sculpture at the Chicago Art Institute and was a graduate of that institution. In 1899, she was chosen to design four panels for the new Soldiers and Sailors Civil War Monument located on the Waukegan courthouse square. She created a different depiction on each panel, one each for the infantry, artillery, cavalry, and navy. Edith turned down a trip to Europe to finish the work. She also worked on Waukegan's Lincoln Monument.[668]

Laura Sprague was the county's first schoolteacher. Starting in 1836, she conducted school in a log cabin in Halfday. It was, of course, a one-room schoolhouse. There were seventy one-room schoolhouses in Lake County by 1861.[669]

155

# CHAPTER 8

## Lake County Women Acting Badly

A woman called Fay-Male lived on the Waukegan flats in 1851 and was known as a bad character. The flats were the area below the bluff and next to Lake Michigan. Everyone thought she was an amazon and worried that sooner or later, she would kill someone. She had been in countless fights over the years, but one fight in August 1851 was a real doozy.

Fay-Male fought a knock-down, drag-out fight with someone (it doesn't say man or woman) for an hour. It was fought with pitchforks, clubs, and brickbats. Brickbats are loose objects like rocks and bricks. When it was over, both combatants were a bloody mess.[670]

The flats were frequently the scene of trouble in 1851. A few weeks earlier, a drunken woman flew into a rage, attacking one of her neighbor's homes. She broke all the windows while cursing at the neighbor and her daughter. The whole neighborhood turned out to watch the spectacle—everyone, that is, except the police. The incident lasted quite a while, and the newspaper thought she should be thrown in jail the next time she pulled a stunt like that.

The assailant is referred to as Mrs. C., whose husband had recently been killed in an accident. Waukegan's citizens had supported her all winter long until they found out he had left her a lot of money.[671]

In 1897, a young woman squared off against another woman and three boys and cleaned their clocks. She tore out almost all the other girl's hair and most of her clothes. The September 30, 1897, *Waukegan Daily Gazette* wrote that the boys' clothes looked like "they had been through a threshing machine."[672]

A strike at the wire mill in September 1919 got out of control fast. The wire mill had hired scabs to take the strikers places. The strikers reacted by throwing stones, bricks, cans, and so forth at the scabs when they tried to leave work. One scab riding in a car fired off a round from his pistol to scare the strikers. No one was hit. The police had to escort scabs home after work. Every car carrying scabs was pelted with debris. A few of the strikers' wives also hurled insults at the scabs.[673]

The September 25, 1919, *Waukegan Daily Sun* wrote that the women and children were now causing more trouble than the men. The men would follow orders, but the women paid no attention and did as they pleased.[674]

The strike was two weeks old when a mob of women and children three hundred to four hundred strong tried to start a riot. The police were escorting a group of scabs home when the women showed up and started harassing the scabs and the police. The police could have arrested a number of the mob but chose not to. The *Daily Sun* mentioned that the strike organizers were able to stop the male strikers from causing trouble, but their wives were out of control. The newspaper thought the police should keep a closer eye on the women.[675]

The next day was even worse. At least a thousand men, women, and children gathered to harass scabs leaving work. The mob tried to attack the scabs, but the police stopped them. The loudest, most vocal members of the mob were three women walking in the front, trying to stir up trouble. The women were having a great time harassing scabs and police. The police finally had enough and arrested two of the women. The other one got away. Arresting the women took the wind out of the mob, and it soon broke up.[676]

In 1912, the women of Zion planned to horsewhip Zion's chief of police if he tore down their signs. The chief had ordered all signs around the city taken down. According to the June 21, 1912, *Waukegan Daily Sun*, the devotees of Wilbur Glenn Voliva had put up signs in their windows that read, "No tobacco, no whiskey, no beer, no pork, no theaters, no doctors, no oysters. A clean city for a clean people."[677] Maybe they should have also added the words "No fun" on their signs.

In 1903, the town of Antioch was in an uproar. An Antioch woman had dealt out some real punishment to a young man from Antioch. The man had been spreading a rumor that he saw the woman's daughter skinny-dipping. The woman wanted to hear the story straight from the horse's mouth and asked the man to come to her home and explain himself. In the meantime, she had bought a red horsewhip in case she didn't like his story. Well, she didn't like his story and attacked the man with her red whip. She gave him a bad whipping in the face, legs, and arms.

The whole episode created more excitement than Antioch had seen in years, and the town split into two camps. One side supported the young man, the other the woman. In 1904, the young man sued the woman for $25,000. A jury trial was held in Chicago, where the young man lost the case. The jury sided with the woman and claimed the young man deserved it. It turns out the young man had witnessed two girls skinny-dipping, but neither one was the woman's daughter.

A horsewhipping occurred in Benton Township in 1872. Some young buck had been spreading disparaging rumors about a young woman there. She attacked him with a horsewhip, beating him. The whole episode caused quite a stir in the area.[678] Stories about women beating men with horsewhips was not that unusual. It occurred in other parts of the country as well.

In 1903, a woman in Waukegan chased a tramp away from her house with a hatchet. A pushy tramp had tried to convince her to give him some food. The newspaper reported that the tramp was lucky to get away with his life.[679]

In 1927, a boarder at a boardinghouse owned by a woman named Paulina fell behind on his rent. Paulina fixed him. She stole all his clothes and then filed a warrant for his arrest. The police arrested him and locked him up in a cell, where the rent and food are free. The man complained that he would have paid the rent but was not able to go to work since he had no clothes.[680]

A man named John Mugwump was attacked by his former landlady in 1924. Mugwump had been a tenant at her boardinghouse for the previous two months. He had paid his rent on time but owed her $20 for some booze he had bought from her. Mugwump decided to stiff the women the $20 and skip town. He slipped away from the boardinghouse and made straight for the train station. There, he paid $16 for a ticket to Youngstown, Ohio.

Somehow the landlady found out he was at the train station and ran all the way to the train station, getting there before his train left. She rushed into the station, and there he was. The confrontation turned into a vicious scrap. The two went at it, and the whole room emptied out to make room for the brawlers. They fought from one side of the room to the other in a combination boxing/wrestling match. During the fight, the landlady ripped Mugwump's ticket from his hands. The desperate Mugwump went nuts and attacked her with everything he had. It wasn't enough, and the landlady tore his ticket into pieces and threw it on the floor.

A policeman for the Northwestern Railroad suddenly appeared and stopped the fight. The landlady took off in a hurry while Mugwump began picking up the pieces of his ticket. The railroad policeman told Mugwump to bring what was left of his ticket to the ticket booth, and maybe they would give him a new one.[681]

A woman pest managed to annoy the men standing in front of the Western Union office in 1918. She walked up to them and began knocking off their hats with a cane. Knocking the men's hats off soon got old, so she tried to rip their clothes instead. One guy had his vest and collar torn. The man then lost his temper, and a wrestling match with the woman ensued. The police were called, but she ran away before they arrived.[682]

A disagreement over ownership of some furniture ended badly for a man in 1915. A woman had worked as a housekeeper for him in Chicago. The man ran off and got married and never bothered to pay her. She took some furniture from the man's house and moved to Waukegan. The man and his new wife came to the woman's home, determined to get it back. A heated argument with the housekeeper turned violent. All parties were supposed to have landed punches, but the former housekeeper got the best of it. First, she hit the man in the head with an iron. Then she slashed him with a knife. A doctor was called to stich up the man's wound. After listening to both sides, the police sided with the housekeeper. The man and his wife were told to leave town immediately.[683]

A 250-pound drunken woman caused a lot of excitement in Highwood in 1931. She had gone to see her husband, an army sergeant at Fort Sheridan. There, she started drinking and got plastered. Her husband couldn't handle her anymore and had to call the police.

Patrolman Clyde Cameron showed up and tried to arrest her. Next, the woman kicked Cameron in the jaw. Her husband came to Officer Cameron's aid, but the woman landed a right cross, knocking him senseless. Cameron tried to get her in the squad car, but she kept on fighting. Next, she kicked him on the other side of his jaw and then kicked him in the side. Officer Cameron thought she kicked him in the shins at least a couple of dozen times. He finally got her in the squad car after an hour-long battle. The husband was still out cold.

The drunken woman still wasn't ready to quit and kicked out two windows in the squad car. The police didn't think Highwood's jail was strong enough to hold her, so they took her to the Lake Forest jail. There, she almost ripped a jail door off its hinges. She was charged with disorderly conduct and public drunkenness. The woman was fined $50 and costs.[684]

Here is another story about a woman who couldn't hold her alcohol. Three women were staying at a hotel in Highland Park in 1906. They wanted some excitement and decided to go barhopping at the saloons in Highwood. The ladies drank in every bar they came to, and all got bombed. One of the three drunken girls was a real heavyweight "fat," who soon passed out. The two other girls tried to waken her, but it was no use. Soon afterward, some men came to the rescue and helped the two women get their friend back to Highland Park. Their friend was too heavy to carry, so the men had to figure out some way to get her back. One man found a wheelbarrow full of lime at a construction site and dumped out the lime. The woman was placed in the wheelbarrow and hauled all the way back to Highland Park.[685]

The October 15, 1924, *Waukegan Daily Sun* wrote about two black women who were carried to the town jail twice. The women were charged with disorderly conduct but refused to go the police station. The police had to physically pick them up and carry them all the way to the police station. The spectacle began on Market Street, and the police had to carry the two women up the bluff. A large crowd was soon on hand, and they all had a good time watching the show.

The two women were let out of jail on Monday morning and told to leave town. They both agreed to go away, but they were later found near the Red Flats apartments on Market Street. The police ordered them to leave town again, but they sat on the sidewalk and refused to leave. Once again, the police had to pick them up and carry them to the jail. Another crowd formed to watch the exhibition, and all had a good laugh.[686]

A woman got even with her brother-in-law in 1909. The brother-in-law was living in their house and owed the husband and wife $98 for rent. The brother-in-law sat for supper but would not take his hat off. The woman told him to take it off, and he responded by cursing at her. He went out on the porch, and the woman followed after him and poured a glass of milk on him. Then he picked up a flowerpot and threw it at her.

The Forgotten History of Lake County, Illinois

His brother ran out and grabbed hold of him while his wife beat the hell out of him. The brother-in-law got two black eyes for his trouble and was also arrested.[687]

In 1910, a furious wife entered a tavern on Washington Street, looking for her husband. He was supposed to be at work but had spent the day drinking instead. She immediately attacked him with a cane. She hit him so many times and with such force that she broke the cane. Then she picked up the pieces of the broken cane and continued the onslaught. Next, she ordered him to go home. After they were gone, everyone in the tavern agreed that the man had gotten what was coming to him.

A drunken Irish woman attacked her Armenian husband in 1904. She hit him over the head with a teapot, leaving a big gash on his head. He picked their baby and ran out of the house and all the way to the police station. The out-of-breath man told the police what had happened. The woman was arrested and spent the night in the county jail. She was charged with disorderly conduct and fined. She told the judge that she would behave herself from now on, and the fine was suspended.

A Hainesville couple had been married for thirty-one years, and for most of that time, the wife had beaten up on her husband. The husband refused to fight back because she was a woman. He finally had had enough and sued for a divorce. He claimed his wife had recently hit him over the head with a piece of firewood. Later, she beat him with a club. She also had threatened to kill him a number of times over the years. The wife repeatedly cursed at him and, to top it off, would not do any housework. The February 20, 1905, *Waukegan Daily Sun* wrote, "Wife Amuses Herself by Beating Him on Head with Club, Etc."[688]

Lake County women probably spent more time fighting with each other than with men. Fighting over a man seems to have been one of the most common reasons for a battle. Women fights were not uncommon.

This angry wife put on a display in 1918. She was seen talking to herself and walking down Genesee Street in a huff. In front of the Globe Department Store, she caught up with the woman who had stolen her husband, and the fireworks started. The wife belted the woman twice, knocking her flat on her back. A woman from the Globe tried to pull the woman away, but the angry wife wasn't done with her victim just yet and took another swing. A store clerk tried to stop her, but she took a swing at him too. The night police captain finally arrived and tried to arrest her. He received a punch in the face for his effort. She raged all the way to the

161

police station and was fined $7.40 for her outburst. She settled down after a couple of hours at the police station and was told to go home. Her fine was canceled.

Two of Waukegan's most prominent women battled it out at a card party in 1911. A bad history between the two was the cause. The fight was so intense that none of the other women were able to separate them. Most of the women, in fact, ran out of the room screaming. When it was all over, the two fighters were covered with bruises and scratches. One had a black eye and the other a bloody nose.

A group of women fought it out after work at the envelope factory in 1905. (Your author worked at the envelope factory for a short time.) It was located at Tenth Street and Sheridan Road. The fight started when one woman made a derogatory comment to another woman about that woman's sister. One of the women was beaten so badly that the spectators had to save her. Another woman was supposed to have cleaned all the other women's clocks. The envelope factory fired them all.[689]

The November 4, 1905, *Waukegan Daily Sun* wrote an interesting account of a woman from Washburn Springs who didn't believe in wasting anything. Washburn Springs was located on the west side of Sheridan Road between Tenth and Fourteenth streets. The woman had raised two pigs for food, but both became sick. The neighbors noticed that the pigs could barely walk all week long. The pig's condition only worsened until they became too weak to get up and just lay in the yard.

The woman put the old expression "Waste not, want not" to good use. She stabbed each pig in the throat and let them bleed out. The pigs were so sick that they could not even get up after being stabbed. After they were dead, the woman dragged the pigs into the house and butchered them.

Besides the woman's family, some boarders also lived at the house. It was time for dinner, but someone had tipped off her boarders that they were about to eat meat from sick pigs. They all fled the house and found other places to live. The ex-boarders returned in a van a couple of days later to collect their possessions. The article doesn't say if her family dined on the pork or not.[690]

## Woman Arsonist

In 1877, the small village of Saugatuck was known for its large number of suspicious fires. Saugatuck was located on Belvidere Road (Route 120) west of Waukegan. I think it was in the neighborhood of Route 21 and Route 120. An old woman named Judith lived in Saugatuck at the time. She doesn't seem to have been very popular, possibly because of her bad habit of filing lawsuits. Some of the village residents thought Judith might be responsible for some, but not all, of the recent fires.

The first of the suspicious fires occurred a couple of years earlier. A rundown hotel named the Warrenton House went up in flames. It never did have much business, and the owner sold whiskey to travelers to make ends meet. The *Waukegan Gazette* newspaper wrote that the hotel was overrun with rats as well. It was well-known by the citizens of Saugatuck that the owner and his wife set the fire to collect the insurance money. Their household goods had all been conveniently packed up and were sitting in the backyard, far from the house, when the fire first started. The owner's story about the origin of the fire sounded fishy as well.

The same night, another fire occurred. An old house situated right across the street caught on fire. At one time, it had also been a hotel, back when Route 120 was the plank road. Saugatuck's residents were able to save the house from completely burning down, but it wasn't easy.

A couple of years later, another hotel burned down in Saugatuck. It was named the Rising Sun and was in poor financial shape. The hotel accidentally burned down, or that was what the owner said. No one believed him, of course.

The next fire burned down a farmhouse, which at one time was the next-door neighbor to the "the Rising Sun" hotel.

Soon after that, a midnight fire burned down a barn containing grain, hay, tools, pigs, and chickens.

Then a different farm had a large amount of hay burned up.

Still, another farm saw its entire supply of hay and grain burned up in an hour.

Suspicion for these last few fires fell on Judith. The fires didn't stop just yet through. Judith's own house was next. It was a small house on the south side of Route 120 and near the site of the old Rising Sun hotel. She also owned a bigger house and a farm a mile east of Saugatuck. Her family lived there, and maybe she didn't need her house in Saugatuck anymore. She had the house insured with the Millburn Insurance Company for $150, the furniture for $150, and her clothes for $100.

163

The second floor of Judith's house caught fire on a Tuesday night between ten and eleven o'clock. Her neighbors rushed to the rescue and quickly put out the fire. The whole time, Judith tried to convince the firefighters that it was too late to save the house. The neighbors all went home to bed after putting out the fire. Her plan ruined, Judith had to find another way to burn down the house. By midnight, the house was on fire again. It was later found that some matches and kerosene were missing from a neighbor. The second attempt almost backfired on her again. This time a dozen young men were coming back from a temperance meeting in Libertyville when they saw the blaze. They rushed into the house to save what they could but found just about everything in the house gone. That was because it was all sitting in the yard. The men did save some doors and windows.

Judith was stressed out. She was despondent over the loss of her clothes, carpet, bed, and furniture located on the second floor. She also told anyone who would listen that the blaze was well under way by the time she was awoken by the smoke.

Something had to be done, so a few men volunteered to get a ladder from one of the neighbors. Judith said it was no use to even bother because none of the neighbors even owned one. Then a couple of men decided to brave the flames and save what they could on the second floor. Judith didn't think that was a good idea and told them to just stay where there were. The men, however, did not listen and ran up the stairs to the second floor. They found the floor empty. They went back down and told Judith that there was nothing there. Judith answered that all those items had burned up during the first fire. The neighbors who had put out the first fire claimed that no such items were destroyed in the first fire.

The house then burned to the ground, and the only thing left to do was to file a claim with the Millburn Insurance Company. The insurance investigator must have rolled his eyes when informed of yet another fire in Saugatuck. The village of Saugatuck had to of been on their radar by this time, so I can't say if Judith was able to collect any money or not. There couldn't have been much left of Saugatuck by this time.[691]

# CHAPTER 9

## The All-Time Worst Lake County Woman

A woman named Kate Bender has to be Lake County's all-time worst woman. Kate was implicated in anywhere from fifteen to twenty murders. Her parents and brother also participated in the crimes. This story has so many twists and turns that it is impossible to know how the story ends.

The murders all took place in the state of Kansas, but the Bender family was supposed to have lived in Lake County before they moved to Kansas. The Benders were such a-holes that they were kicked out of town around 1870 under the heading "general cussedness."[692] The *Waukegan Daily Sun* interviewed some old Highland Park residents in 1908 who knew the Bender family when they lived in the county. They claimed the Benders lived halfway between Highland Park and Deerfield and remembered them as being "shiftless and deadbeats."[693]

I have read several books about the Benders, and not one ever writes that the Benders lived in Lake County. Tori Telfer, author of the book *Lady Killers*, thought the Benders were kicked out of a community of Pennsylvania Dutch. Another source thought the Benders were from Jacksonville, Illinois, by way of Germany. Every other source just writes that they were German immigrants.

I had never heard of the Benders until I found two small articles about the family in the *Waukegan Daily Sun*. The Benders, however, are very well-known in Kansas, probably the most famous family to have ever lived there. I looked for information about the Benders at the Highland Park and Deerfield Libraries but only found the 1910 census record for Mary Jane Bender, a resident of Highland Park. I had better luck at the Lake County Recorder of Deeds in Waukegan. There, I found records of Benders buying and selling land in Highland Park in mid-1860. None of the first names of our subjects matched any of the names recorded, but one name was similar to Ma Bender's first name. Other research found Benders living in Indiana and Iowa.

Highland Park had a large community of German immigrants in the 1860s. The first Benders to settle in Highland Park do not appear to have been the deadbeats spoken about in 1908. In fact, they might have been just the opposite. They owned lakefront property in Highland Park in the 1920s, which would have been some of the most valuable real estate in town. My theory is that our subjects emigrated from Germany to Highland Park because they had relatives there. Their actions would have been a great embarrassment to their German relatives who were probably glad to see them go.

Most of my sources claim the family consisted of Kate, her father, mother, and elder brother. One source claims Kate and her supposed elder brother were really husband and wife. Others thought they were brother and sister in an incestuous relationship.

Old Man Bender, John, spoke little English, and when he did, it was more like unintelligent grunts. He supposedly knew more English than he let on. John was born in the Netherlands but was working in a German bakery before immigrating to America. He was around sixty years old when the family moved to Kansas. One source I have writes that he was short and walked all hunched over. Another source claims that he was taller and had ungodly strength and was compared to a gorilla. It was also said that he could not look anyone in the eye when he talked to them.

Ma Bender, Kate Sr., did not speak much English either. She supposedly knew more English than she let on too. Neither Old Man Bender nor Ma Bender was very friendly, Ma Bender in particular. The local pioneer women referred to her as a she-devil. She was short and dumpy and had masculine features.

The son, John Jr., spoke with a German accent and was not a bad-looking guy. He walked around smiling or laughing to himself, and most people thought he was a simpleton. Junior was a few years older than Kate.

The Forgotten History of Lake County, Illinois

Incredibly, John Jr. and his sister, Kate, attended church and Sunday school. It doesn't look like it did them much good.

Kate was supposed to have been the brains of the family. She was in her early twenties when the family first settled in Kansas. The Bender family creeped everyone out, but Kate was the exception. She was attractive, outgoing, and sociable. Kate was a good dancer and attended all the local dances. She loved to ride horses and was an expert at it. Kate was also a big flirt and always had male callers, though, she seems to have kept most of them at a distance. One more thing about Kate, she was into spiritualism and the occult big time. She placed this ad in the local newspaper in 1872.

## *Prof. Miss Katie Bender*

*Can heal all sorts of Diseases; cure Blindness, Fits, Deafness and all such diseases, also Deaf and Dumbness.*
*Residence, 14 miles east of Independence, on the road from Independence to Osage Mission one and one half miles South East of Norahead Station.*

*Katie Bender*
*June 18, 1872*

The Benders left Lake County around 1870, settling in Kansas. There, they ran an inn/restaurant located on the main road among Fort Scott, Osage Mission, and Independence, Kansas. It was a perfect spot for a traveler's inn. The inn's cabin was only sixteen feet by twenty-four feet and was divided in two by the canvas from their covered wagon. The canvas was supposedly dirty and grimy with stains where the unfortunate guests sat. The front area had a stove, table, and small store. The Bender store sold tobacco, gunpowder, ammunition, candies, crackers, and sardines. The back area was the bedroom. Overnight travelers shared a bed with each other and sometimes with one of the Benders. That was the way it was done in those days, and no one thought anything about it. There was also a small barn, a two-acre garden, and an orchard behind the house.

Hanging on the front of the Bender cabin was a wooden sign with the word "Grocery" spelled on it. John Jr. made the first sign but did not know how to spell grocery, writing "Grocry" instead. Kate had to turn the sign over and wrote the correct word on it.

One of their favorite targets was ranchers returning West with large amounts of cash after selling their cattle. Just about any traveler who looked to have money would do, however. One poor soul was infatuated with Kate and pretended to be rich. Big mistake, he didn't last long. After searching his dead body, they found only 40¢. Kate flew into a rage and repeatedly stabbed the body. His carved-up body was later found buried in the orchard.

Once, they killed a traveler while another traveler slept. The man was awakened by a loud thud and then heard an agonizing cry. He pretended to be asleep when he saw Kate staring down at him. He never suspected at the time that someone had just been killed.

Kate's job was to lure travelers in. Then she would pretend to make them dinner. She always sat them down at the same seat at the table with their backs to the reddish stain on the wagon canvas that divided the inn. The unsuspecting traveler had no clue what was about to happen, mainly because his eyes were always glued on Kate. The stove was located near the table, and Kate flirted with the victim while she cooked dinner. Ma Bender stood guard out front and coughed loudly when someone approached. Some people later realized they had been saved by an approaching traveler. Either her father or brother was hidden behind the curtain with a sledgehammer, waiting for the signal to clobber the traveler in the head with the hammer. Three hammers were found after the Benders were gone, one a six-pound sledgehammer. After they were hit with the sledgehammer, Kate cut their throats. (The Kansas State Historical Society still has the knife.) Next, they dumped the body down a trap door to the cellar. At night, they robbed the victim of his money and clothes and buried the body in the orchard. As daylight approached, Old Man Bender could be found plowing his orchard to cover up another fresh grave. Everyone always wondered why he plowed his orchard so much, but they chalked it up to a Bender idiosyncrasy. It is thought that John Jr. took the victims' wagons and horses and sold them to criminal gangs in Indian Territory. The Benders' story reminds me of crimes committed at Cave-In-Rock in Southern Illinois.

The Benders got away with their misdeeds for two years. No one seemed to notice when travelers disappeared. The Benders' big mistake was to kill a local man.

The man was a doctor named Willian York. York had recently sold

The Forgotten History of Lake County, Illinois

a team and wagon to a friend named George Longcor. Longcor and his young daughter were traveling to Iowa when they disappeared. Longcor had once been a neighbor of Charles Ingalls of "Little House on the Prairie" fame. The Longcor double murders were the Benders' most gruesome crime. Longcor was a German immigrant who was driving a new team and wagon when he stopped at the Bender Inn. The new team and wagon must have caught the Benders' attention, and Longcor was promptly dispatched, along with his young daughter. They might have strangled the little girl. When the graves were later dug up, they found a silk cloth around her neck. An article published in the November 8, 1889, *Chicago Tribune* claimed a pillow was put over the girl's head, and she was buried alive.

Dr. York was determined to find out what happened to the Longcors. There were many missing persons in this part of Kansas by this time, and people were starting to get a little suspicious. York took off on his best horse and brought almost a thousand dollars along for expenses. He found out that Longcor and his daughter had stopped at the Bender Inn and stopped in to investigate. The Benders must have spied his wad of cash and made short work of him. He was never seen again.

York had lived in nearby Independence when he went missing and was from a prominent family. One of his brothers, Alexander, was a Kansas senator. Another brother, Ed, had been a colonel in the Civil War. Colonel York gathered together a search party and went looking for his brother. They stopped at the Bender farm twice, but the Benders were able to fool him both times. Some of York's men, however, came away with doubts. The story of the missing doctor went nationwide and was published in newspapers across the country.

Kansas was still the frontier, and a missing person was not that unusual. The citizens of Cherryvale decided to call a town hall meeting to discuss the matter of Dr. York's disappearance. Old Man Bender and his son found out about the meeting and went there to see what the townspeople were up to. The two Benders heard enough to know it was time to vacate the area and hurried home after the meeting. Bad weather kept the search parties at bay for a while. Phyllis de la Garza, author of the book *Death for Dinner*, wrote that the Benders were not missed for a couple of weeks.[694]

Eventually, a neighbor herding his cattle past the Benders' cabin heard a calf crying out. He stopped in to see what was wrong and found the calf almost dead from starvation. The Benders were nowhere to be found, and it looked like they had left in a hurry.

Word of the Benders' departure soon got to Colonel York. He formed another posse and rode out to the Bender homestead to take a look. First, they searched the house and found Dr. York's glasses. No bodies were found, however. Then they opened the trap door and were overpowered by the smell. A couple of volunteers climbed down into the dark cellar and found themselves standing in a gooey liquid. They soon realized it was putrefying blood. They found no bodies in the cellar either. Next, they pushed the cabin off its foundation to look for bodies under the floor but still no luck.

Colonel York was starting to get discouraged and decided to take a break and sat on his wagon. Then he noticed that something was not right in the orchard. There were a number of depressions in the ground the size of a human body. They began poking an iron rod into one of the depressions and pulled out some human hair. It turned out to be Dr. York's grave. Soon, more graves were excavated and more bodies found. All the victims were men except the Longcor girl and a young woman. The young woman was never identified.

There were so many graves that the posse had to quit for the night and return the next day to look for more. A couple of bodies were found in an unfinished well. A couple more were found in a creek behind the Bender property. Thousands of people showed up to watch the developments. Later, the crowd tore the Bender Inn apart and took pieces home for souvenirs.

Here is where the story gets confusing. After the town hall meeting, the Benders swiftly packed up their possessions into a dog-hide trunk and tied the rest up in a sheet. Then they loaded it all in their wagon and made straight for the train station at Thayer. They might have been carrying up to $50,000 on them. They took a small dog with them but left it behind at the train station. Their wagon was left in a wooded area near the train station with the horses still hitched to the wagon. The wagon was built with scrap lumber. Even their "Grocery" sign was used in its construction. There was also a good number of bullet holes and some blood on the wagon.

Passengers on the northbound train remember seeing four people matching the Benders' description get on the train at Thayer. They bought tickets for Humbolt, Kansas. The Benders split up at Humbolt. Kate and her brother took the train south to Katy. Old Man Bender and Ma took the train to Lawrence, Kansas, and from there to St. Louis, Missouri. It was the last time the Benders were ever seen.[695] John T. James, author of *The Benders in Kansas*, wrote that the Benders took the southbound train from Thayer through Indian Territory to Denison, Texas, and were never seen again.[696] This might be the end of the story but maybe not.

A man named William Wright claimed that he was in a group of vigilantes who followed the Benders' trail to Thayer. The conductor told them the Benders took the northbound train. They telegraphed ahead to the conductor of the northbound train, who said the Benders got off at a town called Chinutte. At Chinutte, the Benders got on the southbound train to Chetopa, Kansas. Chetopa was only two miles from Indian Territory, Oklahoma. The vigilantes rode to Chetopa but missed the Benders by three hours. They thought the Benders were heading for the Grand River some thirty miles away in Indian Territory. They caught the Benders four miles from the river and shot them all and then buried the bodies.[697]

A man named M. Coberly has a different story about the Benders' demise. He was the constable of Havana Township, Montgomery County, Kansas, when the Benders first moved to the state. Coberly claimed that after Dr. York disappeared, an infuriated mob of Cherryvale citizens headed for the Bender residence. On the way, they caught the youngest Bender boy, who admitted that his family had killed York. Most sources I have say there was no young boy in the Bender family. The mob showed up at the Bender house and took Pa, Ma, and Kate prisoner. He never mentioned what happened to the sons or son. Then they began searching around the property and found thirteen bodies buried in the orchard. One grave contained a man holding a baby. It was thought that the baby was buried alive with his dead father. More bodies were discovered the next spring, bringing the total to seventeen.

The mob put the Bender family into their own wagon and drove off. When they got to a place named Reaching Rocky Hill, the procession stopped. The mob all took out their guns, and the Benders were shot to pieces. Their bodies were never buried but left to feed the wolves. Coberly was with the mob, and according to him, Kate Bender was killed that day. The *New York Sun* interviewed Coberly in 1889.[698]

Still, another story is told by three men named Snoddy, Peckham, and Beers. They claimed to have tracked the Benders to the border of Texas and New Mexico. The area was known as a lawless region full of criminal gangs. The three men asked the Texas Rangers for help, but the rangers already had enough on their plate and declined to help. The rangers said it was a very dangerous area and did not recommend going there. The three decided to turn around and go back to Kansas.[699] There are a number of other vigilante stories about the end of the Benders. The following story is one of many.

A man named George Downer gave a deathbed confession about the demise of the Benders in 1908. George was the grandson of the founder of Downers Grove, Illinois. (Your author lives right next door to Downers Grove.) George was a veteran of the Civil War and settled in Independence, Kansas, after the war. He was a member of various vigilante committees and, after Dr. York went missing, joined in the search for him.

Downer said he had visited the Benders three different times and was starting to have his doubts about them. He consulted some of his fellow vigilante friends about his concerns, and five of them, including George himself, decided to take one more trip out to the Bender Inn. The five vigilantes were near the Bender Inn when they saw the Benders loading up their wagon. By the time they got to the house, the Benders were gone. They got even more suspicious when they found the house in disarray. The Benders had obviously left in a hurry.

They all agreed the Benders knew something but decided to wait around for another group of vigilantes, which was on their way. The other vigilante committee showed up an hour later at sunset. They all took off in the dark and soon caught up with the Benders. They ordered them to stop, but the Benders responded by drawing their weapons and firing at them. Soon, a furious gun battle took place. One member of the vigilantes was shot and killed. The vigilantes sped up their horses and closed in on the Benders. Next, Old Man Bender was shot and fell out of the back of the wagon, dead. John Jr. then jumped out of the wagon and started running but was gunned down. Later, Ma Bender was found dead in the bottom of the wagon.

Kate was driving the wagon the whole time, but she abruptly stopped the team and cut her favorite horse loose from its harness and rode away. The vigilantes could have shot her at this point but did not want to shoot a woman. They didn't know at the time that she was the brains behind the whole operation. Kate was a good rider and was making some distance between herself and the vigilantes. Finally, they had no other option than to shoot Kate's horse out from under her. The horse rolled over and pinned Kate under it. They approached Kate, thinking she had had enough, but she was far from giving up. She fought like she was possessed, and it took some doing to finally tie her up. Then they threw her over a saddle and went back to the wagon.

They buried the bodies near the wagon by the light of a large fire and burned all the Benders' clothes. Kate barely talked while they worked and didn't seem much concerned about the dead bodies. Her hair hung down below her waist, and her clothes were ripped and torn from her struggle.

The men asked her what happened to Dr. York, but she refused to talk. Finally, she said she would tell everything if they cut her loose. After being cut loose, she was still reluctant to speak, so they began to tie her up again. She relented and told them everything, where the bodies were buried and how they did it. Someone asked her why she did it, and she answered, "I liked to see the blood come."[700]

The men were so mesmerized by Kate's story that she used the moment to grab a gun from one of the men and shot him in the arm. Someone else immediately fired and shot Kate between the eyes. The vigilantes all agreed that the encounter with the Benders should stay a secret, and everyone made a vow of silence.[701] Only on his deathbed did George Downer break the vow of silence. If George Downer's story is right, then the Benders were already dead before the bodies of their victims were found by Colonel York.

Downer's story had me convinced that he knew what really happened to the Benders, but his story has a slight problem. Nicholas J. Pistor wrote in *Ax Murders of Saxtown* that the location were Downer stated the Benders were buried never turned up any bodies. The site was a cornfield that had been plowed up for years, but no body parts had ever been found there.

Here is my favorite Bender story. In 1877, a story about the Benders appeared in the *Daily Commonwealth* newspaper in Topeka, Kansas. A Mexican sea captain named Pieppo claimed the Benders crash-landed on his ship in a hot-air balloon during a storm in 1873. He was sailing between Brazos de Santiago, Mexico, and Galveston, Texas. Four people matching the descriptions of the Bender family were in the balloon, but three of them were instantly killed when the balloon crash-landed on the ship. Only the young man lived through the crash, but he soon died.

He lived long enough to claim he was John Bender. He said that his family was German immigrants and had worked in Germany as carpenters and hot-air balloon builders. His father could operate them as well. After immigrating to Kansas, they got in some trouble with their neighbors. Old

Man Bender happened to have found a gas spring on his property and went to work building a hot-air balloon to use in case of an emergency.

It did not take long for an emergency to happen, and the Benders took off in their balloon at two o'clock in the morning. Heading south for Mexico, they ran into problems. They were near the Gulf of Mexico when a valve broke, making the balloon hard to handle. Next, Old Man Bender punched a hole in the balloon, trying to let gas out so they could land. Just then, a storm blew in, and the balloon was carried out to sea, where it crash-landed on Captain Pieppo's ship. Captain Pieppo did not know who the Benders were at the time. He told the balloon story to some Mexican newspapers, who then published the story in Spanish.[702]

These types of stories appeared in books and newspapers for the next fifty years. German immigrants thought to be Benders were periodically rounded up, but none ever proved to be the real thing. If the Benders had a long enough head start on the trains, they could have been a long way off when the bodies were found. No one knows what actually happened to them. My own opinion is that they were killed by vigilantes and their money divided up by their killers.

Cherryvale, Kansas, once had a Bender museum. Cherryvale also had a "Back to the 1870's and the Bloody Bender Days" on September 19, 1992.[703, 704, 705, 706, 707, 708, 709]

# CHAPTER 10

## Miscellaneous Lake County Women

### Women's Occupations

For years, I heard that the only jobs available to women before the present time were nursing or schoolteacher. The May 17, 1873, *Waukegan Gazette* newspaper wrote about women's occupations in the United States as listed in the 1870 census.

### *1870 Census*

*The census statistics arrange women's occupations under 72 heads. Domestic servants head the list, in point of number, and strange to say, "Laborers on farms" come next.*

*There are 92,000 seamstresses, 90,000 milliners and dressmakers, and 84,000 teachers. A milliner makes and repairs women's hats. There is a glorious army of 10,170 nurses. There are preachers, shoemakers, journalists, authors, "mechanics" not specified and only 100 "show women." But who would dream of "women" steam boiler makers, 5; "bell founders," 4; hunters and trappers, 2; hostlers, charcoal burners, and miners also figure in the list.*[710]

The May 23, 1907, *Waukegan Daily Sun* claimed that of 303 different

175

breadwinner professions, women worked in all but 9 in 1900.[711] Here's a story about a job that seems to have always been open to women.

## Women Farmers

In 1918, a trade school for women farmers opened in Libertyville. World War I was going on, and the school was established by the Women's Committee of the State Council of Defense.

Women were thought to have a real talent for dairy farming. The school farm had thirty-eight cows, seven horses, four sheep, and a few pigs. Most of the training was on the job, but the students spent one hour a day in the classroom. Courses taught were poultry, animal husbandry, beekeeping, general crops, vegetable gardening, and home economics. The course lasted anywhere from two to six months. A total of fifty-eight women had already taken the course as of October 1918.[712] The school had a dormitory that provided enough lodging for ten women. Only women in good health were considered for the course, and they had to pass a physical. It must have been a very rigorous physical since many women were turned away from the program. The students were on probation for the first two weeks.[713]

Illinois had 10,000 women farmers in 1925.[714] According to the book *A History of Women in America* by Carol Hymowitz and Michaele Weissman, 250,000 women ran farms and ranches in America in 1890.[715]

Here's an interesting piece of trivia. The *Waukegan Daily Sun* newspaper wrote in 1930 that women were in control of over 40 percent of the country's resources.[716]

Here's some interesting information from an article from *Harper's Bazaar* magazine that was published in the *Evanston Index* newspaper on June 24, 1899.

The article shows how girls without means can work their way through college with a little creativity. Girls who sew can repair clothes and darn socks at 1¢ a hole. One girl student sold women's hats. Another made "shirtwaists" and sold them to other students. (I have no idea what a shirtwaist is.) Some girls rehabbed dresses. One girl became a packer. She charged to pack other students' belongings when the school year ended. Still, another girl charged for shampoos. A good writer could become a newspaper correspondent. Tutoring students was a common way to make

*The Forgotten History of Lake County, Illinois*

extra money. Women athletes could teach their girlfriends to skate, swim, or ride a bicycle. Teaching dance or music lessons was another possibility.[717]

## Old Man Lucks Out

In 1906, an eighty-one-year-old man named Daniel T. Kleckman married a thirty-six-year-old woman named Mrs. Emma Franzen. Kleckman lived in Shermerville in Cook County and Franzen in Deerfield.

Kleckman had been a lifelong bachelor and disliked women so much he wanted nothing to do with them. People would ask him when he planned to marry, and he would always answer them with contempt for daring to ask. His own female relatives never felt welcome in his home. Kleckman lived alone and did all his own housekeeping. He was retired but had become a wealthy man after running a stone quarry for a number of years.

Mrs. Franzen was the widow of William Franzen, who had operated the largest grocery store in Milwaukee. After William died, Mrs. Franzen was forced to go out and find a job. She ended up living in Deerfield and working at a store in Shermerville.

It just so happened that Kleckman regularly patronized the store where Mrs. Franzen worked. She was an attractive woman, and Kleckman started falling for her. He even started taking his hat off when he entered the store. Kleckman became smitten with her and let Mrs. Franzen use his chair when they talked. The residents of Shermerville had a field day spreading the news.

Kleckman finally proposed to her, and a date was set for the marriage. Unfortunately, Kleckman got sick when the big day came, and the wedding had to be postponed. The wedding was on again when Kleckman's condition improved.[718]

## Woman Daredevil

A brave woman was lucky she wasn't killed at the 1906 Lake County Fair. Madame La Verne was only seventeen years old and made her living parachuting out of hot-air balloons. She was an employee of the Northwestern Balloon Company and a veteran of forty-eight jumps.

Madame's real name was Ms. Mary Quarttell. Her sister had died doing the same type of work, but Madame couldn't quit because she needed the money.

Friday had always been Madame's unlucky day, and she had a bad feeling about going up in the balloon. The balloon's first attempt to get off the ground ended badly. Madame was not ready when the balloon was released, and her foot got caught in a rope. The balloon carried her away about ten feet above the ground. An eighteen-year-old boy from Chicago came to her aid, but he also got caught up in the rope. The balloon climbed to about twenty feet before the manager got it under control. The young guy fell at the same time but survived without a scratch. Madame fell from the balloon when it was only ten feet above the ground, but it took her several minutes to recover.

I'll come back to our story soon. In 1904, a fourteen-year-old boy got caught in the ropes of a hot-air balloon at the Sparta, Wisconsin, County Fair and carried upside down two hundred feet into the air. The balloon's operator heard the spectators screaming at him and thought the crowd was cheering for him until he looked under the balloon. The operator guided the balloon down slowly, and the boy was not hurt.[719]

I have one more interesting hot-air balloon story before going back to Madame. In 1908, an unusual hot-air balloon parachute jump almost took place in Waukegan. A Professor Robinson was supposed to parachute out of a hot-air balloon accompanied by a lion at the Waukegan Days Festival. The lion was supposed to jump first, and then Professor Robinson would follow. Thousands of people showed up to witness the event, but Professor Robinson was a no-show.[720]

Now back to our story about Madame. She was soon ready for the second try. This time the balloon rose without a hitch, and Madame was two hundred feet above the ground. The manager then fired his pistol in the air, the signal for her to jump. Madame did not think the balloon was high enough, but her fellow workers urged her on. The audience applauded Madame when she jumped. Unfortunately, Madame's parachute didn't open properly, and she went spiraling down to the ground. The audience gasped and ran over to check on her condition. Madame was out cold. The manager ordered everyone back, drawing his pistol on the crowd. Then a policeman came on the scene and disarmed the manager. They later found out the pistol only contained blanks.

The Forgotten History of Lake County, Illinois

What Madame thought was her unlucky day turned out to be her lucky day—she lived. Her only injury was a broken ankle.[721]

An article in the February 14, 1931, *Waukegan News Sun* wrote some interesting things about the Lake County Fair in its early days. Besides hot-air balloons, there were baseball games, boxing and wrestling matches, and horse races. (I would like to see some of these events brought back.)

## Brave Lithuanian Woman

In 1912, a Lithuanian woman living in Waukegan woke up to a big surprise. A large elephant was in her garden helping itself to her cabbages. The elephant had escaped from a carnival in town. She ran out in her nightgown and yelled at the elephant to leave and then hit it with a shingle. The elephant promptly hit the woman in the head with its trunk, knocking her down. Then it stood there stomping the ground. An elephant can easily kill a person with its trunk, so the elephant treated her more like a pest. She wasn't hurt but was too shaken to get up and called to her husband for help. The husband ran out of the house and grabbed a ten-foot-long clothespole. Then he tried to drive the animal away, but the elephant grabbed the pole with its trunk and broke it into pieces. The husband figured the elephant belonged to the carnival and ran there for help. In the meantime, the elephant moved on to the beets. The husband returned with the elephant's trainer, who was able to coax the elephant back to the carnival.

The elephants name was Big Epho and at eighty-five years of age was supposed to be one of the oldest elephants in captivity.[722]

## Wifebeaters

Here's a subject that will get your attention. There seems to have been no lack of wife-beating stories for the newspaper to report. The newspaper routinely criticized wifebeaters, and the act was always frowned upon. Alcohol seems to have been involved in most cases. The offender was usually arrested, fined, and spent the night in jail.

In 1907, someone calling himself Q. Marks, "Question Marks," used the newspaper to survey Waukegan residents about establishing a whipping post for wifebeaters. The January 26, 1907, *Waukegan Daily Sun* published some of Marks's thoughts about wifebeaters whom he considered "the most despicable of all men."[723] The newspaper printed two letters from readers who responded: one from a man and one from a woman. Both were for a whipping post but only under certain circumstances, mainly drunkenness. Both also wanted women to get the same treatment for beating their husbands.[724]

This same conversation was going on in other parts of the country. The city of Baltimore had a whipping post. In 1907, Sen. James A. Henson of Decatur, Illinois, proposed making whipping posts the law in Illinois. A punishment of up to fifty lashes would be dealt out by the police. Thomas Tyrrell, Waukegan's assistant police chief, was all for it.[725] It looks like a whipping post never became a reality in Waukegan; at least I can't find any evidence for it. Assistant Police Chief Tyrrell had a stern warning for a repeat wifebeater in the October 20, 1921, *Waukegan Daily Sun*.

> *The next time you are brought in here I'll give you a thrashing you will remember as long as you live. In my opinion a wife beater is more contemptible than a rat.*[726]

A wifebeater faced danger even without a whipping post. In 1911, one wifebeater got a phone call from an upset woman. The September 29, 1911, Lake County Independent printed the message.

> *Either stop beating your wife or we will wait upon you, dressed in pillow slips, and as white caps, and beat you worse than ever you beat her.*[727]

Wifebeaters had to look out for other dangers as well. In 1911, a man came home drunk and beat his wife and daughter. The patrons of a nearby tavern heard the commotion and rushed out and attacked him.[728]

Beating a woman period was dangerous. In 1908, a Waukegan man beat his daughter mercilessly. A mob of five hundred people formed and almost lynched him. The timely arrival of the police saved the man.[729]

In 1902, one Waukegan wifebeater was beaten up so badly by a group of young men that he offered to pay them to stop.[730]

## Wife Deserters

Here's a problem that Lake County's old-timers couldn't stand. They would never have put up with the current tendency of some men to have children with many different women. A man was expected to take care of his family instead of letting them become wards of the state.

The Waukegan police made conscientious efforts to find wife deserters and bring them back. Deserters were fined from $3 to $5 or sent to jail for ten days. A deserter could be relieved of his sentence if he promised to support his wife and family.[731] In 1912, there were twelve wife abandonment cases in a two-month period. The police wanted to put a thousand-dollar bond on each man to make sure they supported their families.[732] Chicago had 939 cases of abandonment in 1905.[733] One wife deserter in 1910 got thirty days in jail. He was told that if it happened again, he would get six months.[734]

In 1927, Sheriff Doolittle pursued a wife deserter through Oklahoma, Texas, and New Mexico. The man was caught in Roswell, New Mexico, and taken back to Lake County.[735]

# CHAPTER 11

## Miscellaneous Lake County Stories

### Lake County's Lynching Record

I cannot find any record of a lynching in Lake County, not that it wasn't attempted. There were quite a few close calls, but the police were always able to stop them. One time a man was saved when the rope unraveled from a tree limb. Three men were hanged in Lake County, but they had all been sentenced to death by a court of law.

Two of the hangings occurred in 1866 and the third in 1874. A man named John Kennedy was one of the unfortunate men. On November 20, 1864, John and a friend named Corbett stopped at a tailor shop in Cicero. Corbett ordered a tailor named Malone to open the door. Malone declined, so Corbett shot through the door, killing him. Corbett was hanged in Chicago on December 15, 1865. Kennedy was charged with complicity to a murder.

John Kennedy had emigrated from Ireland fifteen years earlier. He worked at a manual labor job and thought he was about forty-two years old. John, an alcoholic, admitted being drunk the night of the crime and could not remember what had happened. John had a wife and children.

John's attorney didn't think he could get a fair trial in Chicago. The attorney felt the newspapers had swayed the public against his client so requested a change of venue. The trial was moved to Waukegan. Unfortunately for John, a Lake County jury found him guilty after deliberating for only one hour. He was hanged on July 27, 1866.[736]

The other 1866 hanging occurred in March. A man named William Bell was convicted of killing Mrs. Braden at Slocum Lake near Wauconda. Bell is the only Lake County man ever hanged in the county. He worked at Mrs. Braden's farm and was cutting down trees when he supposedly killed her with an ax in the barnyard. Mrs. Braden, a widow, was found with her head smashed in and throat cut. A razor was found lying next to her. It was known that Mrs. Braden and Bell had recently argued over Mrs. Braden's daughter, whom Bell wanted to marry. Bell was not seen at the crime scene, but a neighbor told police she saw blood on his boots.[737] A newspaper article from 1921 had a little different ending. It claimed that after killing Mrs. Braden, Bell went back to cutting down trees like nothing had happened but left tracks in the snow. He was arrested, convicted, and hanged inside the courthouse in Waukegan.[738] Supposedly Mrs. Braden's brother-in-law made a deathbed confession to the murder years later.[739]

The third hanging happened on February 27, 1874. Chicago resident Christopher Rafferty was hanged for the murder of Chicago Police Officer O'Meara. Rafferty grew up in the Bridgeport neighborhood in Chicago. He was twenty-six years old, had little education, and hung out with a bad group of characters. He and his friends were well-known to the police. Rafferty was known for his terrible temper, which got even worse when he drank. He worked in a brickyard in the summer and the stockyards in the winter and was a physically powerful man. Rafferty was a military veteran but was discharged after serving time in a military jail.

Officer O'Meara had tried to arrest Rafferty in a saloon on South Halsted Street. Rafferty acted like he would go peacefully and asked if he could get his coat. Rafferty walked toward his coat but then turned around and pulled out his pistol. First, he warned the police to leave him alone but pulled the trigger anyway, killing Officer O'Meara. Rafferty ran away but was caught the next day close to Willow Springs.

Rafferty had three trials and was found guilty at all three. No one could remember anyone ever being hanged after three trials. His first trial took place in Chicago. His lawyer then asked for a change of venue. The second trial took place in Waukegan. The third trial went before the Illinois Supreme Court.[740]

Rafferty was sent back to Lake County for his execution. There was concern that some of Rafferty's hoodlum friends from Chicago might try to break him out of jail. Several Waukegan men volunteered to guard Rafferty the night before his execution. (One was Charles Wetzel. Charles's son George was one of Waukegan's greatest athletes and married to my grandfather's sister.) It was cold and windy the night before the execution, and the guards jumped at every sound.[741]

Rafferty was not hanged in public but inside the old courthouse. A total of fifty people witnessed the hanging, jurors included.[742]

Rafferty never admitted killing Officer O'Meara. Ten years later, a dying man claimed that he had killed Officer O'Meara.[743]

Lake County was the favored place to go to avoid the death penalty. Many in the county thought that William Bell was innocent of killing Mrs. Braden in 1866. (I just wrote about Bell.) In 1881, the lawyer for a career criminal named Mooney got a change of venue from Joliet to Waukegan. Mooney was a convicted murderer and a member of the "Molly Maguire" gang. The guards at the Joliet penitentiary thought he was an animal and were afraid of him. Lake County Sheriff John Swansbrough had to interview 2,500 men before finding 12 willing to vote for the death penalty. Mooney was convicted again but got life in prison.[744]

A number of lynchings were attempted in Lake County, but the police were always able to stop them.

In 1896, a mob threatened to lynch a murderer in Halfday. The police took the murderer away before he was lynched.[745]

A mob of fifty men tried to lynch two horse thieves in Barrington in 1899. A police officer had to draw his weapon to keep them back. The prisoners were then taken to jail in Lake Zurich. Members of the mob said they just wanted to put a good scare into the horse thieves.[746]

Soldiers from Fort Sheridan tried to lynch a fellow soldier in 1901. The man had been drinking in Highwood and was walking back to the fort. He spotted a four-year-old boy and tried to beat and sexually assault him. A guard from the fort saw the crime and saved the boy. The pedophile was thrown in a jail cell with seven other prisoners. When the other prisoners found out what had happened, they tried to lynch the pedophile. The guards heard the man screaming and saved him just in time.[747]

Two Lake Bluff men got into an argument in 1922. They lived next door to each other and had been feuding for some time. One was black and the other white. Each had a large family. The white man had lost both legs in a work accident and had to use crutches to get around. Two of the men's children got into a fight, and both men came out to see what all the ruckus was about. Next, the men started to argue, and tempers became heated. The legless white man must have really been intimidating. The black man apparently had no other option but to pull out his razor and cut the white man's throat. The wound just missed the jugular vein and took twelve stitches to close up.

Lake Bluff's residents were obviously upset over the incident, and a mob began to form. Worried that a lynching was in the works, the perpetrator was rushed out of town by the police and taken to the county jail in Waukegan.[748]

The court really threw the book at the throat cutter. He was given sixty days in jail, the minimum sentence. The reason given was that he was the sole supporter of a large family.[749]

In 1906, a man was nearly lynched in Diamond Lake. The article didn't divulge his crime, but the residents of Diamond Lake were very upset. The man was staying at the Diamond Lake Hotel. A mob formed, but they were too late. The Libertyville police had already taken the man away.[750]

In 1908, a man broke into a woman's home in Highland Park and almost killed her. He was gone before the police arrived. Highland Park's citizens were in a state of uproar and swore to lynch the man if they could find him. It looks like the man got away.[751]

Every police officer and fifty navy recruits searched the rail yards in Waukegan in 1913. An employee of the railroad had kidnapped a twelve-year-old girl. The police were first on the scene, but the navy recruits made their appearance as soon as they heard about it. The kidnapper was lucky the police found him first. The recruits had planned to lynch him. The girl was found with the kidnapper.[752]

There are some other close calls in the county. In chapter 4, I wrote about a black lynch mob in 1906. I wrote about a man who badly beat his daughter in chapter 10. The police had to save him from a lynch mob of five hundred people.

In 1901, a Jewish peddler almost became the first and only person ever lynched in Lake County. He was on his way to Waukegan when two men in a wagon offered him a ride. The two men worked for the Kenosha Ice Company and were headed to the Durkin farm in Benton Township to pick up a load of grain. They also carried a long rope to bring a cow back to a farm near the state line. Both men were drunk, and one of the men began lassoing things along the way. Then the man with the lasso turned around and threw the rope around the peddler's neck. The peddler was sitting in the back. The peddler kept removing the noose until a well-thrown noose landed far down the peddler's neck. Just then, the wagon stopped, and the other end of the rope was thrown around a tree limb; the rope wrapped around the limb a few times. The wagon drove off, leaving the peddler hanging, but luck was with the peddler. The rope slowly came loose, and the peddler fell to the ground uninjured. The driver of the wagon saw what happened and told the peddler it was all just a joke and then offered the peddler a ride to Waukegan. The man politely refused and later claimed that he would never again accept a ride and walk from then on.[753] The peddler later sued the two men, but unfortunately, I was not able to find out the result of the case.[754]

## Fats versus Leans

Here's a sporting event that will likely never be seen again. There used to be baseball games between Fats and Leans. The politically correct crowd would have a fit if the word "Fat" was used now.

I'm not sure when the first Fats versus Leans baseball games took place. The May 9, 1896, *Evanston Index* newspaper wrote about a Fats versus Leans baseball game.

A charity Fats versus Leans game was played at the Lake County Fairgrounds in 1913. A large crowd showed up, and $20 was raised for the Lakeside Cemetery Association. The Leans won 7–6.[755]

In 1910, the Waukegan Elks Club went up to Racine, Wisconsin, to watch a Fats versus Leans game. The Fats were touring the country and were so heavy that an ordinary bus could not carry them. They were hauled around in a theater bus.The Fats infield consisted of first baseman "Baby Bliss." Bliss, from Bloomington, Illinois, weighed in at 640 pounds. Baby Bliss was advertised as the heaviest man in the world. There were actually heavier men around. In 1919, a farmer from Silver Lake, Wisconsin, named David McGuire was 6 feet 7 inches tall and weighed 744 pounds.[756] The Fats should have recruited him. J. A. Brownell was at second base. He weighed 400 pounds and was from Manchester, Iowa. The third baseman was W. B. Hinds. Hinds was from Monmouth, Illinois, and weighed 400 pounds. The shortstop was Ed J. Sheean, who was from Clermont, Iowa, and weighed 390 pounds. E. Holm, from Franksville, Iowa, pitched and weighed 350 pounds.

The outfield consisted of F. C. Knee from Waterloo, Iowa, and was team manager. He weighed in at 450 pounds. Outfielder Harry Vorwold was from Dubuque, Iowa, and weighed 325 pounds. Also in the outfield was Frank Hunt from Wolbach, Nebraska, who weighed 325 pounds. The catcher was C. P. Van Luven from Asage. He was the lightweight of the team, weighing in at only 245 pounds. The umpire was Chicagoan Oliver Kimball. He was only 4 feet tall and weighed 139 pounds. This looks like an early form of the Harlem Globetrotters, only it was baseball.[757]

## The Strongest Man in the County

The January 9, 1914, obituary of George Knesley claimed that he was the strongest man in the county. George was a farmer in Warrenton, which was located on Route 120, a couple of miles west of Waukegan. Those who knew George claimed no other man in the county could come close to George's strength. One man said he saw George pick up the back end of a threshing machine. Another person claimed to have seen him lift a 600-pound pig and throw it over his shoulder. One time he unloaded forty-five wagonloads of ice in one day using a block and tackle. George always volunteered to do the heaviest work at any job he was doing.[758] My grandfather's brother (also named George) was supposed to be the strongest man in Wadsworth.

## The Tallest Man in the County

In 1923, Rollo Rogers was Lake County's tallest man at 6 feet 11inches. Rollo grew up between Antioch and Spring Grove. His four brothers were also tall. The shortest one was 6 feet 4 inches. Rollo had a tough time walking and used a custom-built cane 2 feet longer than a normal cane.[759]

## A Ton of Carnival Freaks

In 1922, five employees of a carnival called a cab. Cab driver Harold Murrie showed up but hesitated for a moment when he saw his passengers.

One weighed in at 560 pounds, another 542 pounds, and a third 521 pounds. The other two were lightweights at 163 and 150 pounds.

Murrie's cab was supposed to be the only cab in the fleet with enough power to haul them up the Madison Street hill in Waukegan. Despite having such a mighty vehicle, Murrie's cab couldn't make the hill, and he had to turn the car around and go up backward.

Going down another hill almost ruined his car. He had to brake so hard that he burned out the brake band (never heard of a brake band). The car sat so low to the ground that the mud flaps got caught under the tires.[760]

## Gypsies

At one time, gypsies were a common sight in Lake County. They passed through the county every spring on the way to Wisconsin and came back through the county in late fall on their way south. (The only place in the county I have ever seen a gypsy was at a carnival or fair.)

Most people in the county thought gypsies were a menace to society. My grandmother said everyone was missing chickens whenever they came through the area. Earl Walsh, a sports writer for the *McHenry Plaindealer* newspaper wrote in his column "So I Hear" that gypsies tried to steal his pony when he was a young boy. He also claimed they would steal anything not nailed down, and their women shoplifted from the stores.

The January 27, 1916, *Waukegan Daily Sun* called gypsies the Second Harbinger of Spring, robins being the first.[761] The *Waukegan Gazette* wrote about them in 1885. Gypsies came into town in covered wagons with a small herd of horses trailing behind. They had a collection of monkeys performing tricks and five bears. They had a rough appearance, and their kids ran around barely clothed.[762] The *Daily Sun* claimed in 1911 that the gypsies had mobs of kids and dogs.[763]

The men were described at times as having unkempt black hair.[764] Gypsy women usually dressed in colorful clothes. A *Waukegan Gazette* reporter wrote an article about a gypsy camp on May 1, 1869. The reporter paid a visit to the camp located on the south side of Waukegan. He claimed the gypsies were very secretive about all their activities. The reporter asked them numerous questions but never could get a straight answer from any of them.

The first thing the women did after arriving in Waukegan was go from business to business and house to house, offering to tell fortunes. When they were done with that, they would hit up people on the street. The men would go door to door, trying to buy or sell things. Both men and woman shoplifted and begged. According to the Racine News, from Racine, Wisconsin, in 1904, they stole items from a store owner right in front of his face and just laughed at him when he said something about it.[765] Another one of their tricks was for a group of them to enter a store. The group would get the owner's attention while one of them would slip away and go behind the counter and loot the place.[766]

There were always a lot of complaints to the police about them. After they left town, items would be missing from people's yards.[767] Waukegan's residents were always advised to lock up their houses and barns whenever the gypsies appeared.[768] One Waukegan resident said he never had any complaints about them. He used to let them camp on his land and said the gypsies never stole anything from him.[769]

Some gypsy tribes were worse than others.[770] As soon as the police got wind of gypsies in town, they usually kicked them out.[771] The favored strategy for dealing with gypsies was to always keep them moving on.[772] By 1915, gypsies were banned from camping alongside roads in the county.[773]

In 1900, a tribe of gypsies was accused of stealing a prize horse from a farm near Ottumwa, Iowa. A dozen armed men showed up to get the horse back. The gypsies opened fire, and the men retreated. There were about two dozen armed gypsies, half of them women. The farmers were soon back; this time their ranks had swelled to fifty men. The gypsies put up such a stiff fight that the men retreated again. They finally decided to call the police. A good number of police showed up. The sight of the police was too much for the gypsies, and all their men ran away except one. The lone man and all the women were thrown in jail.[774]

In 1901, a gypsy tried to sell two girls to another gypsy at Momence, Illinois. One girl was sixteen and the other seventeen, and all involved belonged to the same gypsy tribe. The girls' custodian sold them for $800, but the girls protested and made threats to kill the buyer. Then the buyer took out a warrant on the seller to get his money back. The whole town was upset over the affair and chased the gypsies out of town.[775]

In 1916, a band of gypsies camped in Millburn for two weeks, causing trouble the whole time. They seem to have helped themselves to whatever they wanted. One woman said they stole clothes from the clotheslines. Farmers claimed they stole corn, dug up potatoes, and took chickens or pigs. The town's residents were scared of them as well, and someone finally called the police. A carload of police soon arrived and gave the gypsies ten minutes to leave.[776]

Gypsies were alleged to have kidnapped children, and blondes were their favorite. My grandfather's generation sure believed it. They would run outside and pick up their children any time gypsies were rumored to be in the area, blonde kids being taken into the house first. Any time a child was missing, the first thing the police did was check the nearest gypsy camp.

In 1908, Waukegan police searched a gypsy camp for two missing boys from Chicago. The boys weren't found.[777] In 1911, gypsy camps in McHenry and Volo were searched for a missing girl. Again, the girl wasn't found.[778] The newspapers published quite a few gypsy child kidnapping stories over the years.

Gypsies supposedly preferred to kidnap blonde children. The following story could have been the source or one of the sources for their thinking. In 1857, a band of gypsies showed up in St. Louis, Missouri. One of the gypsies was a stunning blue-eyed blond white girl. Some of the citizens of St. Louis invited her to leave the gypsies and stay in town. The gypsies left immediately after that, taking the girl with them. Some people thought that she might have been kidnapped when young and raised with the gypsies.[779]

Some people ran off with gypsies. In 1932, a sixteen-year-old girl from Chicago ran off and joined a tribe of gypsies. She was found telling fortunes in Paris, Illinois, and taken back to Chicago. She had already married one of the gypsies.[780]

Gypsies were great pickpockets. In 1933, a gypsy band stopped at a farm in Lake Villa. They told the farmer they wanted to buy a chicken. A friend of theirs was ill, and they needed to make some chicken soup. He gave one of them a chicken, but a woman picked his pocket when he handed it over. He tried to get it back, but she ran to the car, and the gypsies made a fast getaway. The man lost $20.[781]

In 1911, Gypsies used what is called a seeress game on an eighty-year-old Antioch farmer. First, you put silver in the gypsies' palm, and they tell you your fortune. If you want to know even more about your fortune, you place gold in their palm. They fleeced the old guy out of $20 worth of gold and silver and then went across the state line. The Antioch police were hot on their trail.[782]

The Forgotten History of Lake County, Illinois

In 1903, a group of gypsies came up to an old man who delivered mail from the train station to the Benton Township Post Office. One woman tried to steal the mail pouch right out of his hands. The old guy had to fight to keep from losing the bag.[783]

In 1937, a carful of gypsies stopped to ask a man from Libertyville directions. The gypsies spied his potbelly and acted shocked. They told him that they could help him out with that. One woman patted his potbelly and another one his side. After they left, he found his wallet containing $260 was gone.[784]In 1911, North Chicago was the scene of a gypsy wedding. A gypsy tribe was camped in North Chicago at the time. The groom was the son of the gypsy tribe's king. His bride was an attractive gypsy woman. They were forced to have two ceremonies, one for the state of Illinois and the other according to gypsy custom.

The first wedding was performed at 9:00 a.m. at the Catholic Church on Fourteenth Street. Afterward, they went back to their campground for the gypsy wedding.

The gypsy ceremony consisted of bundles of branches laid out in a circle about ten feet in diameter. Standing in the middle of the circle was the bride wearing a bright red silk dress. Next, the bundles were set on fire. After the fire was burning well, the groom, also wearing red, jumped through the flames and took hold of the bride. Then the two escaped from the flaming circle and ran away. They were pursued by a raucous mob of gypsies.

After the wedding, it was time to party. There were eight barrels of beer on hand, and two pigs were roasted over the burning bundles of sticks. Two young girls sang and performed traditional gypsy dances.[785]

This is not the end of this story. The newlyweds decided to settle down in Waukegan. The man and his wife were sharing a small two-room house with his mother and ten younger siblings. Then the bride's father showed up. They had only been married a few months, but he wanted his daughter back. The recently wed gypsy went to the police and asked if his father-in-law could take her back. He told the police that he had paid $2,100 for her and was afraid he would lose both his money and his wife. The wedding had cost him $600, and the father-in-law made him sign a document stating he would pay the father-in-law $1,500.

The police told him that his marriage was legal under Illinois law, and the father-in-law could not take her away. The father-in-law wanted to give her to another man. The newspaper never mentioned it, but I think

191

the man probably stiffed his father-in-law of the $1,500. The father-in-law wanted to give (sell) her to someone else. According to gypsy law, the wife had to obey her father even if she was married.[786] I never did find out how this story ended.

A gypsy is supposed to be buried in the Oakwood Cemetery on Sheridan Road in Waukegan. A gypsy caravan was driving through Waukegan in 1934, and the police started following them. A gypsy named Mark Mitchell (which doesn't sound like much of a gypsy name to me) freaked out and sped away. The police took off after him, but Mitchell crashed his car and was killed. His son was also in the car but wasn't hurt. The funeral took place in Waukegan, and gypsies from all over the country attended. A shovelful of dirt was thrown in the coffin so Mitchell could be close to the soil. Then a bottle of wine was poured in the open casket so he could be in good spirits.[787]

## Some Good Lake County Names

In 1933, one of our beautiful Lake County women, age eighteen, married Ray Wawrzyniakowski, age twenty-one, of Milwaukee, Wisconsin. Deputy County Clerk Joe Stanczak spoke Polish but declared that he "couldn't pronounce the name in English or Polish."[788]

In 1906, a Waukegan clerk had a tough time writing these Lithuanian names on a marriage license. Their names were Mikolas Jesinkewiczius, twenty-seven, and Marijona Zawiestaukintie, twenty-one. According to the February 17, 1906, *Waukegan Daily Sun*, the clerk remarked that someone must have "thrown the whole alphabet in the air and caught the letters."[789] He remarked that he might need an extra bottle of ink to finish the job.

A number of foreigners submitted petitions to become naturalized citizens in 1910. One Greek name really stood out. The forty-one-letter name is spelled Andricopoulouis Anastastioious Demetrioious. The November 25, 1910, *Waukegan Daily Sun* commented that the king of Greece must have thought "the greater part of his kingdom has gone."[790]

## The Laflin-Rand Powder Mill Explosion

The year 1911 saw one of the world's largest explosions to date. The Laflin-Rand Powder Mill in Pleasant Prairie, Wisconsin, was blown to kingdom come. The mill was located about eighteen miles from Waukegan. It was owned by the E. L. Du Pont De Nemours Company and produced dynamite and gunpowder. The plant was situated on 190 acres and contained forty buildings, most of which were destroyed in the blast.

A total of 280 tons of dynamite, 180 tons of gunpowder, 1,000 kegs of giant powder, and 25,000 kegs of unfinished giant powder blew up. There were five different explosions that left craters up to fifty feet deep. The second explosion was supposed to have been the worst.

Effects from the blast were felt as far east as Cleveland, Ohio, and as far west as Clinton, Iowa. It was felt as far south as Elgin, Illinois, and Whiting, Indiana. Only a small amount of damage was done north of the plant. It was thought that the direction of the wind and Lake Michigan had something to do with it.

The plant employed forty-five men; most lived in Pleasant Prairie. The population of Pleasant Prairie at the time was five hundred to six hundred people. The plant had recently shut down for a couple of days and was not operating at full capacity. Only about a dozen men were working that day instead of the usual forty-five. Amazingly, only a man named Elden Thompson was killed. A total of one hundred people were injured, some seriously. One old woman in Elgin died from a heart attack.

The Wisconsin towns of Ranney, Bain, Truesdell, and Pleasant Prairie were almost obliterated. Pleasant Prairie, at the center of the blast, lost sixty to seventy buildings. After the first blast, hundreds of citizens rushed out of their homes in their pajamas and left for other parts. A special train carried residents from Ranney, Bain, Trusdell, and Pleasant Prairie to Kenosha. The roads were filled with buggies and cars hauling the wounded to hospitals. No one knew if there would be any more explosions, so most people evacuated the area. A few brave souls did stay to watch over their homes. The police were soon on the scene to guard against looters.

The explosion not only scared the living daylights out of everyone in Lake County but also caused a lot of damage there. The county was inundated with burning debris and half-burned powder. Telephone poles were damaged, and many people lost phone service.

Soldiers at Fort Sheridan were knocked right out of their chairs, and windows were shattered. The thirty-foot-by-twenty-foot front doors of the Great Lakes Naval Base Drill Hall were blown off the building. Two men in Highland Park were knocked to the ground, and some windows were broken. Folks in Zion heard four of the five explosions, and windows were broken all over town. Some businesses lost their plate glass windows. Half the buildings in Antioch had broken windows. Some homes and downtown businesses lost all their windows. Four chimneys were knocked down, and the phones did not work. Two theaters in Grayslake were full when the explosion occurred. Terrified theatergoers rushed out of one of the theaters and almost trampled a nine-year-old girl. Luckily, she was not seriously injured. Some Grayslake businesses lost windows. Buildings in North Chicago lost many of their windows, and plaster fell from the ceilings. One store lost an eighteen-foot-by-twelve-foot window. A store in Russell lost much of its stock after the second explosion when it rained glass and rubble. In Barrington, a large plate glass window was blown out of its frame and deposited in the street. Barrington is twenty-five miles from Pleasant Prairie, but its residents could see the flames shooting up one hundred feet in the air. A passenger train traveling four miles south of Kenosha almost derailed. The first blast smashed some of the windows. The second blast broke all the rest. The city of Chicago had thousands of north-facing windows broken.

Libertyville, Lake Forest, and Highwood suffered little damage. An old Methodist Church in Lake Forest did shake badly. It was thought that one more explosion would have brought it down.

Waukegan got hit particularly hard. According to residents, a powerful gust of wind hit the city right after the first blast, and the sky in the northwest lit up in flames. Next, the earth shook like it was hit by a powerful earthquake. Finally, glass could be heard breaking. The windows on the north side of town broke first, but windows shattered in a southerly direction with the blast. A passenger train traveling through town had twenty-five windows broken.

A show at the Barrison Theater had just started when the first explosion happened and someone yelled fire. Everyone panicked and ran out of the theater. A woman holding a baby was run over but survived without injury.

A play was taking place at the Schwartz Theater. The whole theater shook, and everyone thought it must be an earthquake. The band was able to keep their heads and broke into a song; everyone calmed down.

The Baptist Church was in the middle of a service when the first blast occurred. The March 10, 1911, *Waukegan Daily Sun* wrote that the minister was right in the middle of a sermon and had just spoken the words "And there shall be a great light appearing in the east."[791] (I find it hard to believe he was actually speaking those words when the blast happened, but that is what the story says.) Anyway, his terrified congregation rushed for the exits while the minister begged them to stay. He was able to temporarily stop the exodus until the second explosion happened. Then even he ran out of the church.

Nothing like this had ever happened before. Women fainted. Teams of horses broke loose and started to run. Some thought it was the second coming of Christ and got down on their knees to pray in the middle of Genesee Street. Even some of the prisoners in jail started to pray. Others pleaded to be released from jail. It was too dangerous to stand near any windows, so everyone ran out into the middle of the streets. People ran to the police station or *Daily Sun* office in their pajamas, wanting to know what happened. As loud as the blast was, it still could not stop a fistfight on Market Street.

Most businesses on Genesee Street lost their windows. Many homes also had broken windows. The chimney fell over at the armory as exercises were being conducted. Ceilings fell down. Trees were uprooted and doors ripped off their hinges. Barns were destroyed and livestock injured. Hundreds of clocks stopped working.[792]

The Pleasant Prairie Powder Mill explosion caused much destruction in Waukegan, but at least no one was killed. An incident in 1914 proved to be far worse for Waukegan. The Waukegan Corn Refining Plant blew up, killing fourteen men and seriously injuring many others.[793] The corn refining plant was located on Market Street near South Avenue. Ellen Williams Staben claimed that the blast from the corn plant was so strong that bodies were found in St. Mary's Cemetery. St. Mary's was located on the bluff while the corn plant was on the flats.[794]

## Lake County's Greatest Alcoholic

A German immigrant named John was probably the county's greatest drinker. He worked as a farm laborer at the Rodney farm near Libertyville in 1916. One time, John drank fifteen quarts of whiskey in five days. He ate nothing the entire time, making it a liquid diet. At the same time, he polished off a gallon of 188-proof alcohol that he kept in his room. John died from alcoholism six weeks later.[795]

## Man Never Smoked, Drank, or Swore

James Maloney was born in County Clare, Ireland, in 1824. He immigrated to America in 1838, first settling in Vermont. He later settled in Waukegan and served in the Civil War. James claimed to have never chewed or smoked tobacco, drank, or swore during the eighty-four years he lived on planet Earth.[796] (Your author can never make any of these claims.)

## Buffalo Bill

This is not the famous Buffalo Bill Cody but a different Buffalo Bill. In 1898, a seven-foot-tall man calling himself Buffalo Bill rode into Waukegan on a white pony. He wore a giant straw hat and said he had left Mexico two months earlier, claiming to have ridden his pony all the way from Mexico.[797]

## Why Ride When You Can Push?

A man named Al Smith showed up in Waukegan in 1932. Al was pushing a five-hundred-pound sealed motorcycle across the country. He had already pushed his motorcycle from Seattle, Washington, to New York. He was on his return trip and had walked 7,000 miles and worn out fourteen pairs of shoes.[798] (Al must have been the original Forrest Gump.)

## Physical Fitness Nut

A man named Erhard Riehl arrived in Waukegan in 1914. He was pushing a wheelbarrow through five states in the name of physical fitness. He had already pushed his wheelbarrow 3,250 miles. His goal was to make 4,000 miles. Erhard gave a talk about physical fitness at Waukegan's Elite Theater.[799]

## Five Brothers Serve in the Civil War

Mrs. Sarah Simpson lived in Newport Township from the years 1865 to 1880. Five of her sons served in the Union Army during the Civil War.

Her son Capt. James D. Simpson died at the Battle of the Wilderness. Another son, Thomas, was wounded at Antietam and later died.

Mrs. Simpson's other three sons survived the war. Only her son John stayed in the area. John's son later became Lake County superintendent of schools.[800]

## Too Many Flies

The horse and buggy days had a number of drawbacks, one being gazillions of flies. In 1897, the city of Waukegan had 680 horses. Lake County as a whole had 7,551 horses.[801] Piles of manure were located all around town and were perfect breeding grounds for the insects. Waukegan urged its citizens to leave garbage in garbage cans, not in the street.[802] A hot, humid summer day with swarms of flies buzzing around must have been a nightmare. One strategy to cut down on the pests was more fly swatters.[803] Waukegan's youngsters were the chief administrators of the fly swatter. Hundreds of kids were given "good neighbor cards" and told to start early in the morning and kill as many flies as possible. Each card held 100 dead flies, and the kids were paid 10¢ for each full card.[804] In 1921, Waukegan's children killed 11,000 flies in two weeks and earned a total of $110.[805] The town of Lake Forest paid 50¢ for a pint of dead flies, and the town didn't have much of a fly problem.[806]

A new invention did more than anything to control flies, the internal combustion engine. The more automobiles replaced horses, the less piles of manure were lying around town. It was also found that spreading oil around town killed fly maggots. Then it was discovered that spreading oil on lakes cut down on the number of mosquitoes.[807]

## Rats

If living with zillions of flies didn't gross you out, these stories will.

197

Rats were a real problem before automobiles came along. They are still a problem today but nothing like it used to be. Rats can survive on just about anything, poop included. Rats in Chicago eat dog crap to survive. When everyone had horses, there was always plenty of feed and road apples (horse crap) that supported large populations of them.

In 1914, the north side of Waukegan was invaded by a large army of rats. The area had not had a rat problem for the last twenty years, and no one knew where they all came from. The rats took up residence in every house and business. They were so bold that you could almost pet them before they ran away. Rats were running over people's beds while they slept. Residents of the north side were scared for their children (rat bite), and many people were having trouble sleeping at night.[808]

Also in 1914, Waukegan's commercial fishermen had plenty to say about the rats living among the piers on the lakefront. Gangs of rats came at night and stole their fish. They said the rats were incredibly bold and gigantic in size. The rats would steal their largest fish and sometimes lots of them. Then the greedy rats would hide the fish but not eat all of them, and the piers smelled like rotting fish.[809]

In 1913, an old building was torn down next to a bridge on Genesee Street in Waukegan. Thousands of rats lost their home and stormed up a ravine and onto Genesee Street. Then they marched in one giant mob up the street. The rats were anywhere from babies to large mature rodents, all looking for a new home. Next, they broke off into small groups and began infesting nearby houses. Waukegan was afraid the invaders would overrun the whole city.[810]

In 1916, the city of Waukegan ordered all junk dealers to clean up their yards. A pile of junk on Ash Street had not been moved in years and was home to thousands of rats. Predictably, the neighborhood was overrun. Some rats were the size of cats.[811]

Not to pick on Waukegan, just about every town had rat problems. Lake Forest had a bad one in 1905. Some people had to leave their homes. Finally, the town of Lake Forest went out and hired professionals to rid the town of the unwelcome guests.[812]

In 1919, Lake Forest was overrun with rats again. The residents of Lake Forest accused the town of not collecting the garbage. Rats were taking up residence in people's basements. The town square was absolutely teeming with them. One businessman was killing 100 per day but not making a dent. One Lake Forest telephone operator liked the rats and bragged about feeding them.[813]

The rest of the country was in the same shape. Towns in Mercer, Rock Island, and Whiteside Counties, Illinois, were overrun by millions of rats in 1904. One farmer in Mercer County killed 3,435 rats on his farm in two weeks, but there was still plenty left.[814]

In 1908, every man, woman, and child living in Obed, Illinois, went on a giant rat hunt. Rats were practically taking over the town, and its residents would soon have to move out of their houses if something was not done.[815] Obed is located near Mattoon.

> Here's one of my favorite rat stories. In 1909, the New York City Fire Department was attacked by hundreds of rats. The firemen were trying to put out a fire at a junkshop when hundreds of rats ran out and attacked them. Rats ran up their legs and bit their hands, forcing the firemen to turn their hoses on the rats.[816]

## Trapped on an Iceberg

A really big iceberg is known as an ice floe, which is the term I should have used. In 1899, fifteen people were trapped on an ice floe on Lake Michigan. A total of twelve were students from Lake Forest College who had been out on the ice near the college. The other three were ice-skaters who were trapped on the ice while taking pictures near Rogers Park.

It was the middle of February. The temperature was below zero with a strong, biting wind. The fifteen unfortunate victims were out on the ice about four o'clock in the afternoon when the ice floe broke off and began swiftly floating out into Lake Michigan in a southeast direction. The ice floe extended at least from Lake Forest to Rogers Park and Chicago.

People on shore noticed the event and immediately sent a dispatch to the authorities. Word of the incident spread, and soon, most residents of Lake Forest were on the shore, trying to help, but there wasn't much they could do. They did make sure the stranded students knew that their plight was known and help would soon be on the way. Then they braved the cold after it got dark and waited around shore, trying to signal the students by any means possible. Even though it was a long shot, the crowd was optimistic that the ice floe might float near the pier at Fort Sheridan, making it possible to save the students. But the ice floe had other ideas, and it floated farther out into the lake.

Senator Larned of Lake Forest notified the chief of police and the fire department at four thirty. Captain Smith, captain of the tugboat *Alice*, was also called out. Unfortunately, the *Alice* was frozen fast in the ice. Lake Forest's firemen went to work chopping and sawing the ice, but they soon realized it would take hours to free the tug.

It was decided to call Captain Lawson, head of the Evanston lifesaving crew, for help. The crew was dissolved a month earlier, but Lawson hurriedly contacted his old crew and was soon on the scene. His entire crew was made up of college students, probably from Northwestern University. The tugboat was still stuck in the ice when the crew made their appearance. Captain Lawson would need to haul his own boat from Evanston before anyone could be saved. A team of horses would take too long, so he called the Chicago Police Department and asked if they could supply a train to haul the boat to Lake Forest. The Chicago Police declined to help. Next, he called the superintendent of the Chicago and Northwestern Railroad and asked for help. Strangely, the superintendent also had the last name of Lawson. The superintendent acted immediately and supplied an engine, a caboose, and two flat cars. The train made the eighteen-mile trip to Lake Forest in twenty-three minutes.

Meanwhile in Rogers Park, the Chicago Police Department was out in the lake looking for the three skaters but not having much luck. The three missing skaters were Elmer D. Brothers; his seventeen-year-old niece, Ms. Orel Manney; and his twenty-five-year-old-nephew, Chauncey Manney.

By this time, word had spread all along the North Shore, and other brave souls came to the rescue. Three men from Highland Park—L. O. Van Riper, M. T. Baker, and Frank Perryman—sailed out into the lake in a sixteen-foot boat. The lake was almost covered in ice, but they were able to reach the ice floe and portage across it to a channel in the middle of the floe about a mile and a half from shore. Sailing down the channel, they found ten of the freezing students standing on the edge of the floe. After picking the boys up, they headed for shore. The weight of the thirteen people was almost too much for the sixteen-foot boat, but it managed to make it back to shore at 8:30 at night. Somehow the other two students got separated from the rest, and it was feared they might be dead.

Captain Lawson and crew launched their boat soon after dark. They were notified that ten students were already saved so were determined to

The Forgotten History of Lake County, Illinois

find the other two. The ship spent all night looking for the two students but without luck. They found tough sailing on the way back to Lake Forest and had to chop through the ice part of the way.

The tugboat *Alice* was finally freed from ice at 8:45 and put out to sea. The crew included Capt. William Smith; Capt. Richard Smith; Assistant Chief McArthur; Engineer Henry Buckman; Fireman Jacob Ernst; Deckhands Gus Wantke, William Genett, and Scotty Moss; Prof. A. G. Welsh, the principal of Lake Forest College; nine students from Lake Forest College; and six newspaper reporters. Looks like a full ship.

The *Alice* had to crash and ram their way through ice for most of the trip. The thickness of the ice was anywhere from an inch to six inches. They also had to look for the easiest route (the thinnest ice) so rarely went in a straight line. People on shore tried to signal them, but the sound of the ice breaking prevented them from hearing anything else. The spray from ramming the ice got everyone wet, and their clothes were soon frozen to their skin.

By the time they reached Fort Sheridan, the tug was two miles from shore. They kept sailing south and reached the ice floe five miles south of Highland Park but could not go any farther. The *Alice* had to turn around and made it back to Lake Forest at four o'clock in the morning. Assistant Chief McArthur claimed that if they arrived just one hour later, the harbor might have been frozen over, preventing them from landing.

Others along the North Shore tried to save the trapped people. A Ravenswood man named Albert Fetcher went out by himself looking for the three missing skaters. He had rescued other people on Lake Michigan before but not on this night. He was out for five hours but came back with frozen feet. He was in real bad shape, and the Luther Laflin Mill planned to hold a fundraiser for him.

A rescue party from Chicago went out looking for the three skaters at two o'clock in the morning and was able to locate them in just a few hours. There was a surprise waiting for them. The two missing college students were with the three skaters. In fact, the college students saved the life of the seventeen-year-old girl by carrying her for miles on the ice floe. She was so tired and cold that she was unable to go any farther on her own. The other two skaters were almost as bad off. The two college students had frozen hands and feet but were nowhere near death. They were back in

Lake Forest by noon. It's amazing they were all saved, and everyone lived as far as I know.[817, 818]

In 1935, an Irish setter dog was playing on the ice near Johnson Motors when a piece of ice broke off and carried the dog two miles out to sea. An employee of the Johnson Motors company saw what happened and called the police. Two other employees of Johnson Motors were ready to launch a rescue boat when the police showed up. A tugboat owned by the Smith Company named *My Sweetheart* was put out to sea and the dog saved.[819]

## What Scares a Horse? Answer: "Everything"

Lake County had hundreds of accidents with horses over the years. One thing that seems to be a common theme in many accidents is that the most minuscule and ridiculous things would spook the horse or horses. Some things like cars or a train whistle is understandable, and the next five stories are about this type of accident. Then I will write about some of the most ridiculous ones.

In 1906, a farmer from Wauconda named Peter Jacobson was hired to pull out a car stuck in some mud. The farmer was in the process of hooking up his team to the car when one of the horses freaked out at the sight of the car. It reared up on its back legs and fell backward, dead. The sight of the car literally scared the horse to death.[820]

In 1926, a train whistle scared a team belonging to H. E. Flood of Gurnee. The team went crazy and ran right in front of the train engine. Mr. Flood's hired man was driving the team but was so terrified he could not remember what happened. He survived, but one horse was put down and the other injured. The wagon was completely destroyed.[821]

A street sweeper caused a runaway in 1916. A Waukegan man was driving his horse when the horse panicked at the sight of the street sweeper and took off running. The man was thrown out of the wagon when it hit a curb and seriously injured. Next, the horse knocked over a baby carriage. The baby was not injured. Then the horse ran over a boy on his bike and wrecked the bike. The boy was not badly hurt.[822]

In 1934, a brass band playing in a circus parade scared the daylights out of a horse owned by the Kennedy Ice company of Waukegan. (Your author

The Forgotten History of Lake County, Illinois

is related to the Kennedys.) The horse reared up and smashed its front legs right through the window of a car. The woman driver was not hurt.[823]

In 1913, a horse went nuts at the sight of a steam roller and started to run. The driver, Joseph Blanchard, was thrown out and landed on his head. He died on the operating table.[824]

The following stories show just how crazy some of these runaways could get.

In 1873, the sight of an umbrella was too much for a horse owned by Ms. Elizabeth Clark of Ela. She was driving a horse and buggy when the horse took off at full speed. The buggy overturned, and Ms. Clark was caught in the buggy's wheel and dragged a good distance. Her injuries were so bad she soon died.[825]

In 1900, some clothes drying on a work wagon was all it took to scare a team driven by Mrs. Clark Chandler of Gurnee. Mrs. Chandler's three children were passengers in the wagon. One of the horses lost it and bucked so bad it partially broke the harness. Mrs. Chandler jumped out and grabbed the horse's head. The horse reared up and tossed Mrs. Chandler off and then trampled on her. The harness broke the rest of the way, and the horses ran away. Mrs. Chandler was knocked unconscious but survived.[826]

In 1869, Nelson Landon of Benton Township stayed cool during a runaway. He was driving a team when someone's hat blew off and landed by the horse's feet. The terrified animals started to bolt and ran at full speed. Mr. Landon was able to maintain control and guide the animals into a livery stable.[827]

In 1874, Mr. W. Wenban of Diamond Lake was driving a horse and buggy in Waukegan. It was winter when a small boy came sledding down a nearby hill and scared his horse half to death. The horse started to run. Mr. Wenban only had one hand and found it impossible to get control of the terrified animal. The horse ran over a bridge, where the buggy's wheel hit a post and was smashed to pieces. Mr. Wenban was thrown out but only sustained minor injuries.[828]

In 1907, a man from Racine, Wisconsin, was driving his team when the team was spooked by a car and a piece of paper blowing in the wind. The man held on to the reins for dear life and let the horses run until they got tired.[829]

In 1912, a sixty-eight-year-old Lake Zurich man named Spunner got caught in the lines during a runaway and dragged nearly a mile. He lived,

203

but his wounds were covered with dirt, and he got lockjaw.[830] The *Waukegan Gazette* newspaper regularly cautioned its readers about blowing paper and urged farmers to pick up any papers on their land to cut down on runaways. The September 5, 1885, *Waukegan Gazette* claimed that most horses were afraid of blowing pieces of paper. [831]

In 1882, a pig standing next to the road in Antioch was too much for Mr. and Mrs. Huntley's horse. The horse became uncontrollable and knocked over the buggy. The Huntleys were thrown out, and Mr. Huntley hurt his head and shoulder. He had to be helped into a neighboring house, where he spent the next few days recovering.[832]

In 1874, some sheep scared the crap out of a horse on North Avenue in Waukegan. The two men in the wagon were thrown out when the wagon overturned. One of the men was trapped under the overturned wagon and dragged down the street. He managed to escape from the overturned wagon but not before fracturing his leg in two places. The horse was found the next day west of town.[833]

Here's my favorite runaway story. What was the terrifying object that caused a team of horses to spook in 1870? Why, it was a tree stump. The horrified team, owned by Mr. Cyrus Bryant of Avon Township, took off and ran for a half a mile. You would think the horses had seen a tree stump before. Mr. Bryant and his family were thrown out right away and landed on the frozen ground. The horses were later found, but one had a broken leg and was already dead.[834]

There are a lot more of these stories, and I could probably write a book. Thank God for cars.


## Patriotic Lake County Farmers


In 1863, Union soldiers were not getting a very good diet or enough food. Some were getting scurvy. In October, the Union League of Lake County met in Fremont Township. Lake County had a Union League chapter in each township. It was well-known that the troops needed better victuals, and the Union League wanted to come up with a solution. A man named John G. Ragan from Fremont Township came up with the idea to donate some of their recently harvested crops to help the troops. Lake County had a bountiful crop that year. The plan was to haul the harvest to the great Northwestern Sanitary Fair in Chicago. From there, it would

The Forgotten History of Lake County, Illinois

be sent to the troops. It also looks like some other counties also joined in. Mr. Thomas H. Payne thought school districts would make a great place to ask for donations. Three of Mr. Payne's sons had already joined the army. Two had already been killed and the other one wounded.

The response from Lake County's farmers was immense. The sanitary fair was notified of their plans. The fair officials responded with great enthusiasm and asked them to join the fair parade. Traveling through some bad weather, not quite one hundred teams from Lake County made the trip to Chicago. All their wagons were bursting at the seams with vegetables, apples, and barrels of cider. Each wagon flew a flag with "Lake County" printed on it.

Lake County's wagon train arrived at the fair early in the morning and was led to the parade by a marching band. Lake County was the last county to march in the parade. The front wagon at the head of the wagon train carried a sign with the words "The gift of Lake County to our brave boys in the hospitals, through the great Northwestern Fair." The *Chicago Tribune* remarked, "And last but not least-nay, the greatest and mightiest of all-the sublime spectacle of the Lake County delegation."[835] Thousands of people watched the parade, and the loudest cheering came when Lake County passed by.

The parade ended at the courthouse. Thousands of people congregated there to hear the welcoming address and see the 34-gun salute signaling the opening of the fair. Afterward, the Lake County farmers unloaded their produce and were guided to the Lower Bryan Hall by Mrs. Livermore for dinner. Mrs. Livermore asked John G. Ragan to join her at the front of the line. He also escorted her to her table. The *Chicago Tribune* also wrote the words "God bless the Lake County farmers."[836]

Lake County's women also helped the war effort. Years ago, I found a story in the newspaper about Lake County women meeting in Waukegan with their sewing machines. Unfortunately, I gave the story away, so you will have to trust me. During the Civil War, women from all over the county traveled to Waukegan by wagon with their sewing machines. If my memory is correct, about eighty to one hundred wagons made the trip. In Waukegan, our patriotic women sewed a variety of items useful to the troops.

# CHAPTER 12

## Lake County Hermits and Squatters

### Pair Lives with Poultry

A husband and wife team was found living deep in the woods a mile east of Libertyville in 1915. Their camp was located in a dense thicket on the east side of the Des Plaines River near St. Mary's Road. They lived in an eight-foot-by-ten-foot tent and said they had lived there for three years. Only their nearest neighbors knew they were there and were content to leave them be. The couple did not own the land but were squatters.

Their campsite had about a dozen tents, all used for housing three hundred chickens and turkeys. They shared their tent with about a half-dozen chicken brooders and incubators, leaving only a five-foot-by-ten-foot space for themselves. This space served as a bedroom and kitchen. The tent was heated with a kerosene stove.

They kept to themselves, but the neighbors could no longer ignore the behavior of the wife. She was frequently spotted wandering through the woods half naked, mumbling to herself. She always looked disheveled as well, and it was becoming obvious that she was going mad.

The police were finally called and went out into the woods to visit them. They found the wife sitting next to the stove drinking tea. She told the police that the king of Denmark and the Danish consul of Chicago would soon be there. She needed the king's help divorcing her husband, who had shamed her by uttering the word "damn" in front of her.

After speaking to the husband, the police decided to take his wife to a mental institution. The husband agreed with the police, adding that he also thought she was losing it. He said that lately, he had had to stop her from setting the tents on fire. (I have to wonder if the fumes from the kerosene stove got to her.)

At one time, a railroad ran from Palatine to Wauconda but went out of business in 1919. For ten years afterward, the tracks and right-of-way were basically abandoned. The old railroad was due to be sold in 1929. The railroad depot in Wauconda had been stolen and moved years earlier. Squatters had pitched tents along the railroad right-of-way near Wauconda. They estimated sixty-four people were living in the tents, but all of them would soon be evicted.[837] A website called Shadows of Trains claimed the railroad stopped running in 1924. It began operation in 1912 and ran for twelve years.[838]

In 1923, Lake County owned ten thousand acres of swampland. Squatters moved into much of it around the Fox Lake and Grass Lake areas. County supervisors visited the place in 1923 and found it full of shanties. The squatters had also claimed the land around the shanties and put up "no trespassing" signs. One squatter claimed one thousand acres. The squatters also made a nuisance of themselves by driving away hunters and fishermen.[839]

## Lives in a Sewer Pipe

An employee of a Waukegan scrapyard lived in an abandoned sewer pipe in 1911. The five-foot sewer pipe was located on the flats and on railroad property. The man would block an end of the pipe, depending on which direction the wind changed. One day the railroad police kicked him out and told him to stay away.[840]

## Lives in City Dump

During the depression in 1934, a man lived in a dump once used by the Brumund Dairy Company of Waukegan. He lived in an overturned truck body and nailed scrap lumber around it to make a twelve-foot-by-five-foot home. He made a little money selling scrap metal. The man did not want to be a burden on society and insisted on supporting himself. He mentioned that he used to work in factories but was too old to do that type of work anymore. He kept two dogs for company.[841]

## Old King Cole

A Civil War veteran known as Old King Cole lived in a two-room shack on the south side of Waukegan in 1916. He was eighty-four years old and had lived there for years. The neighbors considered his shack a blight on the community. No one had seen him for a while, and the police were sent to check up on him. It was winter, and they thought they would find him dead. They found him in good spirits, but he was almost dead. The January 20, 1916, *Waukegan Daily Sun* wrote that his face had frozen a few days earlier and was "as black as coal."[842] The police evicted him and sent him to the veterans' home in Milwaukee.

## Two Live in Sand Dugout

In 1909, two North Chicago men made themselves a home hidden in the sand. They dug a hole in the sand and inserted a sheet of tin bent in a circle. First, they covered it with scrap lumber and then covered it all with sand. It looked just like a sand dune and fooled people standing just ten feet away. They didn't fool the railroad police who jabbed a cane into the shelter and forced them out. They were arrested and fined $3 and costs.[843]

# EPILOGUE

The author hopes you enjoyed the book and learned something about the county's history. Lake County's history is second to none in the state. Sorry if I failed to write about your ethnic group. I concentrated on early immigrants to the county, and some groups like the Puerto Ricans immigrated to the area at a much later date.

# NOTES

1. *Waukegan Daily Sun*, June 10, 1919.
2. *Waukegan Daily Sun*, June 11, 1919.
3. *Portrait and Biographical Album of Lake County, Illinois* (Chicago: Lake City Publishing Co., 1891), reprinted by Higginson Book Company Salem, Massachusetts, 353–354.
4. *Waukegan Daily Sun*, January 14, 1909.
5. *Waukegan Daily Sun*, December 20, 1905.
6. Immaculate Conception Church, Baptism, Marriage, and Death records 1848 to 1915. At Church of Latter Day Saints Library.
7. *Waukegan Gazette*, June 5, 1869.
8. *Waukegan Gazette*, January 30, 1863.
9. *Waukegan Gazette*, November 29, 1862.
10. *Waukegan Gazette*, November 22, 1862.
11. *Waukegan Daily Sun*, February 20, 1920.
12. *Waukegan Daily Sun*, February 20, 1920.
13. *Waukegan Gazette*, September 28, 1867.
14. *Waukegan Gazette*, October 5, 1867.
15. *Lake County Independent*, February 3, 1921.
16. *Waukegan Daily Sun*, April 7, 1924.
17. Louise and Julia Osling, *Historical Highlights of the Waukegan Area* (Waukegan, Illinois: North Shore Printers, 1976), 172.
18. *Waukegan News Sun*, July 5, 1961.
19. *Waukegan Daily Sun*, January 14, 1906.
20. *Portrait and Biographical Album of Lake County, Illinois* (Chicago: Lake City Publishing Co., 1891), reprinted by Higginson Book Company Salem, Massachusetts, 353.

21. *Waukegan Gazette*, March 14, 1874.
22. *Waukegan Daily Sun*, January 14, 1909.
23. *Lake County Independent*, January 22, 1909.
24. State of Illinois Agriculture Census for Lake County Enumeration District 235.
25. *Waukegan Gazette*, April 15, 1882.
26. *Waukegan Daily Sun*, July 22, 1911.
27. *Waukegan Gazette*, May 17, 1873.
28. *Waukegan Gazette*, February 9, 1878.
29. *Waukegan Daily Gazette*, April 1, 1905.
30. *Waukegan Daily Sun*, July 29, 1910.
31. *Waukegan Daily Sun*, July 9, 1913.
32. *Waukegan Daily Sun*, April 26, 1915.
33. *Waukegan Gazette*, February 10, 1877.
34. *Waukegan Gazette*, October 23, 1880.
35. *Waukegan Gazette*, March 4, 1882.
36. *Waukegan Gazette*, April 1, 1882.
37. *Waukegan Gazette*, November 4, 1882.
38. *Waukegan Gazette*, April 15, 1882.
39. *Waukegan Gazette*, November 25, 1882.
40. *Waukegan Daily Sun*, November 29, 1902.
41. *Lake County Independent*, December 4, 1896.
42. *Waukegan Daily Sun*, December 14, 1897.
43. *Waukegan Daily Sun*, June 10, 1919.
44. *Waukegan Daily Sun*, December 27, 1897.
45. *Waukegan Daily Sun*, December 27, 1897.
46. *Waukegan Daily Sun*, November 28, 1905.
47. *Waukegan Daily Sun*, December 4, 1903.
48. *Waukegan Daily Sun*, October 15, 1910.
49. *Waukegan Daily Sun*, July 22, 1911.
50. Lands purchased by Frank and Nell, at the Waukegan Historical Society, Nellie Conrad papers.
51. Louise and Julia Osling, *Historical Highlights of the Waukegan Area* (Waukegan, Illinois: North Shore Printers, 1976), 80.
52. *Waukegan Daily Sun*, February 11, 1901.
53. *Waukegan Daily Sun*, March 23, 1901.
54. *Waukegan Daily Sun*, December 3, 1900.
55. *Waukegan Daily Sun*, April 15, 1901.

56. *Waukegan Daily Sun*, January 11, 1901.
57. *Waukegan Daily Sun*, January 5, 1901.
58. *Waukegan Daily Sun*, January 16, 1901.
59. *Waukegan Daily Sun*, December 13, 1901.
60. *Waukegan Daily Sun*, July 9, 1904.
61. *Waukegan Daily Sun*, February 23, 1905.
62. *Waukegan Daily Sun*, May 2, 1907.
63. *Waukegan Daily Sun*, December 23, 1903.
64. *Waukegan Daily Sun*, December 24, 1903.
65. *Waukegan Daily Sun*, January 7, 1904.
66. *Waukegan Daily Sun*, January 22, 1904.
67. *Waukegan Daily Sun*, January 23, 1904.
68. *Waukegan Gazette*, June 19, 1870.
69. *Waukegan Gazette*, February 25, 1877.
70. *Waukegan Gazette*, December 1, 1877.
71. *Waukegan Gazette*, March 25, 1882.
72. *Waukegan Gazette*, March 7, 1885.
73. *Waukegan Daily Sun*, March 15, 1898.
74. *Waukegan Daily Sun*, May 11, 1898.
75. *Waukegan Daily Sun*, April 5, 1899.
76. *Waukegan Daily Sun*, April 7, 1899.
77. *Waukegan Daily Sun*, September 18, 1914.
78. Louise and Julia Osling, *Historical Highlights of the Waukegan Area* (Waukegan, Illinois: North Shore Printers, 1976), 185.
79. Immaculate Conception Church records.
80. Grantee land records at the Waukegan Recorder of Deeds.
81. *Waukegan Daily Sun*, April 4, 1901.
82. *Waukegan Daily Sun*, April 4, 1901.
83. *Waukegan Daily Sun*, February 12, 1910.
84. *Waukegan Daily Sun*, September 17, 1904.
85. *Waukegan Gazette*, January 3, 1880.
86. *Waukegan Gazette*, January 10, 1880.
87. *Waukegan Daily Sun*, October 20, 1911.
88. *Waukegan Daily Sun*, April 29, 1908.
89. *Waukegan Daily Sun*, April 7, 1902.
90. *Waukegan News Sun*, August 10, 1932.
91. *Waukegan Daily Sun*, December 7, 1898.
92. *Waukegan Daily Sun*, December 6, 1898.

93. *Waukegan Daily Sun*, December 22, 1898.

94. *Waukegan Daily Sun*, December 9, 1898.

95. *Waukegan Daily Sun*, December 10, 1898.

96. *Waukegan Daily Sun*, December 20, 1898.

97. *Waukegan Daily Sun*, March 6, 1899.

98. *Waukegan Daily Sun*, March 7, 1899.

99. *Waukegan Daily Sun*, March 13, 1899.

100. *Waukegan Daily Sun*, March 13, 1899.

101. *Waukegan Daily Sun*, December 9, 1901.

102. *Waukegan Daily Sun*, November 11, 1901.

103. *Waukegan Daily Sun*, December 21, 1901.

104. *Waukegan Daily Sun*, December 13, 1901.

105. *Waukegan Daily Sun*, January 4, 1902.

106. *Waukegan Daily Sun*, January 7, 1902.

107. *Waukegan Daily Sun*, June 3, 1903.

108. *Waukegan Daily Sun*, July 2, 1904.

109. *Waukegan Daily Sun*, July 6, 1904.

110. *Waukegan Daily Sun*, July 2, 1904.

111. *Lake County Independent*, November 10, 1899.

112. Louise and Julia Osling, *Historical Highlights of the Waukegan Area* (Waukegan, Illinois: North Shore Printers, 1976), 84.

113. Louise and Julia Osling, *Historical Highlights of the Waukegan Area* (Waukegan, Illinois: North Shore Printers, 1976), 84–85.

114. *Waukegan Daily Sun*, April 10, 1915.

115. *Waukegan Daily Sun*, April 13, 1915.

116. Immaculate Conception Church records.

117. *Waukegan Daily Sun*, May 29, 1914.

118. *Waukegan Daily Sun*, December 14, 1914.

119. *Waukegan Daily Sun*, June 1, 1915.

120. *Waukegan Daily Sun*, May 19, 1914.

121. *Waukegan Daily Sun*, June 1, 1915.

122. *Waukegan Daily Sun*, April 6, 1916.

123. *Waukegan Daily Sun*, April 7, 1916.

124. *Waukegan Daily Sun*, April 8, 1916.

125. *Waukegan Daily Sun*, April 10, 1916.

126. *Waukegan Daily Sun*, May 29, 1917.

127. *Waukegan Daily Sun*, May 29, 1917.

128. *Waukegan Daily Sun*, May 29, 1917.

129. *Waukegan Daily Sun*, April 7, 1916.

130. *Waukegan Gazette*, April 18, 1885.

131. *Waukegan Daily Sun*, October 29, 1918.

132. *Waukegan Daily Sun*, June 10, 1919.

133. *Waukegan Daily Sun*, March 29, 1919.

134. *Waukegan Daily Sun*, September 30, 1913.

135. *Waukegan Daily Sun*, May 4, 1919.

136. *Waukegan Daily Sun*, June 17, 1919.

137. *Waukegan Daily Sun*, March 29, 1919.

138. *Waukegan Daily Sun*, June 17, 1919.

139. *Waukegan Daily Sun*, June 28, 1919.

140. *Waukegan Daily Sun*, June 17, 1919.

141. *Waukegan Daily Sun*, May 23, 1929.

142. *Waukegan Daily Sun*, June 17, 1919.

143. *Waukegan Daily Sun*, June 28, 1919.

144. *Waukegan Daily Sun*, May 23, 1929.

145. *Waukegan News Sun*, July 29, 1949.

146. *Waukegan Daily Sun*, September 13, 1923.

147. Lake County, Illinois, Marriages, Vol. 3, 1881–1901, 83.

148. *Waukegan Daily Sun*, December 2, 1918.

149. *Waukegan Daily Sun*, November 21, 1916.

150. *Waukegan Daily Sun*, March 16, 1916.

151. *Waukegan Daily Sun*, August 22, 1917.

152. *Waukegan Daily Sun*, January 11, 1917.

153. Waukegan Historical Society, Dady papers, March 10, 1905.

154. Waukegan Historical Society, Nellie Conrad papers, May 15, 1909.

155. Waukegan Historical Society, Nellie Conrad papers, August 24, 1917.

156. *Waukegan Daily Sun*, August 22, 1917.

157. *Waukegan Daily Sun*, December 2, 1918.

158. *Waukegan Daily Sun*, February 11, 1911.

159. *Waukegan Daily Sun*, February 11, 1911.

160. *Waukegan Daily Sun*, May 7, 1919.

161. *Waukegan Daily Sun*, April 30, 1919.

162. *Waukegan Daily Sun*, May 7, 1919.

163. *Waukegan Daily Sun*, December 9, 1919.

164. *Waukegan Daily Sun*, November 15, 1921.

165. Robert Dady Will, Number 8458, filed on January 24, 1919.

166. *Waukegan News Sun*, August 10, 1932.

167. *Waukegan Daily Sun*, February 8, 1921.

168. George Rogers Clark, *George Rogers Clark's Memoir: the Conquest of the Illinois* (CreateSpace Independent Publishing Platform, 2015), 1.

169. *Waukegan Daily Sun*, October 5, 1920.

170. *Waukegan Daily Sun*, February 9, 1921.

171. *Waukegan Daily Sun*, December 9, 1922.

172. *Waukegan Daily Sun*, February 16, 1925.

173. *Waukegan Daily Sun*, September 22, 1923.

174. *Waukegan Daily Sun*, November 24, 1924.

175. *Waukegan Daily Sun*, May 22, 1923.

176. *Waukegan Daily Sun*, June 2, 1923.

177. *Waukegan Daily Sun*, December 4, 1920.

178. *Waukegan Daily Sun*, January 26, 1924.

179. *Waukegan Daily Sun*, March 25, 1924.

180. *Waukegan Daily Sun*, May 26, 1924.

181. *Waukegan Daily Sun*, May 10, 1924.

182. *Waukegan Daily Sun*, September 3, 1925.

183. *Waukegan Daily Sun*, February 27, 1926.

184. *Libertyville Independent*, October 7, 1926.

185. *Waukegan News Sun*, January 14, 1935.

186. *Waukegan Daily Sun*, January 10, 1927.

187. *Waukegan Daily Sun*, September 17, 1929.

188. *Waukegan News Sun*, May 5, 1933.

189. *Waukegan News Sun*, May 20, 1933.

190. *Waukegan News Sun*, January 25, 1935.

191. *Milwaukee Sentinel News*, September 10, 1938.

192. *Waukegan News Sun*, January 14, 1935.

193. *Waukegan News Sun*, April 30, 1937.

194. *Waukegan Daily Sun*, February 7, 1929.

195. *Waukegan Daily Sun*, January 11, 1930.

196. *Waukegan News Sun*, November 14, 1930.

197. *Waukegan News Sun*, March 30, 1932.

198. *Waukegan News Sun*, May 26, 1930.

199. *Waukegan News Sun*, July 29, 1949.

200. Al Westerman document.

201. *Waukegan News Sun*, February 9, 1981.

202. *Waukegan News Sun*, February 9, 1981.

203. Al Westerman document.

204. *Waukegan Daily Sun*, February 28, 1905.

205. *Waukegan Daily Gazette*, October 25, 1897.

206. *Waukegan Daily Sun*, January 3, 1906.

207. *Waukegan Daily Sun*, January 3, 1906.

208. *Waukegan Daily Sun*, January 17, 1899.

209. *Waukegan Daily Sun*, July 30, 1901.

210. *Waukegan Gazette*, September 15, 1877.

211. *Waukegan Daily Sun*, April 10. 1917.

212. *Waukegan Daily Sun*, August 3, 1911.

213. *Waukegan Daily Sun*, December 20, 1908.

214. *Waukegan Daily Sun*, June 12, 1905.

215. *Waukegan Daily Sun*, May 9, 1910.

216. *Waukegan Daily Sun*, May 20, 1908.

217. *Lake County Independent*, July 13, 1906.

218. *Lake County Independent*, June 17, 1914.

219. *Waukegan Daily Sun*, July 9, 1925.

220. *Libertyville Independent*, December 10, 1915.

221. *Waukegan Daily Sun*, July 5, 1906.

222. *Waukegan Daily Sun*, July 5, 1906.

223. *Libertyville Independent*, September 6, 1912.

224. *Waukegan Daily Sun*, May 17, 1909.

225. *Waukegan Daily Sun*, May 29, 1909.

226. *Waukegan Daily Sun*, May 19, 1909.

227. *Waukegan Daily Sun*, May 26, 1909.

228. *Waukegan Daily Sun*, May 17, 1909.

229. *Waukegan Daily Sun*, May 20, 1909.

230. *Waukegan Daily Sun*, May 20, 1909.

231. *Waukegan Daily Sun*, May 20, 1909.

232. *Waukegan Daily Sun*, May 18, 1909.

233. *Waukegan Daily Sun*, May 20, 1909.

234. *Waukegan Daily Sun*, January 5, 1910.

235. *Waukegan Daily Sun*, December 10, 1923.

236. *Waukegan Daily Sun*, September 9, 1907.

237. Chicago Commission on Race Relations, *The Negro in Chicago* (Chicago: University of Chicago, 1921), 57.

238. *Waukegan Daily Sun*, June 2, 1920.

239. *Waukegan Daily Sun*, June 2, 1920.

240. *Waukegan Daily Sun*, June 2, 1920.

241. *Waukegan Daily Sun*, June 3, 1920.

242. *Waukegan Daily Sun*, June 4, 1920.

243. *Waukegan Daily Sun*, June 3, 1920.

244. *Waukegan Daily Sun*, June 4, 1920.

245. *Waukegan Daily Sun*, May 29, 1917.

246. *Waukegan Daily Sun*, July 9, 1917.

247. *Waukegan Daily Sun*, August 29, 1917.

248. *Waukegan Daily Sun*, August 29, 1917.

249. Taped interview with Mr. G. Taylor, Waukegan, Illinois, summer of 1974, side A.

250. Chicago Commission on Race Relations, *The Negro in Chicago* (Chicago: University of Chicago, 1921), p. 57.

251. *Waukegan Daily Sun*, June 4, 1920.

252. *Waukegan Daily Sun*, November 28, 1913.

253. *Waukegan Daily Sun*, February 13, 1926.

254. *Waukegan News Sun*, March 14, 1936.

255. *Waukegan Daily Sun*, July 18, 1903.

256. *Waukegan Daily Sun*, July 31, 1905.

257. *Waukegan Daily Sun*, February 24, 1903.

258. *Chicago Tribune*, October 10, 2015.

259. *Waukegan News Sun*, October 7, 1935.

260. *Waukegan Daily Sun*, June 29, 1914.

261. *Lake County Independent*, July 13, 1900.

262. *Lake County Independent*, July 13, 1900.

263. *Waukegan Daily Sun*, May 7, 1906.

264. *Waukegan Daily Sun*, June 29, 1914.

265. *Waukegan Daily Sun*, May 11, 1908.

266. *Waukegan Daily Sun*, June 29, 1914.

267. *Waukegan Daily Sun*, December 3, 1907.

268. *Lake County Independent*, January 8, 1909.

269. *Waukegan Daily Sun*, January 9, 1908.

270. *Waukegan Daily Sun*, January 8, 1908.

271. *Lake County Independent*, August 4, 1913.

272. *Lake County Independent*, November 15, 1907.

273. *Waukegan Daily Sun*, August 31, 1912.

274. *Waukegan Daily Sun*, August 31, 1912.

275. *Waukegan Daily Sun*, November 13, 1916.

276. *Waukegan Daily Sun*, November 13, 1916.

277. *Waukegan Daily Sun*, November 20, 1916.

278. *Waukegan Daily Sun*, November 13, 1916.

279. *Waukegan Daily Sun*, November 16, 1916.

280. *Waukegan Daily Sun*, November 20, 1916.

281. *Waukegan Daily Sun*, November 20, 1916.

282. *Waukegan Daily Sun*, August 27, 1910.

283. *Waukegan Gazette*, October 31, 1885.

284. *Waukegan Gazette*, October 31, 1885.

285. *Waukegan Daily Sun*, October 12, 1914.

286. *Lake County Independent*, June 17, 1904.

287. *Waukegan Daily Sun*, September 30, 1900.

288. *Waukegan Daily Sun*, February 6, 1922.

289. *Waukegan Daily Sun*, February 6, 1922.

290. *Waukegan Daily Sun*, May 12, 1920.

291. *Waukegan Daily Sun*, June 3, 1899.

292. *Waukegan Daily Sun*, June 18, 1910.

293. *Waukegan News Sun*, July 22, 1959.

294. *Waukegan Daily Sun*, August 3, 1911.

295. *Waukegan Daily Sun*, August 3, 1911.

296. *Waukegan Daily Sun*, March 20, 1909.

297. *Waukegan Daily Sun*, August 23, 1910.

298. *Waukegan Daily Sun*, October 8, 1903.

299. Ed Link, *Waukegan, A History* (Waukegan Historical Society, 2009), 154.

300. *Waukegan Daily Sun*, November 22, 1910.

301. *Waukegan Daily Sun*, February 20, 1905.

302. *Waukegan Daily Sun*, November 10, 1909.

303. *Waukegan News Sun*, June 20, 1930.

304. *Waukegan Daily Sun*, July 27, 1906.

305. *Waukegan Daily Sun*, February 20, 1905.

306. *Waukegan Daily Sun*, May 20, 1909.

307. *Waukegan Daily Sun*, August 23, 1910.

308. *Waukegan Daily Sun*, August 23, 1910.

309. *Chicago Daily Tribune*, November 27, 1894.

310. *Waukegan Daily Sun*, February 9, 1918.

311. *Waukegan Daily Sun*, January 24, 1921.

312. *Waukegan Daily Sun*, April 10, 1923.

313. *Waukegan Daily Sun*, September 16, 1927.

314. *Waukegan Daily Sun*, October 28, 1916.

315. *Waukegan News Sun*, July 8, 1971.

316. *Waukegan Daily Sun*, May 5, 1909.

317. *Waukegan Daily Sun*, October 28, 1916.

318. *Waukegan Daily Sun*, March 8, 1919.

319. *Lake County Independent*, May 6, 1920.

320. *Waukegan Daily Sun*, May 25, 1904.

321. *Waukegan News Sun*, September 13, 1930.

322. History of the Slovenian Community in Waukegan-North Chicago, 1893–1952 (Slovenian National Home Society, 1953), 87.

323. Joze Zavertnik, American Slovenian manuscript at the Waukegan Historical Society, 1–2.

324. History of the Slovenian Community in Waukegan-North Chicago, 1893–1952 (Slovenian National Home Society, 1953), 87, 89–90.

325. *Lake County Independent*, March 16, 1906.

326. *Waukegan Daily Sun*, September 20, 1906.

327. *Waukegan Daily Sun*, July 16, 1906.

328. History of the Slovenian Community in Waukegan-North Chicago, 1893–1952 (Slovenian National Home Society, 1953), 89.

329. *Waukegan Daily Sun*, May 14, 1909.

330. *Waukegan Daily Sun*, June 7, 1913.

331. *Waukegan Daily Sun*, January 26, 1914.

332. History of the Slovenian Community in Waukegan-North Chicago, 1893–1952 (Slovenian National Home Society, 1953), 91.

333. *Waukegan Daily Sun*, June 10, 1912.

334. History of the Slovenian Community in Waukegan-North Chicago, 1893–1952 (Slovenian National Home Society, 1953), 92.

335. *Waukegan News Sun*, October 3, 1988.

336. *Waukegan Daily Sun*, May 14, 1917.

337. Louise and Julia Osling, "Frances Burkich Vetrone and Frances Matijevich Van Dyke," in *Historical Highlights of the Waukegan Area* (Waukegan, Illinois: North Shore Printers, 1976), 113, 115.

338. *Waukegan News Sun*, September 17, 1936.

339. *Waukegan Daily Sun*, March 19, 1919.

340. *Waukegan News Sun*, April 6, 1931.

341. Lake County, Illinois History Blog, Amos Bennett, First African-American Settler.

342. *Waukegan News Sun*, June 26, 1935.

343. *Waukegan News Sun*, June 26, 1935.

344. *Waukegan Daily Sun*, July 6, 1928.

345. *Waukegan Gazette*, February 23, 1867.

346. Lake County, Illinois History Blog, Amos Bennett, First African-American Settler.

347. James Dorsey, *The Underground Railroad: Northeastern Illinois and Southeastern Wisconsin* (Sons of Thunder Ministry, 2000), 48.

348. James Dorsey, *The Underground railroad: Northeastern Illinois and Southeastern Wisconsin* (Sons of Thunder Ministry, 2000), 47.

349. *Waukegan Daily Sun*, June 21, 1917.

350. *Waukegan Gazette*, February 13, 1886.

351. *Waukegan Gazette*, March 8, 1879.

352. *Waukegan Daily Sun*, December 10, 1910.

353. *Waukegan Daily Sun*, September 5, 1903.

354. *Waukegan Daily Sun*, April 9, 1918.

355. *Waukegan Daily Sun*, May 10, 1915.

356. James Dorsey, master's thesis.

357. *Waukegan Daily Sun*, May 10, 1920.

358. *Lake County Independent*, April 26, 1907.

359. Louise and Julia Osling, *Historical Highlights of the Waukegan Area* (Waukegan, Illinois: North Shore Printers, 1976), 95.

360. *Waukegan Daily Sun*, March 10, 1915.

361. *Waukegan Daily Sun*, March 10, 1915.

362. *Waukegan Daily Sun*, July 7, 1926.

363. *Waukegan Daily Sun*, December 16, 1925.

364. Louise and Julia Osling, "Curtis L. Dorsey," in *Historical Highlights of the Waukegan Area* (Waukegan, Illinois: North Shore Printers, 1976), 106.

365. *Waukegan Daily Sun*, July 28, 1922.

366. *Waukegan Daily Sun*, July 28, 1922.

367. *Waukegan Daily Sun*, October 5, 1927.

368. *Waukegan Daily Sun*, July 9, 1928.

369. *Waukegan News Sun*, June 11, 1932.

370. *Waukegan Daily Sun*, October 26, 1926.

371. Abraham Davis, *History of the Negro in Lake County*, 2.

372. Ed Link, *Waukegan, A History* (Waukegan Historical Society, 2009), 66.

373. Abraham Davis, *History of the Negro in Lake County*, 2.
374. Louise and Julia Osling, "Curtis L. Dorsey," in *Historical Highlights of the Waukegan Area* (Waukegan, Illinois: North Shore Printers, 1976), 105.
375. *Waukegan Daily Sun*, April 17, 1917.
376. *Waukegan Daily Sun*, March 1, 1916.
377. *Waukegan Daily Sun*, May 10, 1920.
378. Ellen Williams Staben, As I Remember the Southeast Side of Waukegan in the Early 1900s, 3.
379. *Waukegan Daily Sun*, September 19, 1900.
380. *Waukegan Daily Sun*, September 21, 1900.
381. *Waukegan Daily Sun*, September 20, 1900.
382. *Waukegan Daily Sun*, September 22, 1900.
383. *Waukegan Daily Sun*, September 22, 1900.
384. *Waukegan Daily Sun*, October 19, 1902.
385. *Waukegan Daily Sun*, January 3, 1906.
386. *Lake County Independent*, January 1, 1907.
387. *Waukegan Daily Sun*, September 21, 1923.
388. *Waukegan Daily Sun*, October 4, 1907.
389. *Waukegan Daily Sun*, July 2, 1909.
390. *Waukegan Daily Sun*, August 18, 1910.
391. *Waukegan Daily Sun*, June 4, 1921.
392. *Waukegan Daily Sun*, November 7, 1922.
393. *Waukegan Daily Sun*, September 29, 1924.
394. *Waukegan Daily Sun*, September 19, 1924.
395. *Waukegan Daily Sun*, November 7, 1922.
396. *Waukegan Daily Sun*, March 13, 1925.
397. *Waukegan Daily Sun*, November 13, 1922.
398. *Lake County Independent*, December 14, 1922.
399. *Lake County Independent*, April 5, 1923.
400. *Waukegan Daily Sun*, December 4, 1924.
401. *Waukegan Daily Sun*, June 30, 1924.
402. *Waukegan Daily Sun*, September 2, 1924.
403. Lake County Register, September 5, 1925.
404. Lake County, Illinois, Blog, Joice Family of Ivanhoe-African-American Settlers.
405. *Waukegan Daily Sun*, August 1, 1924.
406. *Waukegan Daily Sun*, December 23, 1924.

407. Louise and Julia Osling, "Curtis L. Dorsey," in *Historical Highlights of the Waukegan Area* (Waukegan, Illinois: North Shore Printers, 1976), 105.

408. *Waukegan Daily Sun*, November 8, 1910.

409. *Waukegan Daily Sun*, December 7, 1910.

410. *Waukegan News Sun*, May 5, 1934.

411. Louise and Julia Osling, "Curtis L. Dorsey," in *Historical Highlights of the Waukegan Area* (Waukegan, Illinois: North Shore Printers, 1976), 104.

412. *Waukegan Daily Sun*, February 9, 1912.

413. *Waukegan Daily Sun*, May 8, 1917.

414. *Waukegan Daily Sun*, July 12, 1915.

415. *Waukegan Daily Sun*, July 3, 1919.

416. *Lake County Independent*, October 5, 1922.

417. *Waukegan Daily Sun*, May 20, 1907.

418. *Waukegan Daily Sun*, April 18, 1918.

419. *Waukegan News Sun*, October 17, 1935.

420. *Waukegan Daily Sun*, November 18, 1910.

421. *Waukegan Daily Sun*, October 6, 1908.

422. *Waukegan Daily Sun*, May 9, 1908.

423. *Waukegan Daily Sun*, April 10, 1908.

424. *Waukegan Daily Sun*, May 9, 1908.

425. *Waukegan Daily Sun*, October 6, 1908.

426. *Waukegan Daily Sun*, March 17, 1909.

427. *Waukegan Daily Sun*, March 24, 1909.

428. *Waukegan Daily Sun*, March 25, 1909.

429. *Waukegan Daily Sun*, March 17, 1909.

430. *Waukegan Daily Sun*, April 19, 1909.

431. *Waukegan Daily Sun*, February 8, 1909.

432. *Waukegan Daily Sun*, April 1, 1910.

433. *Waukegan Daily Sun*, May 4, 1911.

434. *Waukegan Daily Sun*, October 3, 1912.

435. *Waukegan Daily Sun*, February 4, 1914.

436. *Lake County Independent*, June 14, 1910.

437. *Lake County Independent*, September 19, 1918.

438. *Waukegan Daily Sun*, June 14, 1910.

439. *Waukegan Daily Sun*, December 18, 1909.

440. *Waukegan Daily Sun*, December 18, 1909.

441. *Waukegan Daily Sun*, May 17, 1910.

442. *Waukegan Daily Sun*, June 14, 1910.

443. *Lake County Independent*, September 19, 1918.

444. *Waukegan Daily Sun*, May 17, 1910.

445. *Lake County Independent*, August 9, 1917.

446. *Lake County Independent*, October 25, 1917.

447. *Lake County Independent*, November 8, 1917.

448. *Lake County Independent*, November 15, 1917.

449. *Lake County Independent*, November 22, 1917.

450. *Lake County Independent*, December 27, 1917.

451. *Lake County Independent*, September 19, 1918.

452. *Lake County Independent*, March 4, 1907.

453. *Lake County Independent*, June 7, 1913.

454. *Lake County Independent*, June 28, 1909.

455. *Waukegan News Sun*, February 7, 1931.

456. Louise and Julia Osling, "Mrs. Irene Haapane," in *Historical Highlights of the Waukegan Area* (Waukegan, Illinois: North Shore Printers, 1976), p 117.

457. Esa Arra, *The Finns in Illinois*, trans. Andrew I. Brask (The Finnish-American Historical Society of Illinois, 1971), 8–10.

458. Esa Arra, *The Finns in Illinois*, trans. Andrew I. Brask (The Finnish-American Historical Society of Illinois, 1971), 10.

459. *Waukegan Daily Sun*, June 25, 1908.

460. *Waukegan Daily Sun*, July 7, 1911.

461. *Waukegan Daily Sun*, July 17, 1905.

462. Louise and Julia Osling, "Mrs. Irene Haapane," in *Historical Highlights of the Waukegan Area* (Waukegan, Illinois: North Shore Printers, 1976), 117.

463. Esa Arra, *The Finns in Illinois*, trans. Andrew I. Brask (The Finnish-American Historical Society of Illinois, 1971), 10.

464. *Waukegan News Sun*, December 16, 1969.

465. *Waukegan Daily Sun*, November 7, 1912.

466. *Waukegan Daily Sun*, April 25, 1927.

467. *Waukegan Daily Sun*, August 29, 1910.

468. Thomas Buck, *Waukegan, A Mini-History*, 1.

469. Louise and Julia Osling, "Herbert Ehnert," in *Historical Highlights of the Waukegan Area* (Waukegan, Illinois: North Shore Printers, 1976), 123.

470. *Waukegan Daily Sun*, June 7, 1913.

471. *Waukegan Daily Sun*, December 27, 1919.

472. Louise and Julia Osling, "Herbert Ehnert," in *Historical Highlights of the Waukegan Area* (Waukegan, Illinois: North Shore Printers, 1976), 122.

473. *Waukegan News Sun*, December 16, 1969.

474. *Waukegan Daily Sun*, February 9, 1917.

475. *Waukegan Daily Sun*, December 13, 1926.

476. Louise and Julia Osling, "Peggy Moraitis," in *Historical Highlights of the Waukegan Area* (Waukegan, Illinois: North Shore Printers, 1976), 126.

477. *Waukegan Daily Sun*, August 27, 1910.

478. *Waukegan Daily Sun*, June 7, 1913.

479. *Waukegan Daily Sun*, February 19, 1926.

480. *Waukegan Daily Sun*, October 7, 1912.

481. *Waukegan Daily Sun*, October 26, 1912.

482. *Waukegan Daily Sun*, January 20, 1917.

483. *Waukegan Daily Sun*, January 22, 1917.

484. *Waukegan Daily Sun*, January 24, 1917.

485. *Waukegan Daily Sun*, February 19, 1926.

486. *Waukegan Daily Sun*, June 7, 1913.

487. *Waukegan Daily Sun*, December 27, 1919.

488. *Waukegan News Sun*, March 15, 1980.

489. Louise and Julia Osling, "Irene E. McCann Murphy," in *Historical Highlights of the Waukegan Area* (Waukegan, Illinois: North Shore Printers, 1976), 135.

490. *Waukegan News Sun*, December 16, 1969.

491. Barbara Apple, *Waukegan News Sun*, March 15, 1980.

492. Barbara Apple, *Waukegan News Sun*, March 15, 1980.

493. Louise and Julia Osling, "Irene E. McCann Murphy," in *Historical Highlights of the Waukegan Area* (Waukegan, Illinois: North Shore Printers, 1976), 135–136.

494. *Waukegan Gazette*, July 25, 1857.

495. *Waukegan Gazette*, July 25, 1857.

496. *Waukegan Gazette*, July 12, 1873.

497. *Waukegan Gazette*, July 12, 1873.

498. *Chicago Daily Tribune*, March 5, 1857.

499. *Chicago Daily Tribune*, November 4, 1857.

500. *Chicago Daily Tribune*, September 12, 1854.

501. *Chicago Press and Tribune*, March 1, 1860.

502. *Chicago Tribune*, September 13, 1868.

503. Louise and Julia Osling, "Rose J. Lidschin," in *Historical Highlights of the Waukegan Area* (Waukegan, Illinois: North Shore Printers, 1976), 142.

504. *Waukegan Gazette*, November 25, 1882.

505. *Waukegan Gazette*, November 25, 1882.

506. *Waukegan Gazette*, September 9, 1882.

507. *Waukegan Gazette*, November 25, 1882.

508. *Waukegan Gazette*, September 9, 1882.

509. Louise and Julia Osling, "Rose J. Lidschin," in *Historical Highlights of the Waukegan Area* (Waukegan, Illinois: North Shore Printers, 1976), 142.

510. *Waukegan Daily Sun*, December 18, 1913.

511. Louise and Julia Osling, "Rose J. Lidschin," in *Historical Highlights of the Waukegan Area* (Waukegan, Illinois: North Shore Printers, 1976), 143–145.

512. *Waukegan Daily Sun*, November 12, 1908.

513. *Waukegan Daily Sun*, September 20, 1913.

514. *Waukegan Daily Sun*, February 14, 1918.

515. *Waukegan Daily Sun*, February 10, 1914.

516. *Waukegan Daily Sun*, October 5, 1914.

517. *Waukegan Daily Sun*, February 14, 1918.

518. *Waukegan Daily Sun*, January 19, 1899.

519. *Waukegan Daily Sun*, February 5, 1907.

520. Waukegan City Directories at the Waukegan Historical Society.

521. *Waukegan Daily Sun*, January 19, 1899.

522. *Waukegan Daily Sun*, January 24, 1899.

523. *Waukegan Daily Sun*, January 19, 1899.

524. *Waukegan Daily Gazette*, June 22, 1898.

525. *Waukegan Daily Sun*, January 16, 1899.

526. *Waukegan Daily Sun*, January 28, 1899.

527. *Waukegan Daily Sun*, June 18, 1901.

528. *Waukegan Daily Sun*, July 19, 1905.

529. *Waukegan Daily Sun*, July 18, 1905.

530. *Waukegan Daily Sun*, July 14, 1905.

531. *Waukegan Daily Sun*, July 19, 1905.

532. *Waukegan Daily Sun*, July 18, 1905.

533. *Waukegan Daily Sun*, May 28, 1907.

534. *Chicago American*, June 23, 1963.

535. *Waukegan Daily Sun*, March 12, 1907.

536. *Waukegan Daily Sun*, February 1, 1910.

537. *Waukegan Daily Sun*, September 3, 1913.

538. *Waukegan Daily Sun*, September 23, 1913.

539. *Waukegan Daily Sun*, September 20, 1913.

540. *Waukegan Daily Sun*, October 24, 1913.

541. *Waukegan Daily Sun*, November 20, 1917.

542. Louise and Julia Osling, "Dr. R. Giniotis," in *Historical Highlights of the Waukegan Area* (Waukegan, Illinois: North Shore Printers, 1976), 149.

543. *Waukegan Daily Sun*, December 16, 1904.

544. *Waukegan Daily Sun*, October 5, 1906.

545. *Waukegan Daily Sun*, July 15, 1907.

546. Louise and Julia Osling, "Dr. R. Giniotis," in *Historical Highlights of the Waukegan Area* (Waukegan, Illinois: North Shore Printers, 1976), 147–148.

547. *Waukegan News Sun*, April 23, 1934.

548. *Waukegan Daily Sun*, March 22, 1929.

549. *Lake County Independent*, April 30, 1909.

550. *Waukegan Daily Sun*, February 4, 1905.

551. *Waukegan News Sun*, August 19, 1930.

552. *Waukegan Daily Sun*, December 16, 1904.

553. *Waukegan Daily Sun*, November 7, 1904.

554. *Waukegan Daily Sun*, December 16, 1904.

555. *Waukegan Daily Sun*, July 17, 1909.

556. *Waukegan Daily Sun*, July 13, 1909.

557. *Waukegan Daily Sun*, July 22, 1909.

558. *Waukegan Daily Sun*, July 26, 1909.

559. *Waukegan Daily Sun*, September 11, 1909.

560. *Waukegan Daily Sun*, April 10, 1916.

561. *Waukegan Daily Sun*, April 13, 1916.

562. *Waukegan Daily Sun*, July 6, 1918.

563. Al Westerman, A History of Waukegan Township Lake County Illinois (1835–1835), 137.

564. Al Westerman, A History of Waukegan Township Lake County Illinois (1835–1835), 68–69.

565. James D. Lodesky, *Polish Pioneers in Illinois 1818–1850* (Xlibris, 2010).

566. *Waukegan Daily Sun*, February 25, 1922.

567. *Waukegan Gazette*, April 4, 1885.

568. *Waukegan Daily Gazette*, November 9, 1897.

569. *Waukegan Daily Gazette*, August 18, 1897.

570. *Waukegan Daily Sun*, April 16, 1898.

571. *Waukegan Daily Sun*, January 27, 1919.

572. *Waukegan Daily Sun*, May 15, 1906.

573. *Waukegan Daily Sun*, November 6, 1903.

574. Waukegan Historical Society church records.

575. *Waukegan Daily Sun*, February 4, 1905.

576. *Waukegan Daily Sun*, April 30, 1907.

577. *Waukegan Daily Sun*, April 30, 1907.

578. *Waukegan Daily Sun*, April 8, 1907.

579. *Waukegan Daily Sun*, March 6, 1914.

580. *Waukegan Daily Sun*, March 18, 1918.

581. Charles W. Estus, Sr. and John F. McClymer, *Ga till Amerika* (Worcester, Massachusetts: Worcester Historical Museum, 1994), 37.

582. *Waukegan Daily Sun*, July 18, 1907.

583. Louise and Julia Osling, "Fred Fortney, Swedish Glee Club Historian and Elmer Anderson (Swedes in Waukegan)," in *Historical Highlights of the Waukegan Area* (Waukegan, Illinois: North Shore Printers, 1976), 156–157.

584. *Waukegan Daily Sun*, June 7, 1913.

585. Louise and Julia Osling, "Fred Fortney, Swedish Glee Club Historian and Elmer Anderson (Swedes in Waukegan)," in *Historical Highlights of the Waukegan Area* (Waukegan, Illinois: North Shore Printers, 1976), 157.

586. Ed Link, *Waukegan, A History* (Waukegan Historical Society, 2009), 154–155.

587. *Waukegan Daily Sun*, March 14, 1898.

588. *Waukegan Daily Sun*, February 16, 1927.

589. *Waukegan Daily Sun*, June 14, 1910.

590. *Waukegan Daily Sun*, October 20, 1910.

591. *Waukegan Daily Sun*, December 23, 1910.

592. *Waukegan Daily Sun*, December 17, 1910.

593. *Waukegan Daily Sun*, December 23, 1910.

594. *Waukegan Daily Sun*, November 24, 1915.

595. *Waukegan Daily Sun*, October 20, 1910.

596. *Waukegan Daily Sun*, January 6, 1911.

597. *Waukegan Daily Sun*, December 9, 1929.

598. *Waukegan Daily Sun*, December 18, 1909.

599. *Waukegan Daily Sun*, June 14, 1910.

600. *Waukegan Daily Sun*, March 20, 1928.

601. *Waukegan Daily Sun*, November 16, 1910.

602. *Lake County Independent*, July 30, 1909.

603. *Waukegan Daily Sun*, November 24, 1915.

604. *Lake County Independent*, July 27, 1906.

605. *Lake County Independent*, April 5, 1907.

606. *Waukegan Daily Sun*, January 29, 1898.

607. *Waukegan Daily Sun*, July 2, 1898.

608. *Waukegan Daily Sun*, March 5, 1902.

609. *Lake County Independent*, December 6, 1917.

610. *Waukegan Daily Sun*, January 27, 1905.

611. *Waukegan Daily Sun*, April 24, 1906.

612. *Waukegan Daily Sun*, February 24, 1922.

613. *Waukegan Daily Sun*, May 28, 1909.

614. Louise and Julia Osling, "Vivian Merlo," in *Historical Highlights of the Waukegan Area* (Waukegan, Illinois: North Shore Printers, 1976), 141.

615. *Waukegan Daily Sun*, August 10, 1910.

616. *Waukegan Daily Sun*, June 7, 1913.

617. *Lake County Independent*, October 25, 1917.

618. *Waukegan Daily Sun*, October 21, 1919.

619. *Waukegan Daily Sun*, April 20, 1926.

620. *Waukegan Daily Sun*, May 10, 1926.

621. Waukegan Historical Society, Immigration to Waukegan Township from Census Records 1850–1900, 4.

622. *Waukegan Daily Sun*, March 4, 1907.

623. *Waukegan Daily Sun*, June 6, 1913.

624. *Lake County Independent*, January 4, 1907.

625. *Waukegan Daily Sun*, June 7, 1913.

626. *Waukegan Daily Sun*, July 8, 1911.

627. *Waukegan Daily Sun*, September 12, 1912.

628. *Waukegan Daily Sun*, March 19, 1915.

629. *Waukegan Daily Sun*, February 24, 1903.

630. *Waukegan Daily Sun*, August 8, 1911.

631. *Waukegan Daily Sun*, February 9, 1911.

632. *Waukegan Daily Sun*, November 23, 1910.

633. *Lake County Independent*, June 16, 1911.

634. *Waukegan Daily Sun*, July 17, 1909.

635. *Waukegan Daily Sun*, July 16, 1909.

636. *Waukegan Daily Sun*, November 24, 1925.

637. *Waukegan Daily Sun*, June 14, 1910.

638. *Waukegan Daily Sun*, October 3, 1912.

639. *Waukegan Daily Sun*, March 29, 1921.

640. *Waukegan News Sun*, September 30, 1937.

641. *Waukegan News Sun*, September 1, 1931.

642. *Waukegan News Sun*, November 21, 1936.

643. *Waukegan Daily Sun*, October 29, 1909.

644. *Lake County Independent*, July 19, 1912.

645. *Waukegan Daily Sun*, June 4, 1914.

646. *Waukegan Daily Sun*, December 17, 1910.

647. *Portrait and Biographical Album of Lake County, Illinois* (Chicago: Lake City Publishing Co., 1891), reprinted by Higginson Book Company Salem, Massachusetts, Illinois, 538–539.

648. *Portrait and Biographical Album of Lake County, Illinois* (Chicago: Lake City Publishing Co., 1891), reprinted by Higginson Book Company Salem, Massachusetts, Illinois, 761.

649. *Portrait and Biographical Album of Lake County, Illinois* (Chicago: Lake City Publishing Co., 1891), reprinted by Higginson Book Company Salem, Massachusetts, Illinois, 733–734.

650. *Portrait and Biographical Album of Lake County, Illinois* (Chicago: Lake City Publishing Co., 1891), reprinted by Higginson Book Company Salem, Massachusetts, Illinois, 289–290.

651. *Portrait and Biographical Album of Lake County, Illinois* (Chicago: Lake City Publishing Co., 1891), reprinted by Higginson Book Company Salem, Massachusetts, Illinois, 207–208.

652. *Portrait and Biographical Album of Lake County, Illinois* (Chicago: Lake City Publishing Co., 1891), reprinted by Higginson Book Company Salem, Massachusetts, Illinois, 308.

653. *Portrait and Biographical Album of Lake County, Illinois* (Chicago: Lake City Publishing Co., 1891), reprinted by Higginson Book Company Salem, Massachusetts, Illinois, 321–322.

654. *Portrait and Biographical Album of Lake County, Illinois* (Chicago: Lake City Publishing Co., 1891), reprinted by Higginson Book Company Salem, Massachusetts, Illinois, 394–395.

655. *Portrait and Biographical Album of Lake County, Illinois* (Chicago: Lake City Publishing Co., 1891), reprinted by Higginson Book Company Salem, Massachusetts, Illinois, 450–451.

656. *Portrait and Biographical Album of Lake County, Illinois* (Chicago: Lake City Publishing Co., 1891), reprinted by Higginson Book Company Salem, Massachusetts, Illinois, 529–530.

657. *Portrait and Biographical Album of Lake County, Illinois* (Chicago: Lake City Publishing Co., 1891), reprinted by Higginson Book Company Salem, Massachusetts, Illinois, 545–546.

658. *Portrait and Biographical Album of Lake County, Illinois* (Chicago: Lake City Publishing Co., 1891), reprinted by Higginson Book Company Salem, Massachusetts, Illinois, 696.

659. *Portrait and Biographical Album of Lake County, Illinois* (Chicago: Lake City Publishing Co., 1891), reprinted by Higginson Book Company Salem, Massachusetts, Illinois, 256–259.

660. *Portrait and Biographical Album of Lake County, Illinois* (Chicago: Lake City Publishing Co., 1891), reprinted by Higginson Book Company Salem, Massachusetts, Illinois, 727.

661. *Portrait and Biographical Album of Lake County, Illinois* (Chicago: Lake City Publishing Co., 1891), reprinted by Higginson Book Company Salem, Massachusetts, Illinois, 778–779.

662. "Man at washtub, wife votes: an election year retrospective." Lake County, Illinois, historical blog.

663. Lake County, Illinois, History, "Bess Bower Dunn."

664. *Waukegan Daily Sun*, October 29, 1903.

665. Lake County, Illinois, History, "Jane Strang McAlister, Millburn."

666. Lake County, Illinois, History, "Beatrice Pearce Dickinson, M. D. County's First Woman Doctor."

667. Lake County, Illinois, History, "Mother Rudd's Temperance Tavern."

668. Lake County, Illinois, History, "Edith F. Sherman, Women Artists and the Civil War."

669. Lake County, Illinois, History, "Laura Sprague, Swan School."

670. *Waukegan Gazette*, August 16, 1851.

671. *Waukegan Gazette*, July 19, 1851.

672. *Waukegan Daily Gazette*, September 30, 1897.

673. *Waukegan Daily Sun*, September 26, 1919.

674. *Waukegan Daily Sun*, September 25, 1919.

675. *Waukegan Daily Sun*, October 10, 1919.

676. *Waukegan Daily Sun*, October 11, 1919.

677. *Waukegan Daily Sun*, June 21, 1912.

678. *Waukegan Gazette*, October 26, 1872.

679. *Waukegan Daily Sun*, August 20, 1903.

680. *Waukegan Daily Sun*, January 21, 1927.

681. *Waukegan Daily Sun*, September 9, 1924.

682. *Waukegan Daily Sun*, November 12, 1918.

683. *Waukegan Daily Sun*, July 3, 1915.

684. *Waukegan Daily Sun*, November 20, 1931.

685. *Waukegan Daily Sun*, August 15, 1906.

686. *Waukegan Daily Sun*, October 15, 1924.

687. *Waukegan Daily Sun*, May 10, 1909.

688. *Waukegan Daily Sun*, February 20, 1905.

689. *Waukegan Daily Sun*, March 15, 1905.

690. *Waukegan Daily Sun*, November 4, 1905.

691. *Waukegan Gazette*, September 29, 1877.

692. *Waukegan Daily Sun*, May 6, 1910.

693. *Waukegan Daily Sun*, May 9, 1908.

694. Phyllis de la Garza, *Death for Dinner: The Benders of (Old) Kansas* (Honolulu, Hawaii: Talei Publishers, Inc., 2003), 68.

695. Phyllis de la Garza, *Death for Dinner: The Benders of (Old) Kansas* (Honolulu, Hawaii: Talei Publishers, Inc., 2003), 112.

696. John T. James, *The Benders in Kansas* (Pittsburg, Kansas: Mostly Books, 1995), 47.

697. *Chicago Daily Tribune*, December 20, 1882.

698. "The Benders." *Chicago Daily Tribune*, November 8, 1889.

699. Phyllis de la Garza, *Death for Dinner: The Benders of (Old) Kansas* (Honolulu, Hawaii: Talei Publishers, Inc., 2003), 114.

700. *Chicago Daily Tribune*, July 12, 1908.

701. *Chicago Daily Tribune*, July 12, 1908.

702. Phyllis de la Garza, *Death for Dinner: The Benders of (Old) Kansas* (Honolulu, Hawaii: Talei Publishers, Inc., 2003), 145–150.

703. "The Fate of the Cruel Benders." *Chicago Daily Tribune*, November 8, 1889.
704. "Kate Bender Dead; Lived in County." *Waukegan Daily Sun*, May 6, 1910.
705. "Old Settlers Are Recalling Bender Horror." *Waukegan Daily Sun*, May 9, 1908.
706. *Wikipedia.*
707. Phyllis de la Garza, *Death for Dinner: The Benders of (Old) Kansas* (Honolulu, Hawaii: Talei Publishers, Inc., 2003).
708. John T. James, *The Benders in Kansas* (Pittsburg, Kansas: Mostly Books, 1995).
709. Tori Telfer, *Deadly Women Throughout History* (Harper Collins, 2017).
710. Waukegan Gazette, May 17, 1873.
711. Waukegan Daily Sun, May 23, 1907.
712. *Lake County Independent*, October 17, 1918.
713. *Lake County Independent*, May 16, 1918.
714. Palatine Enterprise newspaper, January 30, 1925.
715. Carol Hymowitz and Michaele Weissman, *A History of Women in America* (Bantam, 1984), 183.
716. *Waukegan Daily Sun*, January 25, 1930.
717. The Evanston Index newspaper, June 24, 1899.
718. *Waukegan Daily Sun*, January 23, 1906.
719. *Lake County Independent*, August 26, 1904.
720. *Waukegan Daily Sun*, August 15, 1912.
721. *Waukegan Daily Sun*, July 10, 1908.
722. *Lake County Independent*, September 14, 1906.
723. *Waukegan Daily Sun*, January 26, 1907.
724. *Waukegan Daily Sun*, January 26, 1907.
725. *Waukegan Daily Sun*, January 23, 1907.
726. *Waukegan Daily Sun*, October 20, 1921.
727. *Lake County Independent*, September 29, 1911.
728. *Waukegan Daily Sun*, June 24, 1911.
729. *Waukegan Daily Sun*, June 24, 1908.
730. *Waukegan Daily Sun*, October 3, 1902.
731. *Waukegan Daily Sun*, February 15, 1917.
732. *Waukegan Daily Sun*, October 31, 1912.
733. *Waukegan Daily Sun*, April 6, 1907.
734. *Lake County Independent*, November 11, 1910.

735. *Waukegan Daily Sun*, August 18, 1927.

736. *Waukegan Gazette*, July 28, 1866.

737. *Waukegan Daily Sun*, February 19, 1916.

738. *Waukegan Daily Sun*, October 22, 1921.

739. *Waukegan Daily Sun*, February 19, 1916.

740. *Waukegan Gazette*, February 28, 1874.

741. *Waukegan Daily Sun*, February 13, 1924.

742. *Waukegan Gazette*, February 28, 1874.

743. *Waukegan Daily Sun*, February 13, 1924.

744. *Waukegan Daily Sun*, February 19, 1916.

745. *Lake County Independent*, January 24, 1916.

746. *Lake County Independent*, November 24, 1899.

747. *Waukegan Daily Sun*, August 16, 1901.

748. *Waukegan Daily Sun*, August 1, 1922.

749. *Lake County Independent*, November 23, 1922.

750. *Waukegan Daily Sun*, June 4, 1906.

751. *Waukegan Daily Sun*, August 26, 1908.

752. *Waukegan Daily Sun*, November 24, 1913.

753. *Waukegan Daily Sun*, March 21, 1901.

754. *Waukegan Daily Sun*, March 27, 1901.

755. *Waukegan Daily Sun*, June 6, 1913.

756. *Lake County Independent*, June 12, 1919.

757. *Lake County Independent*, January 25, 1923.

758. *Waukegan Daily Sun*, July 22, 1910.

759. *Lake County Independent*, January 9, 1914

760. *Waukegan Daily Sun*, July 18, 1922.

761. *Waukegan Daily Sun*, January 27, 1916.

762. *Waukegan Gazette*, July 25, 1885.

763. *Waukegan Daily Sun*, October 2, 1911.

764. *Waukegan Daily Sun*, April 5, 1912.

765. *Waukegan Daily Sun*, July 22, 1904.

766. *Waukegan News Sun*, May 11, 1936.

767. *Waukegan Daily Sun*, June 3, 1915.

768. *Waukegan Daily Sun*, April 5, 1912.

769. *Waukegan Daily Sun*, December 3, 1897.

770. *Waukegan Daily Sun*, March 11, 1915.

771. *Waukegan Daily Sun*, January 27, 1916.

772. *Waukegan Daily Sun*, August 8, 1914.

773. *Waukegan Daily Sun*, September 14, 1915.
774. *Waukegan Daily Sun*, October 6, 1900.
775. *Lake County Independent*, April 19, 1901.
776. *Lake County Independent*, August 24, 1916.
777. *Waukegan Daily Sun*, May 25, 1908.
778. *Waukegan Daily Sun*, April 14, 1911.
779. *Waukegan Gazette*, January 3, 1857.
780. *Waukegan News Sun*, May 19, 1932.
781. *Waukegan News Sun*, May 17, 1933.
782. *Waukegan Daily Sun*, October 5, 1911.
783. *Lake County Independent*, August 14, 1903.
784. *Waukegan News Sun*, June 7, 1937.
785. *Waukegan Daily Sun*, October 2, 1911.
786. *Waukegan Daily Sun*, December 7, 1911.
787. *Waukegan News Sun*, June 18, 1934.
788. *Waukegan News Sun*, September 7, 1933.
789. *Waukegan Daily Sun*, February 17, 1906.
790. *Waukegan Daily Sun*, November 25, 1910.
791. *Waukegan Daily Sun*, March 10, 1911.
792. *Waukegan Daily Sun*, March 10, 1911.
793. *Waukegan Daily Sun*, November 25, 1927.
794. Ellen Williams Staben, As I Remember the Southeast Side of Waukegan in the Early 1900's, 1.
795. *Waukegan Daily Sun*, June 13, 1916.
796. *Waukegan Daily Sun*, May 3, 1907.
797. *Waukegan Daily Sun*, June 25, 1898.
798. *Waukegan News Sun*, August 20, 1932.
799. *Waukegan Daily Sun*, June 26, 1914.
800. *Lake County Independent*, February 18, 1910.
801. *Waukegan Daily Gazette*, August 5, 1897.
802. *Waukegan Daily Sun*, June 17, 1915.
803. *Waukegan Daily Sun*, April 8, 1915.
804. *Waukegan Daily Sun*, April 30, 1921.
805. *Waukegan Daily Sun*, May 18, 1921.
806. *Lake County Independent*, August 2, 1912.
807. *Waukegan Daily Sun*, July 16, 1920.
808. *Waukegan Daily Gazette*, July 18, 1914.
809. *Waukegan Daily Sun*, November 14, 1914.

810. *Waukegan Daily Sun*, August 20, 1913.

811. *Waukegan Daily Sun*, September 25, 1916.

812. *Waukegan Daily Sun*, December 22, 1905.

813. *Waukegan Daily Sun*, February 10, 1919.

814. *Lake County Independent*, May 6, 1904.

815. *Waukegan Daily Sun*, August 19, 1908.

816. *Waukegan Daily Sun*, April 27, 1909.

817. *Waukegan Daily Gazette* and Register, February 13, 1899.

818. *Waukegan Daily Gazette* and Register, February 14, 1899.

819. *Waukegan News Sun*, December 23, 1935.

820. *Waukegan Daily Sun*, July 3, 1906.

821. *Waukegan Daily Sun*, February 19, 1926.

822. *Waukegan Daily Gazette*, July 27, 1916.

823. *Waukegan News Sun*, June 12, 1934.

824. *Lake County Independent*, September 5, 1913.

825. *Waukegan Gazette*, August 23, 1873.

826. *Lake County Independent*, August 3, 1900.

827. *Waukegan Gazette*, August 21, 1869.

828. *Waukegan Gazette*, January 3, 1874.

829. *Lake County Independent*, March 12, 1907.

830. *Waukegan Daily Sun*, January 13, 1912.

831. *Waukegan Gazette*, September 5, 1885.

832. *Waukegan Gazette*, February 11, 1882.

833. *Waukegan Gazette*, July 4, 1874.

834. *Waukegan Gazette*, February 5, 1870.

835. *Lake County Independent*, April 7, 1905.

836. *Lake County Independent*, April 7, 1905.

837. *Waukegan Daily Sun*, August 13, 1929.

838. Shadows of Trains, "Palatine, Lake Zurich & Wauconda Railroad—PLZW."

839. *Lake County Independent*, December 22, 1923.

840. *Waukegan Daily Sun*, March 17, 1911.

841. *Waukegan News Sun*, August 31, 1934.

842. *Waukegan Daily Sun*, January 20, 1916.

843. *Waukegan Daily Sun*, May 17, 1909.

# AUTHOR BIO

James D. Lodesky was born in Waukegan. He grew up in Gurnee, Illinois, but currently lives in Lisle, Illinois. James is the author of the books *Polish Pioneers in Illinois 1818–1850* and *The Revised Early History of Warren Township High School and Its Sports Teams*. James also has a website about animal stories published in newspapers from the 1700s, 1800s, and early 1900s titled uncledicksanimaltales.com. If you would like to buy any of these books, just google jimlodesk@gmail.com.

The book covers the long-forgotten history of Lake County, Illinois. The period takes place mainly in the late 1800s and early 1900s. The first chapter tells the story of Robert Dady. Starting with nothing and never learning to read or write, Robert would become the largest landowner in the county. His daughter, Nellie Conrad, became one of Waukegan's most successful businesswomen. She built the Times Theater, Roller Rink, two subdivisions, plus miscellaneous other real estate ventures.

The next chapters concern Lake County violence in the form of fights, mobs, and riots. Most kinds of violence were common and accepted in society. Penalties were light for all but the worst crimes.

Ethnic Lake County and North Chicago follows. Profiles for the various ethnic groups are covered. The area had Albanians, Armenians, Blacks, Bulgarians/Macedonians, Croatians, Czechs, Danes, Finns, Germans, Greeks, Irish, Italians, Jews, Lithuanians, Poles, Romanians, Russians, Slovaks, Slovenes, and Turks.

Next are stories about Lake County men who overcame adversity. Most had little education and not many prospects. They overcame it all and became successful men in their communities.

Famous Lake County women follow the men. These women had an

impact on a number of county affairs. One Lake County woman was the first woman to vote in the state. The Lake County Historical Society is named after one of the county's most influential women.

The next chapter concerns Lake County women acting badly. Some Lake County women were anything but meek, and the reader might be surprised at just how violent some of them actually were.

None of the county's women could keep up with Lake County's all-time worst woman. The next chapter tells the story of the Bender family. The Benders lived in the country for a time but were sent packing because of their detestable ways. They soon settled in Kansas and became one of the most famous serial killers in American history. Kate bender was the brains of the whole operation.

The book finishes up with miscellaneous stories about Lake County men and women. Some of the stories covered include Lake County's lynching record, hermits, gypsies, women farmers, and Lake County's strongest man. Also included is the Fats baseball team. The Fats played baseball in the county a number of times and sported a 640- pound first baseman. Located in the ethnic Jewish profile is the story of Meyer Kubelsky, father of comedian Jack Benny. Jack Benny is Waukegan's favorite son but not so much Meyer.

Printed in the United States
By Bookmasters